D0205272

Jane Austen has been read as a novelist of manners, whose work discreetly avoids discussing the physical. John Wiltshire shows, on the contrary, how important are faces and bodies in her texts, from complainers and invalids like Mrs Bennet and Mr Woodhouse, to the frail, debilitated Fanny Price, the vulnerable Jane Fairfax and the 'picture of health', Emma. Talk about health and illness in the novels is abundant, and constitutes community, but it also serves to disguise the operation of social and gender politics. Behind the medical paraphernalia and incidents are serious concerns with the nature of power as exerted through and on the body, and with the manifold meanings of illness. 'Nerves', 'spirits' and sensibility figure largely in these books, and Jane Austen is seen to offer a critique of the gendering power of illness and nursing or attendance upon illness. Drawing on modern – medical and feminist – theories of illness and the body, as well as on eighteenth-century medical sources, to illuminate the novels, this book offers new and controversial, but also scholarly, readings of these familiar texts.

JANE AUSTEN AND THE BODY

JANE AUSTEN
AND THE BODY

'*The picture of health*'

JOHN WILTSHIRE

Department of English, La Trobe University

CAMBRIDGE
UNIVERSITY PRESS

Published by the Press Syndicate of the University of Cambridge
The Pitt Building, Trumpington Street, Cambridge CB2 1RP
40 West 20th Street, New York, NY 10011-4211, USA
10 Stamford Road, Oakleigh, Victoria 3166, Australia

First published 1992

Printed in Great Britain at the University Press, Cambridge

A catalogue record for this book is available from the British Library

Library of Congress cataloguing in publication data
Wiltshire, John.
Jane Austen and the body: 'the picture of health' / John Wiltshire.
p.   cm.
Includes bibliographical references and index.
ISBN 0 521 41476 8 (hc)
1. Austen, Jane, 1775–1817 – Knowledge – Medicine. 2. Austen, Jane, 1775–1817 –
Knowledge – Anatomy. 3. Body, Human, in literature. 4. Medicine in literature.
5. Health in literature. I. Title.
PR4038.M4W5   1992
823'.7 – dc20   91-45042   CIP

ISBN 0 521 414768 hardback

For Ruth and Johnny

'One hears sometimes of a child being "the picture of health;" now Emma always gives me the idea of being the complete picture of grown-up health. She is loveliness itself. Mr Knightley, is not she?'

Emma, chapter 5

Contents

Acknowledgements

I would like to take this opportunity of thanking Arthur Frankland, Jock and Maggie Tomlinson, Tim Kelly and Peter Shrubb who, long ago now, opened my eyes to Jane Austen's lasting greatness, and S. L. Goldberg, whose later work in literature and philosophy I have made use of in these pages. I am grieved to think that neither Maggie nor Sam will now ever read them.

Ann Blake, Gerda Seaman and Kay Torney, among my colleagues, gave me tangible help, and I thank them, especially Kay, with whom I have taught several courses on written versions of illness, and who is a contributor to many parts of this book, especially the chapters on *Mansfield Park* and *Emma*. I am also grateful to David Ellis, Robin Grove and Robert Cole, who gave me the idea that was its germ, to Howard Mills, who was encouraging and energetic over a MS that was, I suppose, its earlier incarnation, and to my wife Zaiga for our conversations about Jane Austen over many years.

I also wish to thank the Librarian of King's College, Cambridge, for permission to study the manuscript of *Sanditon*, Kevin Taylor, my editor at Cambridge University Press, for his encouragement of this project, and, once again, Con Coroneos, my copy-editor, and Richard McGregor, for indexing.

A note on texts

Citations of Jane Austen's novels are made in the text by following quotations with the standard abbreviations and page numbers, viz. (PP 124). The page numbers refer to the text which has been used throughout, the *Oxford Illustrated Jane Austen*, ed. R. W. Chapman, 5 vols. 1923, revised editions, 1965, 1967, *The Works of Jane Austen*, ed. R. W. Chapman, vol. VI: *Minor Works*, 1954, revised editions, 1963, 1965. For *Sanditon*, *Sanditon, an unfinished novel by Jane Austen, reproduced in facsimile from the manuscript in the possession of King's College, Cambridge*, introduction by B. C. Southam, Oxford and London, 1975, has also been used. Where a number of references to the same novel are made, the abbreviated title is omitted after the first citation.

Introduction: Jane Austen and the body

The cover of this book shows the steps at Lyme down which Louisa Musgrove fell that fateful November day. It's a picture of a space, not of a body. And Jane Austen's novels, I will admit, seem among the least likely texts on which to found a discussion of the body. Isn't the body – absent, suspended, at best relegated to the inferior partner in the dyad of mind and body, as all agree is its position in our culture – virtually banished from her work? However we categorise them – as comedies of manners, or narratives of moral sensibility, of domestic politics, of the developing ethical consciousness, of heroines educated out of illusion, of the anxieties of choice, the subtleties of self-deception – these are novels whose titles, *Sense and Sensibility*, *Pride and Prejudice*, *Persuasion*, firmly ensconce them within an august and dominant tradition of moral adjudication, and by 'moral' here we must mean transcending the natural and the immanent. These are novels of a polite society too, in which obvious restraints are put upon the discussion of bodily matters, and the latitude of bodily expression allowed men and women, but especially women, is severely curtailed. 'Even the Maid' who was dressing Mrs Thrale's hair in 1782, 'burst out o' laughing at the Idea of a Lady saying her stomach ach'd'[1] and the lady-like decorum of the age of sensibility is one which this author scarcely seems to infringe or question.

Such at least may explain the reactions of Jane Austen's most notorious detractors, several of whom seem to have focused upon just this absence of the bodily in her writing. 'No glance of a bright, vivid physiognomy' was to be found in her novels, complained Charlotte Brontë to Lewes. Instead they yielded

1

only 'an accurate daguerreotyped portrait of a commonplace face'. Two years later she famously elaborated on this dismissal to W. S Williams, supplying with physiological specificity what she thought Austen lacked. 'Her business is not half so much with the human heart as with the human eyes, mouth, hands and feet; what sees deeply, speaks aptly, moves flexibly, it suits her to study, but what throbs fast and full, though hidden, what the blood rushes through, what is the unseen seat of Life and the sentient target of death – *this* Miss Austen ignores. '[2] Lawrence's response to 'the mean Jane Austen', an 'old maid' who typifies 'the sharp knowing in apartness' was even more visceral, if his meaning was much the same.[3] Another detractor, Cardinal Newman, complained of *Emma*: 'Everything Miss Austen writes is clever, but I desiderate something. There is a want of *body* to the story'[4] (though he might have had something else in mind). 'Her books madden me so much that I can't conceal my frenzy', wrote Mark Twain in a letter of 1898. 'Every time I read "Pride and Prejudice" I want to dig her up and hit her over the skull with her own shin-bone',[5] presumably, like Dr Johnson kicking the stone to refute Berkeley, to remind Miss Austen of the absoluteness of corporeal reality.

The critical tradition has of course taken these cries of dissatisfaction or repugnance seriously enough to answer, or attempt to answer, them repeatedly. It has usually been understood that the body in these condemnations is a metaphor or metonymy, and that what is felt to be missing is overt ardour or warmth or intensity of desire. Amplifying Raleigh's remark that 'the world of pathos and passion is present in her works by implication',[6] critics and writers have made it much of their business to mine the discreet and often understated surface of these texts, and they have repeatedly brought to the surface, made manifest, dramas of some political or sexual intensity. R. W. Chapman turned Brontë's physiological metaphor against her conclusions in his 1948 Clark lectures when he quoted Donne's phrase about 'eloquent blood' and defined the supremacy of *Emma* as being 'above all in the flow of the blood beneath the smooth polished skin: a flow of human sympathy and charity that beats with a steady pulse, rarely – but the more momentously – quickening to a throb that sets our own veins leaping in unison'.[7] Few later critics will have expressed their pleasure in the text so candidly, or unguardedly.

They have usually been governed by more austere purposes, concerned to authenticate Jane Austen's position in the literary canon by showing that her novels, far from being 'hermetically sealed' as Reginald Farrer put it, from 'the vast anguish of her time'[8] were deeply implicated both in the political controversies of her age, and in the literary and ideological traditions through which they were conducted. Jane Austen (increasingly merely 'Austen') was inserted into a strong intellectual tradition, which – adapted and rethought through her position as a woman, and in the mode of the domestic novel – nevertheless was made the vehicle of commentary upon society, and especially of her class, at a crucial period of historical change. It was plausibly argued that Austen, though professing herself 'the most ignorant and ill-informed female who ever dared to be an authoress' to the Regent's Librarian, and though certainly abstaining from the display of learning in her novels, had more than a passing acquaintance with the great moralists and philosophers of the previous century, and if her knowledge and indebtedness could not actually be proven, it became clear that the field in which her novels would henceforth be discussed would be marked out by these figures – almost all of them of course, male – standing sentinel on its boundaries. The abstract language of her novels was seen to marshal a whole hidden discourse of political morality. Austen became the Warrior of Ideas: the pupil of Locke and of Bishop Butler, Samuel Johnson's daughter, the antagonist of Godwin, the peer of Burke.[9]

The recent, more explicitly feminist readings of Jane Austen are a continuation of this tradition (she has now joined Richardson's admirers, become Mary Wollstonecraft's sister) only sharpening the edges of the ironies to be discerned in the novels and explicitly contrasting the self-defining energies to be found in them with their overt adherence to conservative ethics and genteel standards of reticence. No longer merely a warrior, Jane Austen is now a strategist of subversion, indirection and displacement, and the theatre of war is the domestic hearth, the salient issue one of women's relation to patriarchal structures and authority. One problem of this newly politicised Jane Austen is that once the field of politics has been redefined to include the subject of gender difference at its centre, then almost any item can be included in what Claudia Johnson calls 'the lexicon of politically sensitive terms',[10] a word such as 'sensibility' becomes inevitably loaded with controversial reference, and the thesis is self-confirming, even though nothing like an explicit political position is declared or overt allusions are made. These readings position Austen against the conflicting grids of bourgeois individualism and conservative morality and in many ways match the adroitness and skill with which they credit Austen by the tactical subtlety of their own readings. The problems of female destiny in a society governed by disregard for the female come now to the fore of the debate, and the contradiction between Austen's enterprise as an author and the restrictions upon the lady the source of the novels' continuing life.

I have no quarrel with these recent readings, some of which have been among the most brilliant Austen has received. The chapters which follow will in many places confirm, intersect and engage with them. In particular, the emphasis in Mary Poovey and Claudia Johnson on the restrictions upon the open expression of female energy and desire in the novels of Austen and her female contemporaries is relevant to my discussion of the ways in which that desire is represented as doubling back and displaced into women's bodies. But the feminism that is most relevant to this book is not the feminism, or protofeminism, of the later eighteenth century, in which Jane Austen has been situated with so much advantage to our understanding of her work. Much of what has been written about female destiny in the novels overlaps with the concern in this book with occasions in which that destiny is figured as illness or as attendance upon illness; and much of what I shall demonstrate about the novels' interests in hypochondria and hysteria – and other manifestations of power as exerted through the body – belongs to the discussion of women's roles that is situated, necessarily, within a given ideological framework. But contemporary feminist critics of Austen share with their older colleagues an interest in her as a political commentator, however subtle or indirect, however politics is defined. They highlight, in common with the now orthodox tradition, her interactions with her contemporaries, her address to social and historical issues, and that context is not the primary context I offer here. Indeed I find implausibly univocal many readings of the novels which seek to demonstrate their political or social allegiances or 'thought'. But since there are certainly few precedents for a reading which thematises health (or ill health) within Jane Austen's novels, to do so in the present context is to run the risk of being charged with returning the work to a marginal or apolitical status, or to seem foolishly eccentric, out, so to speak, on a limb.

Of course, it is obvious enough how full the novels are of mentions of sickness and ill health. Anyone reasonably familiar with their stories will recall how much the novels are littered with medical incident and props, from sore throats and flannel waistcoats, to thin gruel and headaches and Hartfield arrowroot, gout and Gowlands lotion, right sides and green tea. The paraphernalia of medicine could well be judged to be merely an aid to the effect of domestic realism, merely invisible to earlier critical detection because so obviously on view, domesticated, like the 'several Phials already at home' on the mantlepiece of the hypochondriac Parkers' lodgings at Sanditon. One can see too how Austen makes use of these events of the everyday life to illustrate and develop moral character, as well as to further her plots: if Mrs Bennet sends Jane to Netherfield in the rain and shamelessly maroons her there with a cold and fever, in the hope that she might promote Jane's relationship with Bingley, Austen just as pragmatically uses the same event to display how beautifully flushed her errand across the fields makes Elizabeth and to manoeuvre Elizabeth and Darcy together whilst Jane is on her sickbed upstairs, thus furthering the writer's own designs. The scene of Louisa's fall from the Cobb in *Persuasion* is similarly used to display a range of reactions – hysteria, fainting, shock, resolution and competence – and is clearly designed to be a turning point in the education of the hero. Narratively, Louisa's tumble is no accident. Hosts of similar instances might merely testify to how useful toothache or a sore throat or an enfeebled body can be to a writer who wishes to get a character out of the way or enlist sympathy for a heroine whom no one else regards. At the same time, the physical events or emergencies that are scattered through the novels, arbitrary as they are, like the sudden indisposition of Dr Grant which keeps Mrs Grant away from the final rehearsal of *Lovers' Vows* (MP 171) serve to underpin or underwrite the moral dramas that they so often release – in this instance Fanny's being pressed once again to take a part, and her renewed struggle of conscience. They act as reminders that not everything belongs to the moral world of choice and responsibility, though Jane Austen's capacity to load meaning into the smallest events of life (who sits with whom on a sofa, or in a carriage) might lead one to entertain this gratifying illusion, which comes threateningly close to a hegemonic control over her narrative organisation. But then of course no bodily event is independent of interpretation or ideology: Mary Crawford hints that Dr Grant's 'illness' is just the bon vivant's disappointment with a tough pheasant and a ploy to keep his wife at home.

It's certainly true that Austen's texts are full of enquiries and incidents about health, but these are not to be taken at their own face value as segregated or divided from the novelist's contemplation of social and political realities. Talk about health is seen, in these novels, and paradigmatically in *Emma*, as one way in which a community is constituted. Paying solicitous attention to others' faces and bodies and their symptoms is the means by which human solidarity is confirmed, an expression, to adapt Samuel Johnson's phrase, of that tenderness which by virtue of their common nature one person owes to another. But by the same token concern for the health of others serves to obscure or mask the psychological and social divisions which also traverse that community. Charity to the sick is thoroughly documented: Mrs Norris affects concern for the Bertrams' coachman's rheumatism; Miss Bates, whose mother is herself the blind recipient of Hartfield's benevolence, visits the ailing former ostler of her father, and Anne Elliot calls on the invalid Mrs Smith. It falls upon women, most notably, to heal, or at least to camouflage, the divisions that social and economic determinants inscribe into their world. In a similar fashion, enquiries about other people's health, so abundant in the novels, disguise the operation of a good deal of social and (especially) gender politics. Readings of others' appearance within the apparently non-political, non-controversial, because universalised, ambit of health serve to hide or displace the actually constitutive roles of economic and gendering forces.

Equally, talk about health is to be read in ironic cross-grain against the inner or psychological lives of the figures. In the early work 'Catharine or the Bower' written when Jane Austen was seventeen, Kitty Percival is prevented from going to the ball by an arbitrary, unmotivated interruption, a sudden and violent toothache. Her 'friend' Camilla persecutes her with pity from room to room:

'To be sure, there never was anything so shocking, said Camilla; To come on such a day too! For one would not have minded it you know had it been at *any other* time. But it always is so. I never was at a Ball in my Life, but what something happened to prevent somebody from going! I wish there were no such things as Teeth in the World; they are nothing but plagues to one, and I dare say that People might easily invent something to eat with instead of them; Poor Thing! what pain you are in! I declare it is quite Shocking to look at you. But you wo'nt have it out, will you? For Heaven's sake do'nt; for there is nothing I dread so much. I declare I had rather undergo the greatest Tortures in the World than have a tooth drawn. Well! how patiently you do bear it! how can you be so quiet? Lord, if I were in your place I should make such a fuss, there would be no bearing me. I should torment you to Death.'

'So you do, as it is,' thought Kitty.[11]

There are indeed different kinds of torture, as of cure, and if Jane Austen's focus is on Camilla's talking one, that is hardly the end of this matter. In the later texts, the contrast between a character's experience in and of the body and others' readings of it, sometimes the contrast between the feigned sensibility of fashionable currency and the real sensibility of suffering generates much of the comedy and irony that surrounds Austen's depiction of the whole self in society. The ironic incongruity that opens between Kitty's physical experience and Camilla's response is to be reproduced farcically in the interplay between Marianne Dashwood's distress and Mrs Jennings' ministrations, sombrely in the misconceptions between Fanny Price and Edmund Bertram, to become a structural principle of the relation between Jane Fairfax and Emma, to be deployed repeatedly to mingled comic, ironic and pathetic effect in a host of incidents in the mature novels. And comic or trivial instances to do with health do often of course focus major issues. 'A thoughtless young person will sometimes step behind a window-curtain and throw up a sash, without its being suspected', Frank Churchill teases the flabbergasted Mr Woodhouse, already anxious about draughts on heated bodies if the ball at the Crown goes ahead, but this, too, I suggest, is not merely an amusing incident but a confrontation that itself opens up conflicts and oppositions (between confinement and energy, for example) that are central to the metaphorical structure of *Emma*.

The body is normally merely enabling, transparent, taken for granted: it is only when it becomes painful or dysfunctional that its workings become disclosed to consciousness.[12] We accept it as the ground of our being in the world, unaware, until we fall ill, our teeth ache or our feet blister that in effect our body is between us and the world we inhabit.[13] 'Illness is a voyage of discovery through the body that makes you marvel at how harmoniously it functioned in the good old days, before the virus had begun its withering assault', as a victim of AIDS, Emmanuel Dreuilhe, writes.[14] Our health presumes upon the world, and this phenomenon of being is readily reproduced in most writing in the realist tradition, whose ground is precisely the functional competence of the bodily existence. Naturally then, the health or otherwise of a heroine (or villain) in a realist text is normally just as much an absence, and it is against a background of silence as to this topic that the eccentrically ill (or injured, or deformed) are articulated into prominence. But this – or so I argue – is not the case in Austen's novels. The physical well-being of her figures is, on the contrary, at issue: embodiment, whether it be transcribed as Emma's spirit, or Fanny's debility, or Anne Elliot's loss of 'bloom', is an important given of their life-worlds. Emma's health is the enabling basis of her largesse with her 'powers', her enterprises and miscarriages in Highbury, just as Fanny's physical insecurity is the ground of her fragile construction of a conservative self. In the novels these characters inhabit, the issue of health is, if not paramount, brought actively into play with the educational and courtship narratives that can concurrently be read from, or into, the texts. And indeed if the preceding century's epistemology focused upon the responses of consciousness to the external world, the most significant eighteenth-century medical experiments examined the responses of the body – the bones, the tissues, the nerves – to the external world, and by a variety of agencies, of which the terms 'nerves' and 'sensibility' are but two, that medical understanding entered into general culture. In Jane Austen's novels it is no longer possible to imagine the relation between the human subject and the world as one simply between mind or consciousness and external reality.

The bodily condition of these heroines is not an isolated factor in the play of meanings these novels entertain. If the healthy body is largely passive, unconscious of itself, then the unhealthy body, as a site of anxious self-concentration, is the source of events, of narrative energies. Especially in the novels of the second, Chawton, period, beginning with *Mansfield Park* in 1814, the question of health is brought to the fore and becomes a crucial element in the dynamic of Austen's plots. In Marianne Dashwood, Fanny Price, Henry Woodhouse, Jane Fairfax, Anne Elliot, Mary Musgrove – to list only the main figures – health is a salient factor in their characterisation, an important given of their destinies within the social world. Health, for a woman, may be in the first place a commodity, and the novels pay their due to that part of patriarchal culture in which the question of the woman's body is resolved into its appeal to the male gaze. Fanny Price, pining at Portsmouth, has this touch of sympathy in a letter from Mary Crawford: 'My dear little creature, do not stay at Portsmouth to lose your pretty looks. These vile sea breezes are the ruin of beauty and health'; John Dashwood reminds Elinor that Marianne's illness will mean that she can no longer expect to fetch a high price in the marriage market.[15] This is the simplest and the crudest way in which, as Austen perceives, the body is implicated in social transactions. One other aspect the novels examine is the relationship of bodily preoccupation to the absence of productive work – in one form in Sir Walter Elliot, in another with Mr Woodhouse. This tracing of the relation of the body to other values – of health with romantic courtship, of ill-health with commerce, invalidism with lack of useful employment – is brought to a climax in the dazzling fragment, written in Jane Austen's last months, set in a sea-side town, Sanditon, where Sydney Parker, brother of the gentleman who has abandoned his family's old house, suggests that it might be put to good use as a hospital.

I am suggesting then that the body becomes most visible in Austen's novels not in the framework solely of desire, but in the larger framework of health and illness. I do not mean by this that Austen herself specialises in detailed phenomenological accounts of illness, or – to speak more accurately – of disease. Marianne Dashwood's fever is certainly, as I shall argue, a sequenced and cogent study, but this is a special case. If one were to take only one novel of Dickens, *Dombey and Son*, by contrast, one might find there material enough for a disquisition upon its portrayal of the birth, consumptive decline and early death of little Paul Dombey, not to speak of the startlingly graphic and exact presentation of Mrs Skewton's aphasic stroke and its subsequent clinical course. In the year's time span of *Emma*, on the other hand, there occurs a death and a birth, but very little is made of Mrs Weston's pregnancy, and the birth of little Emma, not actually without significance in the novel, is, very properly, not reported. The 'attack' which brings about Mrs Churchill's demise is unspecified, occurs at two removes, and is pointedly distinguished from the complaints that have made Frank run about the country attending on her. Jane Fairfax is suspected of ill-health, if not of actual sickness, but

Austen makes it quite clear that, though she suffers, she does not suffer from the TB which Highbury fears is her family's only legacy to her. It is not as a source for such dramatic instances of bodily catastrophe that one can discuss Austen's novels: rather it is because the texts are careful to eschew the catastrophic and the abnormal that the field of ill health becomes so interesting. It is, by and large, the everyday and minor complaints, coughs and colds, biliousness, nervousness and fever that fill the novels, just as they fill most doctors' surgeries.

Medical theorists have made a useful distinction between the concepts of disease and of illness. When we fall sick, we experience illness and we define what is amiss, not alone, but according to the norms and terms available within our given culture and social network. Illness is nebulous, indeterminate, its labels approximate and shifting, but when her symptoms reach a certain level of intensity or disablement, the sufferer (not yet a patient) will normally seek some form of professional help. The practitioner listens to the patient's description of her condition and perceives it as a specific diagnostic entity in his profession's nosological system (I am using the pronouns advisedly). 'Through this process illness as lay experience becomes transformed into disease as biomedical explanation, and a clinical entity materialises as a real thing': excessive thirst, urination and hunger, for example, are diagnosed as disordered pancreatic function, breathlessness and chest pain when climbing stairs are reconceptualised into coronary artery insufficiency.[16] Illness is constructed into disease, sickness labelled, validated by the authority of the medical profession, put into circulation, and this public understanding becomes, unavoidably, part of the way the patient now lives and thinks her illness. (One might perhaps go further and suggest that disease functions very much like a male category – stable, defined, inserted into a nosological framework, written up in the case records; and illness like a female one – unstable, fluid, disregarded because unvalidated within culture, unformulated, unwritten.)

Arthur Kleinman, the clinician upon whose work I have principally been drawing here, has consistently called attention to the medical profession's underestimation of the significance of illness in the field of health care.[17] Of course there is overlap between the categories of illness, disease and sickness: the lay experience of illness will be influenced or conditioned by the very terms in which it is thought – many of which will derive ultimately from professional diagnoses. And the traffic, as between folk and official medicine, is not all one way. Typically, such terms have the power to confirm 'reality' upon the sufferer's condition, and then the meaning which attaches to them becomes redirected or (literally) incorporated into the experience of illness. Illness in this instance as in others, becomes inseparable from the wider experience of its meaning. Certain diseases, as Susan Sontag's now classic discussion of tuberculosis and cancer suggested, carry a freight of cultural significance, myths which may alleviate, or – more likely – stigmas which exacerbate the patient's suffering.[18] But the meaning of illness, as Kleinman argues, may, for the patient, exist on another plane, in which the specific disability or illness symptoms may soak up messages from the patient's life, be interpreted as the result of fault or responsibility, for example, or come to function as a metaphor for a life-failure or disaster. (Mary C. Rawlinson calls this particular usage of an organic disease or dysfunction in a life's scenario or narrative, 'appropriation'.[19]) Or illness may serve as an unconscious mode of salvaging self-respect or gaining social leverage.

The body is thus, on this understanding, the site in which cultural meanings are inscribed and illness one of the main means by which the body participates in and is determined by culture. Far from being transhistorical and transcultural, as the premises of biomedicine have it, illness is experienced and may even be produced differently in different social settings. Kleinman is an American-trained psychiatrist and anthropologist whose research work has been in Taiwan and in mainland China. His books emphasise how patients experience their illness, and its alleviation, in differing ways according to the cultural models available. What in North America is experienced as depression, in China is felt as headache, dizziness, exhaustion, an essentially somatic array of complaints which are given the diagnosis, long discarded elsewhere, of 'neurasthenia'. The significance of his thought for my purposes here is not only that he introduces illness as a broader category of health care, and because his work focuses upon the ways in which physical symptoms (not merely mental distress) may be culturally produced. His investigation of illness symptoms offers a way to think about the modes in which other bodily phenomena may be generated through a dialectic of self and life-world. Once illness is thought of as a language – in Kleinman's phrase 'an idiom of bodily complaints' – it enters necessarily into the symbolic orderings of culture. The body is not then something that stands against or opposed to culture, as the brute, animal, or natural mode of the human person, but becomes entrained in an order of cultural expression, or in other words a form of manners, a mode of social interaction. To explain the body as the vehicle of self-expression, Kleinman uses the term 'somatization'.

In somatisation emotions are, so to speak, deposited in the body and there reproduced as illness symptoms. In his *Sudelbuch* of 1789 Georg Christoph Lichtenberg wrote that 'My body is that part of the world which my thoughts can alter. Even *imagined* illnesses can become actual ones. In the rest of the world, my hypotheses cannot disturb the order of things.'[20] But somatisation is not, as Kleinman insists, any form of malingering, nor is it that 'somatic compliance' through which Freud's early patients made use of physical symptoms: it is 'a cultural idiom of distress', the way illness is experienced, in given cultural conditions. Jane Fairfax is a pertinent example. The result of the apparently decisive quarrel with Frank Churchill is that, as Mr Perry, the apothecary who is brought in, declares, 'she was suffering under severe headachs, and a nervous fever ... her health seemed for the moment completely deranged' (389). Jane's symptoms are the somatic product, in Kleinman's terms, of both her local family circumstances and the macro-social forces which compel her, as a single woman, into a helplessly dependent position. Her distress is communicated in a physical mode, because this is required in a specific social situation, one in which, as in Chinese society, the overt expression of the instigating emotions is forbidden. Her symptoms, as well as the community's solicitude about her bodily well-being, serve to obscure the economic and political factors which produce them.

The condition of the somatising patient is experienced as a bodily complaint, though it may be very plausibly explained as the result of social inequities and pressures. By locating the origin of the distress within the body, conceiving of the body as its field, and by naming it (often with the co-operation of health care professionals) as a disease, typical patients can avoid impugning the social system or the local network of support or facilitation in which they are suspended. Their illness may express a disguised political criticism, but it is thought of as organic, non-cultural, independent of their life-world. This process can be seen at work in the construction of hysteria in the nineteenth century. In Julia Kristeva's terms, the hysteric mimes her illness in a masculine mode, thereby rescuing something of her own desire.[21] Kleinman's writings, which emerge from within the medical, not the psychoanalytic, profession, are especially interesting because they offer a reading of the body as acculturated. Illness, so he argues, is the result of 'a dialectic between social world and person, cultural values and physiology'.[22] Neither a conventional understanding of physiology, nor the notion that these conditions originate in the isolate mind of the patient, can adequately account for their genesis.

Another mode of theorising the body is offered by contemporary feminism. Indeed one way of organising the vast and contesting varieties of this feminism is as a 'return to the body',[23] for it is certainly true that what Adrienne Rich called 'the possibility of converting our physicality into both knowledge and power'[24] inspires much recent feminist theory and criticism, as a response both to the denigration of the body in the 'malestream' of philosophical thought, to the eliding of the bodily, the natural, into the female, and to the specific consequences of that denigration as they are enacted in our culture. This is not the place for a survey of the varieties of feminist readings of 'the body', an abstract term which has a great range of referents, but – to simplify the issue drastically – one could say that most discussion of the body in contemporary feminism is regulated by sexuality, and that sexuality is always already installed in its discourse. On the other hand, sexuality was as far as possible not brought into play in the advocacies of eighteenth-century feminism. 'In everything not connected with sex, woman is man', wrote Rousseau, the source of many of Mary Wollstonecraft's arguments.[25] 'Do not consider me now as an elegant female intending to plague you,' declares Elizabeth Bennet to Mr Collins, 'but as a rational creature speaking the truth from her heart'. For early feminists, like Wollstonecraft, the starting point was that women are, as Elizabeth insists and as Mrs Croft too berates her brother Frederick Wentworth for forgetting, 'rational creatures'. The body, as was common in the rationalistic tradition, was silenced – the neutral background of the sexually indifferent 'creature' – what mattered was woman's participation in, and access to universal rights and a universal reason. To treat women as 'elegant females' or as 'fine ladies', as distinct by virtue of their sex, was to justify oppression under the cover of esteem and solicitude. It is a familiar case, and still continues to be an active force within feminism.

The so-called 'third phase' of feminism, though, has 're-membered' the body (as a Lacanian pun has it) since ignoring the body's biological specificity is now thought to have been a mode of male domination: and since one of the prime modes of male domination and the intersection of female bodies and male minds has been medicine, part of the feminist project is necessarily a rewriting of medical history and a rethinking of those relationships of power that have the body as their site. But this feminism does not interest itself in broken bones, diabetes or coronary failure except in so far as the medical context in which these are lived through and discussed is seen as a version of the power contests between the sexes. Feminism has been organised around the fact of sexual difference, and in seeking to theorise the body in society, finding no help (indeed an enemy) in orthodox medicine and philosophy, turned to psychoanalysis as the only available system of thought which problematised the body in its relation to language and culture. 'His majesty the ego', to use Freud's famous phrase, could not tell by what indirect and crooked ways he met his crown of normality. When her majesty succeeded to the throne, the routes to normality became ever more intricated, more lined with pitfalls. In all its forms, whether Freudian, Kleinian or Lacanian, psychoanalysis could support a conception of the bodily self, of sexuality, as a cultural product, a system which did not consider the body an inert self-explanatory given, but was interested in selfhood as an evolving principle whose pathway to definition was beset by vicissitudes in all its stages and relationships.

Thus along with its psychoanalytic inheritance contemporary feminist theory brought a disposition to frame questions of the body under the rubric of desire. Denise Riley in her meditation on the history of women's movements, *Am I that Name?*, suggests that 'anyone's body is – the classifications of anatomy apart – only periodically either lived or treated as sexed, therefore the gendered division of human life into bodily life cannot be adequate or absolute. Only at times will the body impose itself or be arranged as that of a woman or a man',[26] but this caveat is a rare one. Bodily life for the most articulate and sophisticated contemporary feminism is sexed life, whether it be Luce Irigaray's reinvention of biological essentialism in the attempt to subvert phallocentricism, or Kristeva's positing of the 'chora', the realm of 'pre-Oedipal' bodily energies which traverses and disrupts the symbolising power of language. In such a collection of texts as Jane Gallop's *Thinking Through the Body* (1988),[27] the body is thought through as inevitably caught in relations of inter-subjectivity, and thus the prime, the determinant fact of the body is assumed to be its desire. 'The body' is sexually saturated. Just as in medical writing and transactions, the question of sexuality is (or is supposed to be) in abeyance, so, in this feminism, mortality is suspended – that is part of its exhilarating quality, no doubt: the implied female subject in such writing is young, bold and free, menstruates regularly and without discomfort, never suffers from lower back pain or ulcers, and not even her reading of Derrida and Lacan can give her a headache.

In orthodox Western biomedicine, the body is excluded from notions of subjectivity, personhood or identity, and is treated as an observable entity, an organic ensemble of functions. But another branch of contemporary feminist philosophy addresses itself directly to the rethinking and contesting of biological and physiological understandings of the body. This is the discussion of the ways in which culture imprints the self with its meanings. Taking its origin from the notion that gender is a socially ascribed category, not a given of bodily difference, this order of feminist thought investigates the ways in which cultural factors inscribe themselves upon the human body. There are obvious instances (tattooing, slimming, fashion) in which the body surface is the receptor of cultural forces and is decorated or moulded by culture – instances in which the process is mediated by consciousness – but more interestingly, this discussion un-covers the ways in which the body is a receptacle of gendering forces, in a sense hospitable to them, making the 'lived body', to use the phenomenological term, an acting through of social determinations, without the intervention of consciousness.

Elizabeth Grosz has been the foremost theorist of this 'corporeal feminism'. Drawing – if rather remotely – upon Foucault and Merleau-Ponty, Grosz's project is to construct a theory of the body's interiority which is more inclusive than the male models of biology and physiology, and which makes biology accessible to rethinking in a reformist mode. 'Only human bodies create culture', she writes 'and in the process transform themselves *corporeally* (as well as conceptually). Human biology must be *always already cultural*, in order for culture to have any effect on it. It is thus a threshold term between nature and culture, being both natural and cultural. Or, formulated more paradoxically, it is *naturally social*.'[28] Grosz is a separatist feminist, whose work is designed to clear space for a challenge to orthodox scientific constructions of the body, but there is, I think, a convergence between her work and the work of the school of psychiatric anthropology of which Kleinman is representative. She writes that 'this understanding of the body as a *hinge* or *threshold* between nature and culture makes the limitations of a genetic, or purely anatomical or physiological account of bodies explicit.'[29] Kleinman speaks of 'the symbolic bridge, the socio-somatic reticulum that ties failure to headaches, anger to dizziness, loss and demoralization to fatigue',[30] and both insist that what they are speaking of are not 'psychosomatic' phenomena, originating in the mind. The lived experiences of the body are dialectically produced by the interaction of desire and social forces.

From two widely different sources, then, this discussion of the body in society can be funded. I shall position Jane Austen's dealings with the body in its social relations exactly at this interface between physiology and culture – and indeed, in some signal instances, it is precisely the face that is this 'hinge' or threshold. Consider what Austen means when, in reference to Fanny Price, she speaks of 'the modesty of her nature'. One of the signs of this modesty is that Fanny, under a variety of duresses, is prone to colour, to blush. Austen is not alone in the use of this topos, which is so frequently deployed by her contemporary novelists, of all persuasions, because, one suspects, it conveys the presence of desire, and especially of female desire, whilst dramatising it, precisely, as propriety. It declares sexuality in the very form of its denial, and thus makes obeisance to decorum whilst simultaneously heightening whatever erotic tensions may be latent in the conversation or interchange in which it occurs.

The blush is not a straightforward phenomenon of the body, rather one of the acutest signs of the bodily enigma,[31] and its deployment in Austen's narratives is governed by her awareness of its problematic nature, and of the possibility of exploiting this for dramatic purposes. Not only women blush, of course, and the same bodily symptom or signal may stand for a range of inner processes. Does the blush arise from pride? From embarrassment? From anger? Emma archly suggests, perhaps against her own better judgement, that Mr Knightley's 'admiration' of Jane Fairfax might take him by surprise. 'Mr Knightley was hard at work upon the lower buttons of his thick leather gaiters, and either the exertion of getting them together, or some other cause, brought the colour into his face' (E 287). Sufficient hint, that 'some other cause'; but what it might be is left indeterminate, to generate in secret its own ultimate narrative surprises. The blush is no unequivocal guide to emotion, and may be misread – indeed more often than not is misread – to ironic effect. Its phenomenology is puzzling and its signification is problematic, but it does, in all its varieties, represent clearly a form of the juncture between the body and culture, and functions as a miniaturised version of hysteria, the embodied correlate of a social affect.

So it is too with the symptom that is perhaps the most banal example of the interchange between body and culture – the headache. Headaches are not often merely the result of physiological processes, of the autonomous workings of a person's biology. 'As richly overdetermined as dreams',[32] headaches are understood to be physiological, psychological as well as social products. They mark the interiority of the body with the signs of social tension – what we speak of under the ample rubric of 'stress': the headache in the novels, as when Fanny Price retires to the sofa after a day picking roses in the heat, can be understood purely on the physiological plane – and the Bertrams, like most people in Austen's novels, are not sophisticated about the interactions of mind and body – or, as the narrator intimates, as the repository of psychological tensions which reach deeply into her relations with her adopted family. Fanny Price's body here reproduces social tensions – a fact which is intimately connected with her lack of standing, of social leverage within the family.

Indeed such an understanding of the body cannot be disentangled from thought about power relations, both within the family, and in the larger community. Illness can be seen both as the result of lack of power, and as (sometimes compensatively) confering power. Since its 'reality' is forever concealed in the unreachable interiority of the subject, illness is an especially plausible instrument for the exercise of domestic tyranny. 'My sore throats, you know, are always worse than anybody's', whines Mary Musgrove, thereby conferring on herself at once a right to consideration and an instrument of dominance. The very indefinability of illness is the source of its potency, its infinite usefulness as a vehicle of covert manipulations. The ill person (or the person who complains of being ill – which may amount to much the same thing in texts, and even in practice) lays friends and relations under tribute. They respond with solicitude, nursing or indifference, as the case may be. But if the ill person has access to other sources of power – if he or she is older, richer, less scrupulous in the exercise of the ego – then illness becomes a mode of compulsion – as Mrs Churchill exacts from her husband and adopted son not merely an unwilling compliance in, but an internalised acceptance of, her illness's 'reality'. In the socially less privileged, illness or debility, or merely physical weakness may function in a parallel way, to gain a minimal social leverage, consideration or opportunities otherwise denied. Austen has nothing – or almost nothing – to disclose about the phenomenology of illness, but about its performance, about illness appropriation, the novels say a good deal.

Take Mrs Bennet. 'When she was discontented she fancied herself nervous', remarks the narrator curtly at the close of the novel's first chapter. Dramatically, however, Mrs Bennet's nervousness is seen to be the correlate of her anxiety over her five unmarried daughters, and is always produced as a 'complaint' at moments when both her obsession with their futures has been brought specifically out as an issue, and her powerlessness within the family, the futility of her schemes, has been bluntly reinscribed in her consciousness. Her most violent outburst comes after her husband has staged a particularly humiliating rebuff of her as manager of the family's fortunes in front of his favourite daughter Elizabeth (PP 113). Her nerves (to take them seriously for a moment – no one else does) thus function in two ways – as real distress, the result of anger, humiliation and powerlessness – and as modes of recuperation – an attempt to rescue herself as a centre of attention, if not of actual authority. Illness becomes a vehicle whereby the ego-gratification that her youth and spirits once brought her can be salvaged as the consideration now due to the injured parent. 'Mr Bennet, how can you abuse your own children in such a way? You take delight in vexing me. You have no compassion on my poor nerves.' Mr Bennet's famous reply, 'They are my old friends – I have heard you mention them with consideration these twenty years at least', discloses when Mrs Bennet's complaints (to use that usefully ambiguous term) began. Since this is just after the Bennets' marriage, a correlation between 'nerves' and sexuality seems to be implied. To use Freud's famous comparison between neurosis and desire, Mrs Bennet's nerves are related to her spirits, as vinegar is to wine.

The novel of course promotes our reading this as comedy. But this is because Mrs Bennet's complaints are maladaptive: she only increases her daughters' dislike and her own isolation within the family by converting frustration into illness. The proliferation of 'nervous' disorders at the end of the eighteenth century, as I shall suggest in discussing *Emma*, is the result not only of developments in the history of physiological experiment, but of related developments in the history of individualism and self-consciousness. Mrs Bennet appropriates a new mode of representing the self, and her complaints are instances of a whole process by which nerves in the later eighteenth century became available as metaphors of powerlessness. The novel rather cruelly shares in the dismissal of her complaints, Jane Austen not being ready to recognise that the position of women in her society may be such that illness symptoms can be one of the few means available of social protest. 'I have no pleasure in talking to undutiful children. – Not that I have much pleasure indeed in talking to any body. People who suffer as I do from nervous complaints can have no great inclination for talking. Nobody can tell what I suffer! – But it is always so. Those who do not complain are never pitied' (113). Represented in a comic, self-contradictory mode, Mrs Bennet is hence segregated from the self-aware and ultimately self-reflexive Elizabeth. This is one means whereby the problems of female destiny that are implicit in Mrs Bennet's own dilemma are prevented from impinging too closely upon the romantic narrative of her daughter.

Illness features then in the novels of Austen as a mode of social circulation. The society depicted in these texts is not (to use the work of Kleinman again) psychologically sophisticated. It resembles oriental society, as Lionel Trilling long ago intimated, because of the premium placed upon outward decorum, the stylisation of manners, and the consignment of distress to a private area, and indeed because the body is the only area of true privacy allowed. It is a 'sociocentric' not a psycho- or ego-centric society like the West today, but such a society, it can be plausibly argued, was only constituted in the nineteenth century, and Austen's novels themselves are part of the process whereby individualism and individual consciousness became valued and dominant. (Consider for example, Austen's virtual invention in English of that mode of representing internal processes known as free indirect speech.) What is known to the novel – and hence to the reader – is, in many instances, psycho-logical stress and disturbance: visible to the inhabitants of the novel, on the other hand, are somatic symptoms and physical complaints. Attentiveness to others is expressed as care for their physical health, with an effect that is often productive of much irony. There is thus a continuing tension and interplay in Jane Austen's fiction between society's attention to the body and the dramas of interpersonal tension that use the body as their vehicle.

'Health' is an ideal, a meta-physical, quality but it is a nearly indispensable term in any discussion which focuses on the life of the whole self in society. The word slides easily from the physical sphere to the moral, and hence any picture of health will be a portrait of the enabling conditions of its production, and of the ways it (and ill health) are enacted. Health is intimately related to enablement and fulfilment, illness to frustration, anger and defeat. To discuss health in Austen's novels is to suggest that one way – as I would argue, a main way – in which she framed her interest in the moral life and in imagination was through seeing how these are enacted in and by the body, not only through picturing a string of hypochondriacs and invalids, but in the more subtle ways that structure the novels, in the facilities of care and attentiveness that make up in fact a large part of what we understand by a community. Nor is Austen's investigation of the ways people relate to, and make use of their bodies distinct from her sceptical consideration of romanticism: in *Sanditon*, excessive championing of romantic 'illimitable ardour', for instance, is glimpsed as the other side of a perversely minute attention to the body's ills, and the institution of invalidism is seen as the culmination of the culture of sensibility.

This book, then, reads Jane Austen's novels as pictures of health, a phrase which the novelist herself uses more than once. Perhaps I should rather say 'maps' of health, for to take up only the issues of body, of health and illness, in these texts is certainly to abstract from them a theme or meaning which leaves much else unregistered, even whilst it brings out some features that might have passed before unregarded. But I have stuck with the phrase 'the picture of health', partly because of George Eliot's emphatic declaration that novels are pictures not diagrams, and that if they lapse from one to the other they become pernicious[33] (and because I hope to reflect this truth in these readings, however selective of the material in the novels they are) and partly because I have convinced myself – in the way of critics – that this approach to Jane Austen's texts does bring one close, in the other meaning of 'picture', to the symbolic centre of her enterprise. In the chapters that follow I take up aspects of health and the body in some individual texts as a mode, as an option, to open them up to readings which respect – what 'picture' also suggests – each novel's self-framing design.

CHAPTER 1

Sense, sensibility and the proofs of affection

'Can he be a sensible man, sir?' Elizabeth Bennet asks her father after hearing him read aloud Mr Collins' letter. 'No, my dear, I think not,' he replies, 'I have great hopes of finding him quite the reverse' (PP 64). So it turns out: 'Mr Collins was not a sensible man' declares the narrator roundly herself (70), but other men, in other books, on their first appearance, are quickly endowed with this salient virtue. Mr Knightley is introduced with this commendation as 'a sensible man of about seven or eight-and-thirty ... '(E 9), and though Henry Crawford has 'sense and temper' (MP 45), it is intimated, these will scarcely inhibit his future flirtations. Even Edward Ferrars, in a novel called *Sense and Sensibility*, certainly not handsome, and diffident in manner, is generously praised by Marianne Dashwood for the same quality. 'I have the highest opinion in the world of his goodness and sense', she declares, and Elinor in her own style reiterates 'Of his sense and his goodness ... no one can, I think, be in doubt, who has seen him often enough to engage him in unreserved conversation' (20). 'Sense', 'strong, manly good sense', tends in the novels of Jane Austen and her contemporaries to be a masculine attribute, and its association in this novel pre-eminently with one of the heroines is a clue to its organisation. Actually, though, on the sisters' first introduction, sense itself is attributed to Marianne Dashwood ('she was sensible and clever' (6)) and this is one of the many indications that one is not to take the two heroines as merely antitheses. But that the 'sense' of the novel's title is to be largely assigned to Elinor Dashwood – as is apparent in the regard for objective evidence in the speech just quoted – is not really to be doubted.

Masculine 'sense' is strongly associated with masculine 'reason': Elton, Mr Knightley tells Emma, is 'not at all likely to make an imprudent match. He knows the value of a good income as well as anybody. Elton may talk sentimentally, but he will act rationally' (E 66) and Elinor's good sense is revealed as in part a shrewd assessment of the tactical realities of life in the social world. *Sense and Sensibility* gives its first pages to making clear the Dashwood family's social and financial position. Elinor and Marianne are the daughters of a widow, Fanny Dashwood, whose husband's death has left them, and their younger sister Margaret, if not exactly in poverty, since they still have two maids and a manservant, in a financial situation where they must be careful of money. They are at least to some degree dependent upon the goodwill and hospitality of their connections, and it is a silent imperative that they must marry – well, if possible. The family's social position is buffered by the gentlemen who offer them assistance – Colonel Brandon, Sir John Middleton – as well as by Mrs Jennings. But these are distant connections, and as the action of the novel unfolds, the task of negotiating the social world on behalf of herself and her sister (and indirectly on behalf of the family) falls increasingly upon Elinor's shoulders. Mrs Dashwood, though a very kind and sensitive woman, is as romantic, as impulsive, as little inclined to calculation and caution, as her daughter Marianne.

Sense and Sensibility is often envisaged as a point-by-point comparison of the temperaments, opinions and consequent histories of these two sisters, girls of roughly the same age, each in the same position towards life, each confronting the 'world', each with suitors.[1] I suggest, rather, that they are best seen as making part of a family triangle, for Mrs Dashwood, though neglected in many readings,[2] is a significant contributor to their conversations and arguments, and more fundamentally, to the psychological dynamics which produce the two sisters' divergent personalities and attitudes. (Margaret is little more than a plot convenience, to provide a companion for Mrs Dashwood whilst her elder sisters are in London.) Mrs Dashwood is sympathetically and almost continually present in the novel's first volume. In the second, set in London, she is a significant absence through the delegated mother-figure, Mrs Jennings, whose tactless and intrusive attentions Marianne continually, if implicitly, compares with her mother's sympathy. This part of the novel climaxes with Marianne's illness on the return home at Cleveland, and her pleas for her mother's presence: when Mrs Dashwood arrives at her daughter's bedside and returns to the novel, she is reinstated in the family group, and the tripartite conversations of the first volume on matters of ethics and behaviour are resumed. Mrs Dashwood is generous and warm-hearted, on good terms with all her daughters, but it is her affinity in temperament and opinions with Marianne that is continually underlined. She sees her younger self reflected in Marianne, and since she offers herself very much as Marianne's sympathising sister, it is no wonder that it is Elinor who finds herself *in loco parentis*, who keeps an eye on the family finances, and who finds herself occasionally saying the unsisterly thing. At one point, when Elinor suggests that it would be sensible simply to ask if Marianne is engaged to Willoughby, Mrs Dashwood refuses, on the grounds that an unwelcome question might put her own relationship to the daughter in jeopardy (84–5). In this community of women, something is amiss. The alliance of mother and younger daughter forces Elinor into a position where she must appear older than her years, to assume, along with responsibility for keeping within the budget, the mantle of ironic rebuke. It is as if inside the family group the emotional life is apportioned or split: Elinor takes upon herself the role of compromiser, arbitrator, and sage (she even disconcerts the much older Brandon in the firmness of her conviction that more knowledge of the world would put Marianne's ideas to rights) because Marianne is herself so little open to compromise and so utterly committed to her opinions and actions. And by making her the vessel of wisdom and prudence, the actual mother and Marianne are licensed to become the free champions of spontaneous feeling. Elinor is the masculinised daughter, forced by these psychological dynamics to introduce values tradition-ally associated with the male into this domestic circle.

Elinor's real father is absent from the text, but her literary father is Dr Johnson. She often speaks in a measured, stilted prose that reminds one of the eighteenth-century moral essay. When Edward Ferrars and Marianne discuss the picturesque, for example, Elinor pronounces with the typically balanced cadence of Augustan writing her adherence to a judicious mean: 'I suspect... that to avoid one kind of affectation Edward here falls into another' (97). Elinor-Imlac (for Elinor is found occupying the juridical position notably taken by Imlac, the elderly guide and 'sage' in Johnson's *Rasselas*, who comments sceptically on the enthusiasms and assumptions of his two younger charges) arbitrates disputes, interjects words of moderation, and functions, in effect, as the conscience of the family. Her position of authority is increased because she is often in possession of more knowledge than the other members of the household – as, for example, when Willoughby confesses his still abiding love of Marianne to her. She keeps this, and other, secrets to herself, only gradually and partially disclosing them to either her mother or her sister.

Elinor's specific and recurrent concern is with 'propriety', as when she famously censures Willoughby's 'slighting too easily the forms of worldly propriety' (49). Marianne, on the other hand, says too frankly what she thinks, and is careless of whether she gives offence to others: 'It was impossible for her to say what she did not feel, however trivial the occasion; and upon Elinor therefore the whole task of telling lies when politeness required it, always fell' (122). Although in such comments as these the narrator lodges her explicit sympathy with Elinor, the tartness or bluntness of the phrase 'telling lies' evinces within the distribution of values a latent leaning towards Marianne's. Elinor's is the point-of-view that the narrative adopts increasingly by giving us access to her thoughts and unspoken reflections: in contrast (and it is a salient fact about this novel's construction) Marianne's history is given rarely but in dramatic form. In fact the narrative's collusive relationship with Elinor's point of view and its incessant criticisms of Marianne are what for many modern readers make this novel unattractive, even 'especially painful'.[3] Elinor's concern always to pour oil on troubled social waters, to be cautious and tactful, to suppress her real responses, is particularly uncongenial to we who live in an ego-centric culture that privileges frankness, honesty and the pursuit of individual goals and tends to regard all diplomacy or voluntary self-suppression as a sign of weakness, mean-spiritedness or hypocrisy. A more awkward aspect of the narrative manner, to my mind, is that its comedy makes capital out of the follies and pettiness of such characters as Lady Middleton whilst at the same time commending Elinor's tactful politeness, as when for example she praises Lady Middleton's piano ('it is the very best toned piano-forté I ever heard'[4]) very much to the same tune as Lucy Steele's flatteries. Mrs Ferrars' and Fanny Dashwood's tantrums are handled with contemptuous ridicule and yet Elinor is shown paying these women dutiful service. So that while the narrator's wit takes pleasure in deriding the nullity, the vacuousness, the petty and mercenary motives that seem to govern most of those whom the sisters chance to fall among, this trenchantly dismissive satire is at odds with the judicious compromising and accommodation that is simultaneously, it seems, being advocated. The reader's responses are hence strongly encouraged to side with Marianne, who treats all pettiness with disdain, whilst at the same time the argument of the novel is that one should disapprove of this in practice, and instead approve of the sense, the tact, diplomacy and judicious silences of Elinor.

There seems to be only one passage where the narrative clearly takes on the inflections of Marianne's voice, and it occurs after the receipt of her mother's advice to stay in London:

> Marianne had promised to be guided by her mother's opinion, and she submitted to it therefore without opposition, though it proved perfectly different from what she wished and expected, though she felt it to be entirely wrong, formed on mistaken grounds, and that by requiring her longer continuance in London it deprived her of the only possible alleviation of her wretchedness, the personal sympathy of her mother, and doomed her to such society and such scenes as must prevent her ever knowing a moment's rest. (214)

Marianne's intolerance is exposed in these angry rhythms, but her assessment of the likely alleviations from the society of the

Steeles and Mrs Jennings, on the evidence the novel gives us at this stage, could hardly be more correct.

If Elinor is effectively the family's head, Marianne, on the other hand, is the feminised daughter, her mother's 'darling child'. Early in the novel, Marianne is 'wholly engrossed on the most affectionate principle' (20) by her mother. A deeper inference may also be drawn, for such a symbiosis, such an affinity exists between these two (who both regard Elinor's more prudential ideology with dislike) that Marianne can be said to rely upon her mother to an extent that actively inhibits her social adjustment. Marianne's attachment to her mother is one of the fostering elements in her expressiveness and vivacity, but it is also seen, more subtly, as a contribution to her eventual illness. For Elinor's 'sense' bears interpretation as adulthood, maturity, the necessary self-preservation of an independent being, and Marianne has not yet weaned herself from her mother. To put Austen's perception in modern terms, she has not developed an internal model of a care-giving self. Joyce McDougall describes patients in psychoanalysis whose infantile relationships have failed 'to give rise to an internal representation with care-taking functions ... such patients act as shockingly careless parents towards themselves'.[5] Marianne's disregard of elementary social politics, her carelessness of her appearance, and her violently physical enactment of her disillusionment with Willoughby (whose courtship is of course connected with the continuity of her mother's presence in their lives) is not precisely analogous to the experience of McDougall's patients but one element in it is her underlying bondage to her mother, a still infant-like dependence which inhibits her resumption of the social world on her own terms and makes her react with hostility to all Elinor's urgings, however tactfully delivered, that she should. If Marianne is, in fact, incapable of taking care of herself, an element in this is her attachment to her mother, whose sympathetic inner presence, besides validating the opinions through which Marianne consciously defends her behaviour, offers her always an unconscious motive or indemnity.

Thus when Marianne receives Willoughby's letter, Elinor

urges her to keep her distress from being noticed 'For my mother's sake and mine', and Marianne replies 'I would do more than for my own'. The upshot though is that Marianne declares 'Elinor, I must go home. I must go and comfort mama. Cannot we be gone tomorrow?' (190) regarding, it seems, her own misery and her mother's as one, and with the imperiousness of infant demands, completely forgetting her own obligations. (In this light one can see what the novel's rather stilted comedy about spoiled children and their doting parents may be intended to illuminate.) A key element in Marianne's decline is her estrangement from her mother, her pining for that 'only possible alleviation of her wretchedness', her mother's sympathy, as she calls it in the passage I have already quoted. For, repudiated by Willoughby, Marianne also feels herself (less cruelly, of course) rejected by Fanny Dashwood, who writes to urge the sisters to remain in London. Marianne's scorn of the society which she will thus be forced to keep is easily interpreted, in this passage which brings her reactions clearly into focus, as a displacement of the rage she evidently feels at her mother's rejection. Thus, in general, Marianne's disassociation from society, her refusal to draw any comfort from the people, including Elinor, with whom she is surrounded, can be seen not only as an intelligent person's accurate assessment of that society's nullity (as it is interpreted by readers and critics sympathetic to Marianne's romantic position) but as linked to her overdependence on her mother, an overdependence in which her love of, or infatuation with, Willoughby is inextricably intertwined. Marianne's longing for the 'air, the liberty, the quiet of the country', which her prolonged imprisonment in London leads her to over-indulge, contributes materially to that illness where, in her delirium, she calls out repeatedly for her 'mama' (311). Marianne's deepest need, and still deepest love, it is hence suggested, is for her mother, not for Willoughby as he fondly and vainly imagines[6] (though the fear of 'London' she expresses is certainly an indirect manifestation of his still existing power).

Identified then with Mrs Dashwood, who is quite obviously fonder of her younger daughter than of Elinor, and who certainly speaks her language, Marianne is the bearer of romantic theories of the self, a believer in intuition, in the innate moral sense, in the natural goodness of the human soul. More importantly, her ideology is bound to her bodily intensity. Her ideas, her convictions about poetry and music, her scorn of mere politeness and diplomacy, her disregard of conventions, are presented as not just ideas or beliefs but as physiologically conditioned or even determined. The 1797 edition of the *Encyclopaedia Britannica* defined 'sensibility' as 'a nice and delicate perception of pleasure or pain, beauty or deformity. It is very nearly allied to taste; and as far as it is natural seems to depend upon the organisation of the nervous system'.[7] Sensibility as presented in Marianne is both an ideology and a physical condition. Her belief in intuition, her trust in feeling rather than in rational appraisal, her love of the wild and romantic: these ideas are underwritten, as one might say, by her bodily nature. Isabella Thorpe, in Jane Austen's other early novel, *Northanger Abbey*, speaks with the accents of sensibility too, but hers is merely an affectation, an insincere jargon ventriloquised to establish herself as delightfully feminine. Marianne's sensibility is, by contrast, authentic, sincere and unconventional, not so much a matter of language, or opinion, as of eager, impulsive actions.[8] Her physical warmth and ardour, her health, spiritedness and quickness to respond are demonstrated in the first scene where she goes rambling on the hills at the back of the cottage, rejoicing in the wind that blows in her face. Sensibility is both a system of values and an innate property of the self, and it is the interplay between the ideology and her nature that this novel has seized upon (and ultimately, perhaps, is seized by). *Sense and Sensibility* is not simply a debate between contrasting systems of value: by tying Marianne's ideas so deftly to her bodily vitality, it introduces a whole complicating dimension, weaving together discourse and physiology, nature, nurture and nerves.

An important thread of the novel is concerned with contracts and covenants. Sense and reason require that documents verify the transactions of feeling by introducing them into the public world. The set-piece dialogue in the novel's second chapter between the sisters' half-brother and his wife over his father's dying commission prefaces the novel's main narrative to bring this thematic into view. On his death-bed Mr Dashwood has made John promise to take care of, to 'assist', his mother and half-sisters. Since there is no will, under the law, John, as the son, inherits all the estate. At first he intends to carry out the spirit of his father's request by giving the women each a thousand pounds (which he can, of course, well afford). But this understanding between the two men, forged in the heat of an intense emotion (we presume) is shown to be vulnerable to later denial and forgetting. It's this failure of authorisation that enables Mrs John Dashwood to pervert the meaning of her husband's promise to, or his understanding with, his father and, by playing on his loyalty to her and his natural tight-fistedness, to persuade him step by step, that his word means in the end only that he should find a house for his mother and sisters and make them an occasional present of game. That which belongs only in the realm of feeling, so it seems to be implied, can be undone by feeling, and Mrs John Dashwood moulds her husband's passions till she makes *his* will. Without formal authorisation, without a document, or a contract, feelings are undependable, will be open to siege, to attrition by other feelings, displaceable by other passions, like greed. The law of the father, which enforces contracts, which erects feelings into prescriptions, provides security against the encroachment of dangerous feeling, or on the other hand, the coldness of heart which can forget its promises. The dialogue is about the importance of warmth of heart, but it is equally about the supplementary importance of contracts.

There are lovers' contracts, too, but these are labile, misleading, inhabiting a space somewhere between the legal and the sentimental worlds. Willoughby begs a lock of Marianne's hair: Elinor, contrary to her own precautions against reading too much into appearances, reads into the plait of hair Edward Ferrars wears in his ring the assurance that he has purloined it from her, and thus, harbouring the conviction that he must then love her, is deeply mortified, at the climax of volume I, when it proves to be Lucy Steele's. There is something peculiarly intimate about this consignment of a bodily property into the lover's possession, but since these tokens are invested with the meanings of sexual promise only by lovers, they can be disinvested when the lover's passion no longer creates significance in the now inert, inanimate object. By wearing the ring Edward Ferrars seems to make a public, if covert, acknowledgement of that engagement to which he is honourably 'fettered'. He seeks to use it as an amulet or charm to protect himself from forming any other attachment, for as he declares to Elinor, 'the consciousness of my engagement was to keep my heart as safe and sacred as my honour' (368), but besides failing to guard Edward's heart, the talisman has little meaning for Lucy herself, who carelessly allows him to keep the ring when she is married to his brother. On the other hand, the return of such tokens, when not called for, has an especially wounding effect, for it is as if some part of the lover's self were being repudiated, as is the effect of Willoughby's summary return of that lock of hair for which he had once beseeched Marianne. Objects then, do not serve to fix and objectify passion: open declarations and legal covenants are more wise.

In an argument which Elinor has with her mother the polarities on which so much of this novel turns are firmly set up:

'I want no proof of their affection,' said Elinor; 'but of their engagement I do.'
'I am perfectly satisfied of both.'
'Yet not a syllable has been said to you on the subject, by either of them.'
'I have not wanted syllables where actions have spoken so plainly. Has not his behaviour to Marianne and to all of us, for at least the last fortnight, declared that he loved and considered her as his future wife, and that he felt for us the attachment of the nearest relation? Have we not perfectly understood each other? Has not my consent been daily asked by his looks, his manner, his attentive and affectionate respect?' (79–80)

In the event, of course, Elinor, though persuaded by her mother in this conversation that her suspicions are ungenerous, is proved right. Marianne and her mother need no such formally spoken words – they rest their faith on intuitive understanding. Looks and gestures are, for them, guarantees, and body language constitutes a direct avenue to the unlying 'heart' of another. Elinor, on the other hand, requires spoken language: she requires, at least for others, that feelings be brought into the symbolic system, be articulated into contracts. One view privileges language, written or spoken, the other the knowledge of the heart, the intuitive, instinctive rapport between two people whose hearts respond alike. Mrs Dashwood and Marianne's persuasion – shown as the result of their temperaments – is unregenerate. When Willoughby's true character is revealed Mrs Dashwood declares to Elinor that 'there was always, a something – if you remember – in Willoughby's eyes at times, which I did not like' (338). Mrs Dashwood has revised her opinion of Willoughby, but what is comically noticed here is the unrevisability of her conviction that the moral character must inevitably be revealed in the face.

Like much else in the novel this remark underlines the treacherousness of subjective impressions as guides. But in its central drama, the story of Marianne Dashwood and John Willoughby's love, something much more sophisticated and ambitious is embarked upon. John Burrows' analysis of Marianne's idiolect goes to show that she is, as he writes, 'not so much a character as a succession of loosely-fitting roles – the enthusiast, the victim, the regenerate'.[9] This is a verdict based upon the rigorous statistical analysis of Marianne's speeches, but Marianne is a figure notably exhibited also in the mode of the physical, in the language of gesture and bodily display. If Marianne has something of a continuous life in the narrative this is because it is transmitted through her bodily reactions – they may vary, of course, with the vicissitudes of her romance, but their intensity and latitude remains consistent throughout. Marianne's inner life is communicated in instantly readable physical signs: when she is well and happy, walking against the wind, 'resisting it with laughing delight' (41), rapture 'beams' in her 'sparkling' eyes, when she is miserable, her despair is shown in white face and lips, and played out ultimately in sleeplessness, agitation, loss of weight and bloom. Unable to account for Willoughby's absence and non-communication in London, she is 'wholly dispirited, careless of her appearance' (175).

At the party, she sits 'in an agony of impatience, which affected every feature'. When she catches sight of Willoughby 'her whole countenance glowing with sudden delight, she would have moved towards him instantly, had not her sister caught hold of her' (176), but when he, forced into shaking hands, treats her coldly, she reacts with the characteristic bodily intensity which abolishes awareness of others, recklessly displaying herself as a woman, rather than conducting herself as a lady. 'Marianne, now looking dreadfully white, and unable to stand, sunk into her chair, and Elinor, expecting every moment to see her faint, tried to screen her from the observation of others, while reviving her with lavendar water' (177). Later, ardently moved to sympathy for her sister, she publicly shifts her chair, puts one arm around Elinor's neck, and bursts into tears (236). Even when Marianne is 'regenerate', and is trying to be discreet, she listens to Mrs Jennings' praise of Lucy Steele 'with only moving from one chair to another, and when Mrs Jennings talked of Edward's affection, it cost her only a spasm in her throat' (265). When Elinor tells her at last the truth about Willoughby's love 'She trembled, her eyes were fixed on the ground, and her lips became whiter than even sickness had left them. A thousand inquiries sprung up from her heart, but she dared not urge one. She caught every syllable with panting eagerness; her hand, unknowingly to herself, closely pressed her sister's, and tears covered her cheeks' (347–8). There may be an element of convention in Austen's rendering of this excited and susceptible personality; plainly though it is not possible to take up any simple attitude of censure to what is displayed with such vivid physical presence and sympathetic freedom of gesture.

If the central narrative interest of the book is Marianne's romance with Willoughby, it is counterpointed by the carefully guarded, secret and painful story of Elinor's love for Edward Ferrars. Marianne expresses feeling, in the full sense of the verb: it is freely displayed, but Elinor's feelings are kept within, revealed to the reader only through free indirect speech or 'character narrative'. 'Careless of her appearance', Marianne's misery is enacted outwardly, and Elinor is horrified that she gives herself away by the transparency of her face and gestures.

'Pray, pray, be composed', Elinor urges her sister at the London party, 'and do not betray what you feel to every body present' (176). Elinor, on the other hand, seeks to keep up appearances. Especially when sparring with Lucy Steele, she carefully guards her countenance, so that while Lucy's 'little sharp eyes' (146) signal the pettiness of her scheming nature, Elinor presents a seemingly unconcerned and bland surface, and thus defeats her would-be tormentor. She speaks to Lucy 'with a composure of voice, under which was concealed an emotion and distress beyond any thing she had ever felt before' (135), she smiles, too, so as to conceal 'very agitated feelings' (150) and this address – like her address in pleasing Lady Middleton – is implicitly commended. 'Are you ill, Miss Dashwood? – you seem low – you don't speak; – sure you an't well' Lucy attacks her (239), and the dialogue leaves unregistered the turbulent feelings, the anger and contempt that Lucy's flattery of Mrs Ferrars may be presumed to have aroused in her victim, and which Elinor deals with only by preserving silence. 'I *will* be calm. I *will* be mistress of myself', she declares at a moment of crisis (358). Her struggles are always to preserve the appearance of ordinary good spirits and decorous behaviour: if she is, as Tony Tanner memorably described it, concerned with erecting screens,[10] her effort is essentially a discipline of physiological control, exerted over her own face and body. 'Elinor perfectly understood her, and was forced to use all her self-command to make it appear she did *not*.' (217–18) Sometimes the contrasting physical demeanours of the two sisters are illuminatingly juxtaposed. Marianne at last receives a letter

which she eagerly caught from the servant, and, turning of a death-like paleness, instantly ran out of the room. Elinor, who saw as plainly by this, as if she had seen the direction, that it must come from Willoughby, felt immediately such a sickness at heart as made her hardly able to hold up her head, and sat in such a general tremour as made her fear it impossible to escape Mrs Jennings's notice. That good lady, however, saw only that Marianne had received a letter from Willoughby ... (181)

The physiological cost of Elinor's self-command is here vividly made plain. Too often her success in mastering her emotions and presenting an untroubled appearance to her mother and sisters is simply commended, as if the end result of her struggles (and its monitory contrast with Marianne) were what counted for the narrative, and the process through which it is achieved left uninvestigated.

The novel does begin by emphasising not Marianne's bodily vitality but her naive and romantic prejudices or opinions – about Edward Ferrars' reading, about picturesque scenes, about first attachments – and through this introduction to the figure, invites a reading of Marianne's physical expressiveness as a code of manners, a cultural product, and for it (and its pathological propensity) to be tied to the cult of 'sensibility': sensibility is understood to license such expansiveness of emotion, such ardour and warmth, as the 'natural' expression of a virtuous heart. Yet at the same time, and as the figure becomes dramatically involved, the novel asks for Marianne's physical volatility to be read as a natural endowment, a given of her physical nature, which may indeed be supported by a currently fashionable code, but which is intrinsically hers, as an efflorescence of her youth, her ardour, her impulsiveness. The text vacillates between those modalities of viewing the figure, and the very word 'sensibility' is the focus of this indeterminacy. When Willoughby leaves Barton after the first stage of their romance, Marianne spends a sleepless night, and the narrator comments that 'She would have been ashamed to look her family in the face the next morning, had she not risen from her bed in more need of repose than when she lay down in it. But the feelings which made such composure a disgrace, left her in no danger of incurring it' (83). The hostile wit seems to twist itself round to an acknowledgement that Marianne does have genuinely intense feelings – a contortion of narrative stance that is exemplified too in the contemptuous exclamation that closes the paragraph: 'Her sensibility was potent enough!' Whether this means that 'sensibility' is a physiological or a cultural product is unclear: the narrator wants to claim it is the latter, her material forces her into an unwilling admission that it must be the first. Constantly then Marianne's feelings are censured by such words as 'indulged', 'excessive' (as if the spirit were an economy, and measuring of outgoings were dictated by external forces). A 'moral' reading (one which conceives of the self as to some degree a self-determining or limiting ethical agent) runs concurrently with a broader appreciation of the exigencies of physiological or constitutional necessity. The ironic remarks that sometimes attach to manifestations of the character's bodily proclivities (such as the moment just quoted when putting up with Mrs Jennings' cant sticks in Marianne's throat) are peculiarly jarring for this reason.

The Elinor-view of the personal life is contradicted by the reader's attention being drawn to the dynamics of another mode of being. The presentation of the actual history of Marianne's engagement and subsequent illness also tends to subvert the moral commentary that is, sometimes insistently, appended to it, and voiced in Marianne's own declarations of repentance after her recovery. But to consider this fully one needs to recall the intertextual nature of so much of this first of Jane Austen's novels to be published. Uneasy and fretful in London, even before the meeting with Willoughby, Marianne's decline from the early beauty which made her brother so sure she would fetch a good price in the marriage market is difficult to date precisely, but certainly the crucial moment in her history is the cruel letter Willoughby sends in response to her notes, in which he denies any interest in her, says that she herself has mistaken his behaviour, and returns to her the lock of hair 'which you so obligingly bestowed upon me' (183). This letter, though so momentous for Marianne's fate, was not, it turns out, actually composed by Willoughby.

Forged, or at any rate deliberately misleading, letters are important in the novel's prehistory. Robert Lovelace, the hero-villain of Richardson's *Clarissa* (1747–8), notoriously forged a letter of Anna Howe, in order to further his designs on her friend Clarissa. Clarissa, almost as notoriously, sent Lovelace a misleading allegorical letter saying she was going to her father's house, and thereby frustrated his scheme to visit her after the rape. In Fanny Burney's *Evelina* (1778), the rake, Sir Clement Willoughby, one of the many literary descendants of Lovelace, forges a letter to Evelina that forms a crucial turning point in her history just as the letter of John Willoughby (whose surname makes clear just whose son he is) does in Marianne's. An ingenuous young lady of Marianne's age, Evelina is introduced into London society, where she is 'admired' by the handsome and patriarchal, though young, Lord Orville, and in turn shyly, unconsciously, admires him. Their relationship progresses until she receives a letter from him in reply to one of her own (a letter Sir Clement has intercepted) which takes hers to be a declaration of love for him, and suggests a secret meeting. At first Evelina is gratified to find her desire mirrored; after only a moment, though, she is shocked to perceive that it presents her as a desiring subject, and thus that it compromises her value as a marriageable young woman. It is 'improper' and 'impertinent'. 'I cannot find one sentence that I could look at without blushing', she declares. Disappointment and disillusionment with the character of Lord Orville, (as well as, one suspects, the revelation of her own desires at the moment of their being thwarted) lead her to illness. 'Every body I see takes notice of my being altered, and looking pale and ill', she writes.[11] Like Marianne, Evelina is shocked by the overthrow of the emotional foundations of her world: in her case, the idol of gentlemanly refinement seems to have been revealed as having feet of clay. She plunges into a decline. 'Your affliction seems only to augment – your health declines – your look alters', laments her guardian Mr Villars. She becomes 'very ill', and is sent to recover her health – and appearance – at Bristol Hotwells.

Marianne's history, of course, follows a similar course. Like Clement Willoughby's forgery, John Willoughby's letter insults its recipient by attributing amorous overtures to her: like his, it is aimed at destroying her fantasised longings. Marianne never recovers from the shock of this shaming and brutal repudiation. But the ambiguous status of the letter in Jane Austen's novel is crucial, and much is made to depend upon this. It is not forged, but, equally, it is not written by Willoughby: and this indeterminacy serves to generate Marianne's subsequent decline as well as to augment and interlace the novel's central propositions. For Marianne is made 'nervously' ill not solely by disappointed love, she is made ill by a disturbance given to the moral foundations of her world, by a denial of what, through the senses, she is sure she 'knows'. As she reads the letter over, Marianne, characterised as 'shuddering over every sentence', exclaims 'Willoughby, where was your heart, when you wrote those words?' (190). Marianne repeatedly expresses her conviction that the letter could not have been written by Willoughby – not written by the Willoughby she knows. 'He *did* feel the same, Elinor – for weeks and weeks he felt it. I know he did. Whatever may have changed him now, (and nothing but the blackest art employed against me can have done it,) I was once as dear to him as my own soul could wish. This lock of hair, which now he can so readily give up, was begged of me with the most earnest supplication. Had you seen his look, his manner, had you heard his voice at that moment!' (188–9). For Marianne is certain that she cannot be mistaken in these indications of Willoughby's heart, that there is an unfalsifiable bond between bodily signs and emotional commitment. She insists that someone other than Willoughby is responsible for the letter. 'Is there a creature in the world whom I would not rather suspect of evil than Willoughby, whose heart I know so well?' Even Elinor is startled by the contrast between the person revealed by the letter and the Willoughby she has known, as she reflects on its 'hardened villany' and 'on the depravity of that mind which could dictate it' (184). (In the verb, of course, the future author of *Emma* has planted her clue.) Marianne can only account for it through the desperate idea that 'blackest art' has been used against her. Yet the letter is written in Willoughby's hand, signed by Willoughby, and breaks off their relationship with all the finality of a formal document.

This follows the famous and painful scene in which Marianne, overwhelmed with grief, 'almost screamed with agony'. Elinor in these moments shares her sensibility. Moved by the sympathy for her sister which has marked her behaviour in the whole of this episode, she 'took her hand, kissed her affectionately several times, and then gave way to a burst of tears' and it is Marianne who, Elinor-like, restrains herself, 'covering her face with her handkerchief' (182) so as to repress her screams of agony. Now, though, the novel's narrative method – viewing events through

Elinor's eyes – shows its limitations. Marianne's misery is represented only in a series of stereotypical moments depicting the profile of the female hysteric. 'No attitude could give her ease; and in restless pain of mind and body she moved from one posture to another, till growing more and more hysterical, her sister could with difficulty keep her on the bed at all, and for some time was fearful of being constrained to call for assistance' (191). Soon she is found repeatedly in the characteristic posture of the melancholic, 'leaning, in silent misery, over the small remains of a fire' (197).[12] Thus is enacted the conventional trajectory which asserts that votaries of sensibility should be brought, by their excesses, to a state of benumbed insensibility.[13]

This restlessness, this 'most nervous irritability' (180), this wearing away of the emotions in constant attrition, is to be the keynote of Marianne's forthcoming decline, a decline brought about not simply by disappointment, but by a profoundly disturbing violation of her deepest intuitions.[14] What can it be about the letter which gives plausible grounds for this healthy girl's collapse into 'nervous' illness? She 'knows' that Willoughby did not write the letter, and yet he did. She cannot accept that her relationship with Willoughby is over, that, for her, he is dead, because she trusts in her feelings, and that knowledge is in some way that the novelist does not investigate, final, absolute. 'I know him' (or 'her') when said with this intensity, is a statement in which the subject is so implicated in the object that the destiny, perhaps even the life, of one is involved in the destiny of the other. 'My life upon her faith!' Othello exclaims in response to Brabantio's challenge, and the tragedy that results comes precisely from 'blackest art' intervening to destroy just such a relationship of mutual assurance. Willoughby's letter is not pathogenic merely because it breaks off an engagement and declares that Willoughby is engaged elsewhere. It is pathogenic because it seems to repudiate the whole basis of Marianne's world – that knowledge of others is gained indisputably by the body, that the body is the agency of indisputable knowledge of the heart – and it therefore strikes a blow, not only at the beliefs of the person, but, as the logic of the novel insists, at that body which receives it. Marianne's body now becomes, to use Tony Tanner's phrase,[15] the 'expressive vehicle' of her conflicted feelings and disappointed hopes. What makes her ill – to underline the point – is not that her ideas or beliefs about Willoughby are proved to be mistaken, as that however she may intellectually accept the facts, she is the victim of intolerable psychological conflict. As Elinor unsympathetically notices, Marianne's longing to believe in Willoughby 'irritates her mind more than the most perfect conviction of his unworthiness can do' (211). Her mind is soon to be 'settled', by the recital of Willoughby's criminal treatment of Eliza Williams, but she settles, or sinks, into a state of melancholia, a withdrawal which is quickly perceived by her step-brother to damage her prospects:

At her time of life, any thing of an illness destroys the bloom for ever! Her's has been a very short one! She was as handsome a girl last September, as any I ever saw; and as likely to attract the men. There was something in her style of beauty, to please them particularly ... I question whether Marianne *now*, will marry a man worth more than five or six hundred a-year, at the utmost, and I am very much deceived if *you* do not do better ... (227)

The intensity of Marianne's feelings now becomes pathological, though to describe her as either 'manic' or 'mad' as two recent writers have done illustrates rather the uncertainty of terminologies in this realm of the human subject then as now, than any acuteness of critical perception. Her feelings are volatile, uncontrollable, she moves restlessly and without motive; at a slight to her sister she bursts into tears in public. Her illness, and the carelessness of herself that makes part of it, form, of course, an indirect protest at the exchange of women, the market which determines women's 'value' in the patriarchal system for which John Dashwood is here the spokesman. Arthur Kleinman writes that

Depression ... is an emotion that poses a threat to social arrangements and symbolic meanings, and not just when, as part of a serious depressive illness, it leads to suicide. Demoralization, despondency, hopelessness, withdrawal, and loss of interest in the social environment are a-social. They call basic norms and relations and institutions into question, undoing the ties of the symbolic reticulum that connects person to society.[16]

The text of the novel becomes almost silent about Marianne for many chapters, leaving her in a kind of stasis of disintegration, foregrounding instead, as if to underwrite the oppositional stance implicit in her sickness, the folly, spitefulness and sheer nullity of the world about her. Her hysteria is a kind of negative calling into question, since she plays out in her body (over which alone she has power) the distress that, despite her sister's efforts, she will not, or cannot, express in language. She is plunged into melancholia since she can neither recover nor relinquish the lost object of her knowledge. Attention is now focused on Elinor's affairs of the heart, as Lucy Steele's fortunes seem to be advancing and she insinuates herself into the Ferrars household; the narrator is still unremittingly critical of the indulgence said to mark Marianne's behaviour. When Elinor, for example, discloses her own long-kept secret and disappointment, the reader is told that

Her narration was clear and simple; and though it could not be given without emotion, it was not accompanied by violent agitation, nor impetuous grief. – *That* belonged rather to the hearer, for Marianne listened with horror, and cried excessively. Elinor was to be the comforter of others in her own distresses, no less than in theirs... (261)

'Excessively': the word may pass for neutral, and mean no more than greatly, but what slips in is the pre-eminence of the social, the application of a standard of measurement to emotion that judges Marianne's as exorbitant.

As Jocelyn Harris has shown, Marianne is metonymically linked to the figure of Clarissa Harlowe, the most famous of betrayed heroines, through the device of the two Elizas whose stories are narrated by Colonel Brandon to Elinor. The first Eliza, whom Brandon himself loved, was married off to his brother and, her youthful idealism being succeeded by worldly cynicism, eventually died, abandoned by all but the Colonel, of consumption. He himself points out her resemblance to Marianne: the implication here too, is of the danger of bodily intensity – now more explicitly of sexual intensity – of Marianne's type. Her illegitimate daughter, the second Eliza, has been seduced by Willoughby: thus both stories illustrate the fate of women at the hands of men. (They also reveal that Brandon's present 'cheerless gravity' is the consequence, like Marianne's decline, of disappointed and disillusioned love.) 'Though Jane Austen does not permit her heroine to be actually ruined by Willoughby, the way that the two Elizas are surrogates for Marianne, together with her public commitment to him, her forwardness, her secret correspondence, and her agony of distress when she is rejected, make her look very much as if she has been', as Harris writes.[17]

But it is as a contrast with *Clarissa* that Austen's treatment of Marianne's decline is most to be noted. Drugged and raped by Lovelace, Clarissa seems to resolve to die, and spends the subsequent weeks preparing for her death. She makes Belford her executor, sells her sumptuous dresses to buy a coffin, has the coffin brought to the house, and, growing weaker by the day, uses it to lean upon whilst she writes her last will and testament, as well as the ten or so letters to be delivered to her relatives and friends after her death. What Clarissa actually dies of is not important: she is simply 'ill', and the blurring word is repeatedly used to indicate that it is the movement away from the encumbering body, ('I shall be happy', she writes to Anna Howe, 'Yet how this *body* clings! How it encumbers!'[18]) and not the body's own processes of degeneration which is the focus. It is hence impossible to be certain from what Clarissa actually dies. Margaret Anne Doody suggests 'galloping consumption'[19] and there is one hint of that, but Richardson is simply unconcerned to articulate the processes through which the body is brought to the state of pure spirit. Like James, in *The Wings of the Dove*, as Doody suggests, he 'takes it for granted that a mortal illness can be a datum for which specific causes and medical details need not be supplied'.[20] If we are to pick up the crumbs of information about her symptoms he almost inadvertently drops we must conclude, though, that not consumption (for there is no mention of coughing) but gradual starvation is the road that leads Clarissa to her death. Like the saints of the early

Church, Clarissa Harlowe achieves her immortality, recovers her status within the family, and takes her revenge upon men, by a form of holy anorexia.[21]

Marianne Dashwood's illness career, on the other hand, is given with specific medical detail. Hers is not the generalised sickness of exacerbated sensibility, a simple extrapolation from the moralist's conviction of its 'dangers' to its physiological apotheosis, and Marianne does not fall simply victim to her feelings, as if feeling alone, indulged, intensified, and engorged, could bring about destruction. The theme or idea 'excessive sensibility is dangerous, and may be mortally dangerous' is certainly inscribed in the plot here: but the novel rethinks the convention of the young heroine as a victim, both of male vice and of her own femaleness, in a number of ways. Marianne is not a 'victim of her feelings' in the straightforward way her analogues are, and nor is she the martyr of the broken heart that Clarissa, the great exemplar, is. The decline and sickness of the heroine from wounded sensibility is entailed upon Austen by her predecessors: by Johnson's persuasion of the awful destructiveness latent in passions once indulged; by Richardson's grand portrayal of the wasting away of his disillusioned and betrayed heroine; and by the death from excessive sensibility predicted and illustrated in the novels of her (mainly female) contemporaries.[22] But, given this overriding pattern (which is, after all, what makes Marianne's mistakes culminate in sickness, in a death-bed tableau) Austen's working of the inner details is quite different.

Marianne's sickness is articulated as a sequence of quite specific, and physiologically plausible reactions. Firstly, Marianne's distress and 'nervous illness' under Willoughby's rejection (with its torturing complication), secondly, her wilful wandering about the grounds of Cleveland in the long wet grass (an activity 'of precious, of invaluable misery' analogically linked to her earlier indiscretions), thirdly the infection which is the result, not of one of these preceding conditions, but of both of them combined. The sequence is as coherent today as when it was written: and it is followed by a very exact record, or diary of the illness from day one, when Marianne sits about listlessly, or shivers over the fire (307), through the crisis (310–14) to day eight (314) when she begins to recover. William Buchan, whose *Domestic Medicine* was probably the most widely used handbook of the period, divided fevers into continual, remitting and intermitting, and Marianne's is evidently presented as the 'remitting' type.[23] 'This fever takes its name from a remission of the symptoms, which happens sometimes sooner, and sometimes later, but generally before the eighth day', Buchan advises.[24] 'A day spent in sitting shivering over the fire' then a 'very restless and feverish night' is followed by several days in bed, but Marianne is 'materially better' on the morning of the third day after Mr Palmer's departure, about a week after the onset of illness (310). 'But in a few hours the fever returns', as Buchan predicted. 'Towards the evening, Marianne became ill again' and her remission only precedes delirium and crisis. Marianne is not suffering here a 'hysterical' or 'nervous' illness, but one authenticated by contemporary physicians and her author's insistence on the clinical detail is a means of suggesting (not altogether successfully, since it occupies attention of itself too much) that ideas or convictions alone cannot bring about serious physical illness, not even an ideology so powerfully lived as sensibility. The illness is overdetermined – prolonged unhappiness, including estrangement from her mother, sleeplessness and weight loss, has made Marianne vulnerable, and negligence of various kinds has done the rest. Austen does not accept the ideological premise that excessive sensibility, acting through the body's heightened vulnerability, can of itself bring about destruction. Yet at the same time, Elinor's ideal of the body being brought under the control of the will is here forced to its greatest contradiction and challenge.

The disease takes its own course: but concurrently the novel makes play with the different emotional reactions, the vacillating hopes and fears and coping strategies which surround the inexorable bodily phenomenon. Buchan emphasises the importance of early medical attention. 'There is reason to believe, if the efforts of nature, at the beginning of a fever, were duly attended to and promoted, it would seldom continue longer than twenty-four hours; but when her attempts are either neglected, or counteracted, it is no wonder if the disease be prolonged.'[25] Elinor, through her commonsense and optimism, her minimalisation of the physical, plays down the significance of the early signs of Marianne's disease; Marianne, careless of her own body, tries to pretend she is well, and thus the illness is neglected in its first few days. The apothecary is sanguine when he is eventually called to examine Marianne, but 'by pronouncing her disorder to have a putrid tendency, and allowing the word "infection" to pass his lips, gave instant alarm to Mrs Palmer on her baby's account' (307).[26] Drawing on the work of the military doctor Sir John Pringle, who, incidentally, noted the importance of damp ground in causing 'putrid' fevers,[27] Buchan emphasised the significance of 'infection' in diseases, and declared that 'Every person ought therefore, as far as he can, to avoid all communication with the diseased. The common practice of visiting the sick, though often well meant, has many ill consequences.'[28] So Mrs Palmer, and babe, and eventually Mr Palmer too, decamp, and Colonel Brandon, though remaining in the house does not, of course, visit the patient. He, who has been earlier 'astonished at Elinor's composure' now tries to argue himself out of fears 'which the different judgement of the apothecary seemed to render absurd' (309). What is demonstrated is how different temperaments and degrees of affection for Marianne determine a whole spectrum of imaginative responses to her condition.

The second crucial revisioning is that Marianne's is not a death-bed scene at all. The novel alludes to the conventional sick-bed of sensibility in the dialogue in which Marianne complains of Colonel Brandon's rheumatism and flannel waistcoats. 'Had he been only in a violent fever, you would not have despised him half so much', Elinor rather tartly, as is her style, replies. 'Confess, Marianne, is not there something interesting to you in the flushed cheek, hollow eye, and quick pulse of a fever?' (38) This is illness as metaphor, consumption as the badge of superior spiritual elevation. The naming of Marianne's illness as 'putrid fever' rules out such symbolic auras. Elinor later regrets her misjudgement in minimising the symptoms, but her fears at the bedside are exorbitant when compared with the apothecary, Mr Harris, who preserves his confidence that Marianne will recover, with only one slight moment of hesitation, throughout the course of the illness, and she does recover. Marianne's fever does come to a crisis in the frightening period of delirium when she asks for her mother, but attention is given here to the fears of Elinor as she visualises the impact of Marianne's death upon their mother. The word that is so consistently appended to Marianne's feelings is now transferred to Elinor, whose 'apprehensions once raised, paid by their excess for all her former security' (312); within the calculus of emotions it is as bad apparently to be too sanguine as it is to be too imaginative, and Elinor is now besieged by the fears she had earlier excluded. But Marianne's death exists only in the imaginations of others, for as Claudia Johnson has shown,[29] both Willoughby and Mrs Jennings take some satisfaction in the fantasy of the young girl dying of a broken heart.

Yet within these parameters of realism, and in describing a plausible and authentic manifestation of the illness, Austen finds a point of entry into a realm which, in approximating to the unconscious, is analogous to the Gothic:

Marianne, suddenly awakened by some accidental noise in the house, started hastily up, and with feverish wildness, cried out -
'Is mama coming?-'
'Not yet', replied the other, concealing her terror, and assisting Marianne to lie down again, 'but she will be here, I hope, before it is long. It is a great way, you know, from hence to Barton.'
'But she must not go round by London,' cried Marianne, in the same hurried manner, 'I shall never see her, if she goes by London.'
(310–11)

Marianne continues to talk 'wildly of mama'. Cleveland is in Somerset, a few miles from Bristol, Barton is in Devon, and the sisters are *en route* to their mother. Since it took them two and a half days to get to Cleveland from London, and Barton is eighty miles further on, to imagine that her mother might go 'by London' to come to them is a fantastic aberration of a disordered and fevered mind which suggests that her mother will have to retrace the route she herself has taken. It is in

London, though, that Marianne has experienced that shock which has led to her present misery, there that she has felt totally alienated from the social world. 'London', the scene of disconfirming experience, becomes a symbolic site. Her unconscious (one might claim) unlocked by fever, Marianne now reveals another manifestation of her identification with the mother, for in its logic, if Mrs Dashwood is to 'go by London' as her daughter did, she too will be vanquished by Willoughby, by that repudiation which is here felt to be the origin of Marianne's present despair.

Marianne's decline and illness thus derive from and allude to the topos of young heroine dying of sensibility and a broken heart but at the same time as its broad schema is a traditional one, Austen consistently reworks its inner details so as to transform the result. Marianne's recovery leads, as another convention dictates, to self-reappraisal and conversion. But here too, within the general form of convention, a quite radical redrawing is going on: Austen's conception of Marianne is firm enough to mark the consistency of her nature at the very moment when she testifies to her past mistakes. 'We always know when we are acting wrong', she had pronounced in a Shaftesburian moment early in the novel, but now she elaborates on this as a truth which explains her sickness. As I have argued, the 'moral' reading of this text (one which conceives of the self as to some degree a self-determining or limiting ethical agent) runs concurrently with a broader appreciation of the exigencies of physiological and psychopathological necessity. Marianne's regenerate speech on recovering from her serious illness seems to make just this kind of sense out of sensibility:

'Do not, my dearest Elinor, let your kindness defend what I know your judgment must censure. My illness has made me think – It has given me leisure and calmness for serious recollection. Long before I was enough recovered to talk, I was perfectly able to reflect. I considered the past; I saw in my own behaviour since the beginning of our acquaintance with him last autumn, nothing but a series of imprudence towards myself, and want of kindness towards others. I saw that my own feelings had prepared my sufferings, and that my want of fortitude under them had almost led me to the grave. My illness, I well knew, had been entirely brought on by myself, by such negligence of my own health, as I had felt even at the time to be wrong. Had I died, – it would have been self-destruction ... ' (345)

Elinor has been pleased to see that Marianne's mind has been 'awakened to reasonable exertion' (342): she must surely be delighted to see Marianne reflecting back to her what has been her own reading of the case. In fact, the emphatic, balanced, deliberate cadences suggest a kind of ventriloquism: Marianne is now using Elinor's terms and speaking with Elinor's voice. Yet this announcement of her conversion to the 'moral' view of her history, in its intensity, or exaggeration ('my illness, I well knew, had been entirely brought on by myself') reveals that Marianne is Marianne still:

'Had I died, – it would have been self-destruction. I did not know my danger till the danger was removed; but with such feelings as these reflections gave me, I wonder at my recovery, – wonder that the very eagerness of my desire to live, to have time for atonement to my God, and to you all, did not kill me at once ... ' (345–6)

Thus at the moment when Marianne is confessing her misconduct, she is also expressing the very intensity of her nature – the very eagerness of her desire to live – which makes her reform a new enactment of her embodied self, not the assumption of an Elinor-like sobriety.

The secret problematic at the novel's heart, that Willoughby did not write the letter he wrote, that Marianne's intuition is correct, that the face and body do give proofs of affection, undoes (and deliberately undoes – this is not a deconstructive reading) the sovereignty of sense. In the novel's most remarkable scene, Willoughby arrives at night, thinking Marianne is on her death-bed, and reveals to Elinor the true circumstances of the damning letter's composition. To pen the letter, at his wife's dictation, he says, cost him almost as much pain as it did for her to receive it. Her agonies in London, when he refuses to acknowledge her attentions, we now gather, were matched by his:

'With my head and heart full of your sister, I was forced to play the happy lover to another woman! – Those three or four weeks were worse than all. Well, at last, as I need not tell you, you were forced on me; and what a sweet figure I cut! – what an evening of agony it was! – Marianne, beautiful as an angel on one side, calling me Willoughby in such a tone! – Oh ! God! – holding out her hand to me, asking me for an explanation with those bewitching eyes fixed in such speaking solicitude on my face!' (327)

And he tells her that the letter which has brought about Marianne's miseries was not in fact composed by him. 'Willoughby, where was your heart, when you wrote those words?' Marianne had cried (190). Now she is vindicated: he inscribed the words, true, but 'my heart was never inconstant to her ... at this moment she is dearer to me than ever' (330).

By this device, the novel vindicates Marianne's trust in Willoughby, and underwrites that part of her romantic ideology which insists there is a language of the body which cannot lie. More significantly, in a touch which has occasioned some raised eyebrows, the narrator shows Elinor as susceptible to his attractions as her sister. With his eagerness, warmth and energy, the decisiveness and vehemence of his manner and language, he succeeds in winning Elinor over despite her initial hostility and despite the flimsiness of some of his excuses. She is compelled by the powerful charm of his presence to acknowledge to herself that 'reason' somehow does not seem to have quite the force she has been used to attribute to it. This is precisely analogous to the reader's response to Marianne as compared with Elinor's code of conduct: the bodily presence of one dramatically positioned figure tends to counteract, and for some readers to overwhelm, the undeniably cogent and eminently reasonable values of the other.

Sense and Sensibility is, as A. Walton Litz said, a novel over which hangs an air of depression.[30] Partly this must be because two of the main male figures are themselves lacking in spirits, having their own unhappy, disillusioned and secret pasts. Marianne, too, is unhappy for the central volume of the novel, so is Elinor, who has, besides, to guard her own sorrows in silence, and to withstand the barbs of the sadistically inclined rival Lucy Steele. The comic scenes and figures which intercept the novel's main narrative and diversify its mood tend to be hard-edged and unforgiving; figures like Robert Ferrars and Fanny Dashwood are conceived in too theatrical a mode to be brought effectively into relationship with the more subtle and nuanced inward dramas of the heroines. Yet it is possible to see ways in which this stylised and limited comedy does comment on issues opened more fully in the romantic part of the book, and to see that here Jane Austen is announcing preoccupations which are to be worked over more subtly in later texts.

Elinor spends much of the novel guarding or protecting her sister from pain and painful notice, in activities that, in one way or another come under the rubric of nursing, and of course she figures as a full-blown nurse in the sick-bed sequence. Her activities are paralleled and commented upon by a continual comedy of illness coping. When Lady Middleton's spoiled child is scratched by a pin from her mother's dress, she screams lustily until 'Lady Middleton luckily remembering that in a scene of similar distress last week, some apricot marmalade had been successfully applied for a bruised temple, the same remedy was eagerly proposed for this unfortunate scratch, and a slight intermission of screams in the young lady on hearing it, gave them reason to hope that it would not be rejected' (121). From here it is but a short step to the comedy of Mrs Jennings' efforts to soothe Marianne's broken heart by treating her 'with all the indulgent fondness of a parent towards a favourite child on the last day of its holidays' (193). When all else fails Mrs Jennings remembers that she has some fine old Constantia wine in the house, and she brings a glass for Marianne, saying, 'My poor husband! how fond he was of it! Whenever he had a touch of his old cholicky gout, he said it did him more good than anything else in the world. Do take it to your sister' (198). Elinor smiles at this absurdity. It is not felt to be amusing however when Elinor herself administers hartshorn and lavendar drops as well as glasses of wine to Marianne in social emergencies construed as medical ones.

Many variations on this comic motif are to be played in Jane Austen's later novels, for it reflects a persistent dilemma and challenge to appropriate response. That care of the body is often a clumsy and second-best substitute when attention to the spirit is needed is dramatised in a whole variety of occasions. That people comfort themselves as well as the recipients of their attention by attending to physical symptoms and thus denying the more disturbing problems posed by mental pain is a knowledge Jane Austen's texts seek to reconcile with appreciation of what is genuine and valuable in such communal attentiveness. Kindheartedness and moral obtuseness are so often linked. Mrs Jennings represents an early statement of the problematic: her kindness and well-wishing are not to be questioned, but with kindness comes vulgar possessiveness and with well-wishing the invasion of privacy. Marianne is irritated and exasperated by her interference but the sympathy given to the sufferer is balanced by the narrator's acknowledgement that Mrs Jennings is, after all, well-disposed, and that Marianne is intolerant in rejecting help however misguided are the forms it takes. Presented at first as a vulgar and inadequate chaperon, Mrs Jennings' good qualities are gradually uncovered by the narrative, and when she stays during Marianne's sickness and helps Elinor with round-the-clock nursing, her genuine warmheartedness and concern for the sisters is made to redeem her earlier clumsy attempts to minister to miseries she cannot understand and to form a minor but important element in the education of Elinor, who comes now to 'really love' a woman whose suitability as chaperon for such genteel young ladies as herself and her sister she had earlier and ungraciously questioned. Used in something of the same way that Shakespeare uses Emilia, Mrs Jennings is seen in the end to be the blunt enactor and advocate of values the novel seeks to put at the centre of its schema: her demonstration of genuine warmth of heart is an essential supplement to the novel's critique of that form of sensibility, which is its synthetic, fashionable, self-regarding imitation.

Mrs Jennings is the spokeswoman, too, for one of the most farcical scenes in *Sense and Sensibility*, which nevertheless also predicts a theme which is to recur in later novels. Her daughter's doctor, called to attend to a child's ailment, has smirked and simpered as he hints that 'For fear any unpleasant report should reach the young ladies under your care as to their sister's indisposition, I think it advisable to say, that I believe there is no great reason for alarm; I hope Mrs Dashwood will do very well' (258). What this means is brought out as Mrs Jennings recounts the happenings in the household when Lucy Steele's secret engagement to Edward Ferrars is inadvertently revealed by her sister. Thereupon Mrs John Dashwood, as Mrs Jennings reports to Elinor,

'fell into violent hysterics immediately, with such screams as reached your brother's ears, as he was sitting in his own dressing-room down stairs, thinking about writing a letter to his steward in the country. So up he flew directly, and a terrible scene took place, for Lucy was come to them by that time, little dreaming what was going on. Poor soul! I pity *her*. And I must say, I think she was used very hardly; for your sister scolded like any fury, and soon drove her into a fainting fit. Nancy, she fell upon her knees, and cried bitterly; and your brother, he walked about the room, and said he did not know what to do. Mrs Dashwood declared they should not stay a minute longer in the house, and your brother was forced to go down on *his* knees too, to persuade her to let them stay till they had packed up their clothes. *Then* she fell into hysterics again, and he was so frightened that he would send for Mr Donavan, and Mr Donavan found the house in all this uproar. The carriage was at the door ready to take my poor cousins away, and they were just stepping in as he came off; poor Lucy in such a condition, he says, she could hardly walk; and Nancy, she was almost as bad.' (259)

Fanny's 'illness' (her 'indisposition' requires the attendance of the apothecary and solicitous enquiries from her friends – including Elinor) is merely a manifestation of thwarted power. To complete the farce, Mr Donavan goes back to Harley-street, to be within call when Mrs Ferrars is told the news, for 'your sister was sure *she* would be in hysterics too'. Because of their social position such women can force others to attend to as a sickness what is a manifestation of snobbery and greed, and Fanny's exhibition seeks to appropriate to herself the sympathy that might be given to Lucy (a gambit Mrs Jennings refuses). This, and John Dashwood's subsequent clucking over his wife and mother-in-law's misfortunes, is a savage farce which has analogies in the comedies of Ben Jonson (especially *Volpone*) where figures driven by mercenary and power-hungry designs behave with all the plaintive self-righteousness of victims. The moral superiority with which John Dashwood and Robert Ferrars in their different ways invest inverted value-systems prompts the same comparison.[31] If illness, in Marianne's case, is intimately related to lack of social power, here one form of power itself is seen to take the guise of sickness – a pattern repeated most notably in Mrs Churchill of *Emma*. When, a few chapters later, Marianne reacts with hysterics on being given the same news of Edward's engagement, the relationship between the two manifestations is not entirely lucid: Marianne is not manipulative, and yet the symptom seems to reflect a dislike of extravagant shows of emotion on the author's part that seeks to discredit all such appearances as factitious. Fanny is to suffer 'agonies of sensibility' (371) at Robert's marriage to Lucy Steele: and once again the term, here used with brusque contempt, confuses the judgement that is sought upon Marianne's own 'agonies'.

But the most searching and difficult question, or series of questions, the novel poses concerns the relation of the body to moral worth. In practice, and as dramatised, people continually make equations between the body and the moral character, between vigour and comeliness and worth. At the comic end of this spectrum is Sir John Middleton's amazed reaction to the news of Willoughby's deceit. 'Such a good-natured fellow! He did not believe there was a bolder rider in England!' (214). At the other is Elinor's remarkable response to Willoughby himself which I have mentioned. 'His influence over her mind', she feels, 'was heightened by circumstances which ought not in reason to have weight; by that person of uncommon attraction, that open, affectionate, and lively manner which it was no merit to possess' (333). Jane Austen is to repeat this latter formula, as if to guard herself against an error she yet unconsciously and inadvertently represents as truth, which she shows her characters operating upon, and which she is herself continually drawn by. If the rational thought 'To be beautiful is not necessarily to be good' seems irrefutable, what of the closely allied idea 'attractiveness and vitality have no relationship to goodness'?

If presence might be a factor in the assessment of the moral life this proposition *Sense and Sensibility* seeks to dramatise most openly in the scene of Willoughby's interview with Elinor. The figure's freedom of expressive movement and boldness of speech gesture towards a sense that a male may have a physical life, equivalent, even in its tendency towards the hysterical, to those female intensities upon which the novel has dwelt. Later novels will have more to say, too, about the relation of an open nature to moral worth, and assess the process of judging of character more problematic. What relation a handsome face and body have to moral character and value is a question Austen will take up most thoroughly in *Persuasion*, but here it is worth noting how convenient as a narrative device it is to assume that there is a simple equivalence between physiology or physiognomy and character. 'Mrs Ferrars was a little, thin woman, upright, even to formality in her figure, and serious, even to sourness, in her aspect. Her complexion was sallow; and her features small, without beauty, and naturally without expression; but a lucky contraction of the brow had rescued her countenance from the disgrace of insipidity, by giving it the strong characters of pride and ill-nature' (232). Jane Austen never, I think, permits herself so unquestioning a use of physiology as moral character in her later work as here,[32] but she is nevertheless continually teased by the evident plausibility of the equivalence, the germ of truth in what might seem a vulgar and reactive assessment. In *Persuasion*, a novel which questions on almost every page the tie between beauty or physical vitality and moral goodness, Captain Wentworth, the hero, is tall, energetic and handsome, and Captain Benwick, less of a hero, is also less tall.

Another aspect of this problem is touched on in the presentation of Mr and Mrs Palmer, whose incompatible natures – she foolish and cheerfully silly, finding everything droll, and he, morose, uncommunicative, rude – pose the question, which the novel cannot solve, given its chosen manner of presentation, of what each finds in the other. Mr Palmer is a taciturn man who never demonstrates anything but contempt for his silly wife and garrulous mother-in-law, but

Elinor was not inclined, after a little observation, to give him credit for being so genuinely or unaffectedly ill-natured as he wished to appear. His temper might perhaps be little soured by finding, like many others of his sex, that through some unaccountable bias in favour of beauty, he was the husband of a very silly woman, – but she knew that this kind of blunder was too common for any sensible man to be lastingly hurt by it. (112)

'Unaccountable': the uneasy, even arch irony reflects everything that cannot be said about the relations between men and women and yet it is this, the unaccountable, which drives the relationships of this text. Mrs Palmer, as her mother makes embarrassingly clear to the sisters on her first presentation, is pregnant. The Palmers came round by London on account of business, Mrs Jennings whispers loudly to Elinor, but 'it was wrong in her situation' (197). Soon Mrs Palmer is described as being a 'fine size' (163). Such vulgar explicitness is frowned upon by the Dashwood sisters but like the 'natural daughter' Lady Middleton is censured for not enduring to hear spoken of, it points to urgencies and appetites understood to govern, if tacitly, the world the novel constructs. It's unaccountable in the novel's presentation too, where the relation between two caricatured figures is left as a gap, for to articulate a relationship is beyond the convention it adopts. The novel can only admit sexual power here, defensively, ironically, in the code of rational calculation, as a 'blunder'. 'Men of sense, whatever you may chuse to say', Mr Knightley is to tell Emma sternly, 'do not want silly wives' (E 64): yet if Austen's novels represent anything more frequently about marriage choices it is that men certainly take them. 'Sensible men' like Mr Palmer (and like Mr Bennet, Sir Thomas Bertram and Knightley's own brother) and women, like Lady Elliot, 'unaccountably' take partners they find sexually attractive, leaving their good sense to cope with the consequences.

Inheriting certain Lockean preconceptions about the mind and about conduct, the novel, on one plane, seeks to organise its material as an argument that epitomises and advocates the values of sense, but by shifting the term 'sensibility' towards a more amplified meaning, in which to understand the body's

urgencies is necessarily here to understand elements of psychopathology as agents in the formation of the self, it tends
to deconstruct its own rationalist epistemological premises.
Marianne's sensitivity, ardour and impulsiveness suggest a
heightened being-in-the world that is, manifestly, a heightened
sexuality. Furthermore, Austen shows that to understand
Marianne's sexuality entails understanding something at least
of what Freud and, after him, Melanie Klein referred to as the
family romance – that Marianne's mode of bodily existence, the
formation of her selfhood is related to the enabling, or
disenabling, role her mother has in her life, to the loss of her
father, and to her sister's taking upon herself the function of
moral censor and governor of conduct.

But if sexuality is at the heart of the book, it is a sexuality that
is necessarily censored, or screened. It is plain that the energy
that circulates in the novel is sexual, but also that explicit
acknowledgement of this is avoided. Talking to Elinor, after her
recovery, of Willoughby's possible 'designs' on her Marianne
says that her peace of mind would be doubly restored if she
could be sure that Willoughby was '"not *always* acting a part,
not *always* deceiving me; – but above all, if I could be assured
that he never was so *very* wicked as my fears have sometimes
fancied him, since the story of that unfortunate girl" – '(344).
She is concerned that, led on by him, she may have exposed her
own desire. '"What in a situation like mine," she asks, "but a
most shamefully unguarded affection could expose me to" – '
(345). Marianne's questions are left unfinished, for they allude
to the same treacherous matters as are brought into the novel
only by irony, or circuitously, by the extended regressions
entailed in the link of Marianne to the second Eliza, of the
second Eliza to the first, of the first Eliza to Clarissa. (The
similarities between the two Elizas – 'the unhappy resemblance
between the fate of mother and daughter!' (211), otherwise
almost redundant, and re-enforced by the otherwise odd
identity of their names – is another, displaced, hint at the
dangers that attend too close an identification between mothers
and daughters.) The novel's failure fully to acknowledge, to
give space to the sexual energies it releases in the character of

Marianne, is most apparent, of course, in her final marrying-off to Colonel Brandon.

From the moment when that gentleman comes to fetch Mrs Dashwood to her daughter's bedside, and confesses his love for Marianne to her mother as they travel (336), it is made evident that Mrs Dashwood has set her heart on his marrying Marianne. She tells Elinor that Brandon's manners, besides being more pleasing to her than Willoughby's ever were, are 'more accordant with [Marianne's] real disposition than the liveliness' of Willoughby (338). Elinor silently doubts this, for to her, of course, the memory of Willoughby is still recent. Confusing what she wishes with what is, and what she herself feels with what her daughter might feel, this middle-aged lady soon detects in Marianne's behaviour to the thirty-seven year old Brandon on her recovery the dawning love that suits her own fantasies and schemes (her own removal to a cottage nearby makes part of them). When the women meet together to censure Willoughby's maltreatment of Eliza, she takes the opportunity of bringing Brandon's name forward, but her eulogies of him as 'the dearest of our friends, and the best of men!' (350) are unheard by Marianne, who has, one might imagine, other things on her mind. One is led, then, to think with irony of Mrs Dashwood's enthusiastic and unself-reflexive ability to confuse her own desires with those of her daughter, and of the way this matches that daughter's identification with her, but this train of thought is hardly encouraged further by the narrative, which, after being intercepted by Edward Ferrars' return and Elinor's engagement, abandons the irony towards Mrs Dashwood's schemes and allows, in fact, her fantasies to shape its conclusion. (So that one wonders indeed whether one is not reading back modern anxieties into a relationship between mother and daughter the novel itself approves, even applauds.) Stressing now the impartiality of Mrs Dashwood's wish 'to give up' her daughter to her 'valued friend' (376) the narrator shows Marianne's wishes being usurped by her mother and sister ('What could she do?') as she is handed over to Colonel Brandon, as a 'reward' (335), 'with no sentiment superior to strong esteem and lively friendship' (378), scarcely less an item in the politics of the family than she is in her brother, John Dashwood's, designs. The narrative merges itself with Mrs Dashwood's dreams, Marianne's desire is obliterated: the novel's buried allusions to *Clarissa* culminate, perhaps, in the final unintended irony of Marianne becoming the creature of her family's purposes.

If the deep affinity and relationship between Marianne and her mother is transacted first through 'our dear Willoughby' (85) and then through Brandon (it is significant that Willoughby expresses love for the home the women have established together, and thus almost as much love for the mother), one might suggest finally, that *Sense and Sensibility* is a novel pervaded by forms of female homosocial desire.[33] The letter that Marianne receives from Willoughby is not from him, but from Miss Grey: he is the vehicle through which one woman communicates to another. An analogous phenomenon can be discerned in the representation of Elinor's love for Edward: Elinor's attraction towards the object of her love is a poor thing, emotionally and representationally, compared to her relationship with the rival for his hand, Lucy Steele. The contest between the two takes up several important chapters, including the climax of volume I, and puts Elinor on her mettle, for real issues of social prestige and moral authority are in play here, whereas the emotions that Edward arouses are pretty much taken for granted. In this novel the repartee between potential lovers that makes *Pride and Prejudice* so exhilarating is displaced into contests of wit and cunning between sisters and rivals, between women.

A further narrative problem, an inadvertent schematisation of *Sense and Sensibility*, is that though Marianne is allowed a very sufficient measure of good sense and Elinor's strong feeling and acuteness of perception carefully touched in, there occurs an imbalance in the quality of bodily responses given to the two sisters. Of course, Elinor is given her normal portion of blushes, confusions and dashes from the room, but the novel's dramatisation of the cost of a moral wound, so vividly and extensively portrayed in the figure of Marianne, leaves a significant aspect of Elinor underdeveloped. The repercussions upon Elinor's inner life of Marianne's more dramatic story are conscientiously noticed, but for much of the second volume, whilst Marianne's crises are played out, Elinor is not much more than a pure consciousness, attending to and recording her sister's miseries. It is as if all that were to be known about the spirit's exactions upon the body were loaded into the figure of Marianne, leaving Elinor's consciousness upon the plane of pure rationality, as if her secretly cherished love for Edward Ferrars, and the need to bury her secret, exacted no physiological tax at all. If Marianne's body is eloquent, Elinor's is, in this instance, very nearly silent. This, if it is an oversight, is one that is to be amply made good in *Mansfield Park*.

CHAPTER 2

'Eloquent blood': *the coming out of Fanny Price*

'Miss Catherine is put upon the Shelve for the present, and I do not know that she will ever come out',[1] Jane Austen told her niece, Fanny Knight, who had enquired about the fate of the manuscript later published by her brother and known to us as *Northanger Abbey*. The phrase is perhaps in the nature of a pun, for 'coming out' in the sense of 'a young lady's entrance into the world', to borrow the subtitle of Burney's *Evelina*, is very much at issue in *Northanger Abbey*, which shows the seventeen year old country girl Catherine Morland being introduced into the society of Bath.

The phrase 'the world', like 'coming out', is resonant with multiple possibilities. In one of the very first dialogues of *Mansfield Park* a discussion takes place which invites us to consider the destiny of its much less robust young heroine in this light, or rather under the multiple lights and headings the phrase brings together. 'Pray, is she out, or is she not?' asks Mary Crawford of 'Miss Price': 'She dined at the parsonage, with the rest of you, which seemed like being *out*; and yet she says so little, that I can hardly suppose she *is*' (48) and her question gives rise to a lively discussion about the conversational manners to be found among young women who are or who are not 'out'. The question evidently bears upon both Fanny's maturity and her social status. To be 'out' in Mary's sense is not only to 'have the age and sense of a woman' as Edmund Bertram puts it, but to belong to the social class which employs the ritual of coming out as a certification that its young women are marriageable and have sound family connections. In that social class, 'coming out', as the ensuing dialogue between Tom

Bertram and Mary Crawford suggests, bestows the freedom to speak, to express oneself, to take part in unembarrassed social intercourse with the other sex. 'A girl not out, has always the same sort of dress; a close bonnet for instance, looks very demure, and never says a word', Mary declares. On the other hand Tom recounts a meeting with a Miss Anderson, just '*out*': 'She came up to me, claimed me as an acquaintance, stared me out of countenance, and talked and laughed till I did not know which way to look'. This war of 'looks' is to be crucial in *Mansfield Park*. Evidently at this point in the novel Fanny is not 'out' in either way: she is remarkably reserved, and she does not belong to the same class as her cousins. In *Mansfield Park* Fanny is eventually promoted, and accorded the ball that ratifies her social status, but she retains the manners of a girl not out, shyness, silence, embarrassment and reserve: it is a question indeed whether either before, during, or after this ceremony she ever really does, in speech – or in any other than a ritual sense – 'come out'.

Fanny Price is the only one of Jane Austen's heroines whose body is frail, 'debilitated' or 'enfeebled' and, partly because of this, the character is notoriously an obstacle to the appreciation of *Mansfield Park*, and not only among those readers, naive perhaps, who seek a heroine to identify or to flirt with. Fanny is also the only heroine whose childhood is given deliberate and extended treatment. She is introduced into the novel in chapter II when she is 'just ten years old', and reaches eighteen in chapter IV. The whole remaining action of the novel takes place during her nineteenth year. One way round the obstacle of Fanny Price's unloveableness is to think of her as a study in developmental psychology, in the power of formative influences, suspending for a while (as much as possible) the question of the patterning of valuation in *Mansfield Park*. The first part of this chapter, then, will be concerned with psychology, and the second with the way that the psychological study is inserted into the novel's argument, with its sexual and social politics.

The term 'psychology' though, may be misleading if it fosters the assumption that the mind or psyche is an independently functioning part of the self, for it is impossible to separate

Fanny's psychosocial development from her bodily and sexual condition. She is born in 1790, the second child of a woman whose first-born, a son, is scarcely a year old. She is soon followed by two other sons. Being, in her mother's words, 'Somewhat delicate and puny' (11) she is neglected in this very male-oriented (and male-valuing) household of a Lieutenant of Marines, and when, late in the novel, she looks back on her childhood with her father 'she had never been able to recal anything approaching to tenderness in his former treatment of herself' (389). Her mother, too, is indifferent: 'Her daughters never had been much to her' (389). Fanny's early history, deliberately set forth in the narrative, is one of maternal, and paternal, neglect. Her emotional attachment is to her elder brother William, the apple of his parents' eye, 'her advocate with her mother (of whom he was the darling) in every distress' (15). Her inferiority, both physical and sexual, seems indelibly inscribed in her (weak, feminine) body.

At the age of ten she is adopted by her rich relatives, the family of Sir Thomas Bertram, at Mansfield Park. Her mother, though 'surprised that a girl should be fixed on, when she had so many fine boys' (11), sends her off without regret, and only William tells her, apparently, that he will miss her (16). The little girl is conveyed by coach to the splendidly large Bertram mansion, where the grandeur of the rooms makes her feel her insignificance still more intensely, and introduced into the family that is to be hers for the rest of her formative years, a family where the most active influence is her Aunt Norris, who for social and libidinal motives of her own, makes Fanny a degraded object. At Mansfield Park, her physical inferiority, her small size and lack of vigour, provide everyone with a sign of her subordinate social and moral status. Her cousins are 'a remarkably fine family, the sons very well looking, the daughters decidedly handsome, and all of them well-grown and forward of their age' (13). Within this family 'handsomeness', spirit, bodily ease and capacity are valued as the natural endowments of those born into the ruling classes. Lady Bertram, supine on her sofa, is described at one point as 'the picture of health, wealth, ease and tranquillity' (126). Neither this Aunt Bertram, nor her cousin Tom, is unkind, but one calls Fanny a 'poor little thing' and the other 'creepmouse'. Her lack of energy and confidence, her small size, her liability to tiredness, confirm her as inferior, in their eyes and in her own.

Fanny is at first very miserable at Mansfield. Severed from 'the brothers and sisters among whom she had always been important as playfellow, instructress, and nurse' (14), daily reminded of her inferior state, she clings to her cousin Edmund, the only one of the family who offers her more than cursory notice and kindness, and invests him with the emotional value attributable to one who replaces all her primary attachments. He rescues her from despair by talking to her of William, and provides her with materials to write to him, thus initiating the recurring pattern of their relation. In fact, Fanny's early emotional history is set out with the kind of clarity and cogency that would not be out of place in a case-history of a twentieth-century object-relations analyst. To Edmund, who is a replacement for William (himself, of course, a replacement for the mother) Fanny forms what John Bowlby calls an 'anxious attachment'.[2] Never having been confident of the love of her mother, the attachment she feels for Edmund is the more intense and clinging because she can never be sure that he will not betray her, as she has been betrayed in her previous dependencies – and one way of reading the novel is as the history of the realisation of her fear. Fanny's love for Edmund – a love that is tenacious, possessive and funded by primary psychological urgencies – shapes the novel, but, for reasons I shall explore, it has rarely met with answering attention from readers. The reception of *Mansfield Park* has been marked by uneasy questions about Jane Austen's intention in the creation of a heroine so weak and illness-prone, and by a related and consequent obliteration of Fanny as the subject of desire.

An exception was Richard Whately, writing in the *Quarterly Review* in 1821, whose account gives some clues as to why what is for him so striking a part of the novel should have been so disregarded:

Fanny is, however, armed against Mr Crawford by a stronger feeling
than even her disapprobation; by a vehement attachment to Edmund.
The silence in which this passion is cherished – the slender hopes and
enjoyments by which it is fed – the restlessness and jealousy with
which it fills a mind naturally active, contented and unsuspicious –
the manner in which it tinges every event and every recollection, are
painted with a vividness of which we can scarcely conceive any one but
a female, and we should add, a female writing from recollection,
capable.[3]

When she is seventeen, Edmund arranges for Fanny to borrow
his mare so that she may ride for her health, a gift she
appreciates with an emotional fulsomeness which the narrator
treats, as she usually does Fanny's girlish enthusiasms, with
affectionate irony:

She regarded her cousin as an example of every thing good and great,
as possessing worth, which no one but herself could ever appreciate,
and as entitled to such gratitude from her, as no feelings could be
strong enough to pay. Her sentiments towards him were compounded
of all that was respectful, grateful, confiding, and tender. (37)

The novel is to show these sentiments maturing (if that's the
word) into adult and sexual passion. It is a 'silent' passion,
because the very gratitude and respect Fanny conceives for
Edmund, and which is so engrained in her attitude to her
adopted family, rules out its expression. Once that feeling
becomes known to the subject as more than the intense gratitude
and adoration of an adolescent, it becomes, by the same token,
unspeakable. Fanny has been taught, from her first introduction
to the family, that she is an outsider. To love Edmund, to desire
Edmund, to wish – even – to marry Edmund is to transgress the
fundamental social code that organises her world. It is to make
a claim for herself which everything in her temperament and
upbringing condemns. Her love must be silent too, because
Edmund is himself not a perceptive person (far from it) and
because his sincere affection for Fanny has remained the love of
a brother. 'The distinction proper to be made between the girls'
has occupied Sir Thomas even before her arrival. 'They cannot
be equals. Their rank, fortune, rights, and expectations, will
always be different', he emphasises (10–11). Her love is taboo

not only because it seems to occupy the same area as incest, but because in the eyes of the family it would seem a monstrous usurpation of privileges belonging to another caste – and Fanny has adopted the views of the family as her own. All the same Fanny's need for Edmund is, to use Whately's term, 'vehement'. In these circumstances, Fanny's desire, unable to be communicated in words, is expressed, experienced within and displayed covertly upon her body. 'A frame and temper, delicate and nervous like Fanny's' (391) is an especially transparent medium for the expression of emotional turbulences, and it is through Fanny's body that the intensity of her feeling is communicated to the reader.[4]

To reconstruct, to retell Fanny's history, to extract it from the novel, as I have been doing, however, is to distort the balance between the figure and the other aspects of the narrative. *Mansfield Park* is a novel in whose first volume dramatic, ensemble scenes predominate, and in which the life of its heroine is marginalised, to be understood only in glimpses, in 'tinges', in reactions, by small touches and implications. And although Fanny's point of view is most frequently employed, it is by no means the only one. Sometimes an independent narrator's voice intercedes, the tougher, riper wit of an older woman amused at the sober naiveté of her heroine, at others the point of view of other figures, like Mary or Edmund, whose beliefs and hopes are quite different from Fanny's, is allowed to carry the narration, with immense gains in irony and suspense. Fanny's reticent social demeanour is reflected in the marginal and ancillary position she is allotted in the depiction of many of the first volume's events. But she is restored to narrative predominance and moral authority in those passages of self-communing and self-questioning which are set apart both scenically and structurally from the social gatherings. In the East room Fanny's recuperative meditations exemplify her as that self-reflexive moral being, with that ability to 'discuss' her feelings and conduct with herself, which (it is repeatedly suggested) it is the crucial failure of other characters to be without.[5] Thus occasions in which Fanny Price is retiring, reticent, backgrounded, are balanced by passages in which the nuances of her behaviour in the ensemble scenes are picked up and amplified. Conscience, one can say, exercises both the character and the novelist's skills, for Fanny is displayed to the reader less in speech, in dialogue, than through a dramatic rendering of her introspective processes that has no precedent in Austen's earlier, pre-Chawton, work.

In *Emma*, Mr Knightley is first alerted to the nature of his feelings for Emma, whom he has been used to think of as a sister, by his jealousy of the new arrival, Frank Churchill. In an analogous way, Fanny's feelings towards Edmund first become disclosed as sexual, through her jealousy of Mary, the overtly sexual object. The difference is that, due to the force of her internal taboo, Fanny's passion is so silenced that it can hardly be admitted even into her consciousness. Mary has never ridden before, and Edmund asks Fanny if Mary can borrow her mare for half an hour before Fanny's ride. On the second of these outings, Mary, under the supervision of Edmund, enjoys herself so much that Fanny is all ready to ride and the horse has not been returned. Fanny is used to neglect, but not to neglect from Edmund. Nagged out of the house by her Aunt Norris, she looks across the distance of the Park, and sees, framed as in a picture, Edmund teaching Mary to ride. The standpoint is not neutral, for in the prose rhythms, slackening and then festinating with the turbulencies of Fanny's attention, the lineaments of her inner life, for the first time in the novel, are disclosed:

in Dr Grant's meadow she immediately saw the group – Edmund and Miss Crawford both on horseback, riding side by side, Dr. and Mrs. Grant, and Mr Crawford, with two or three grooms, standing about and looking on. A happy party it appeared to her – all interested in one object – cheerful beyond a doubt, for the sound of merriment ascended even to her. It was a sound that did not make *her* cheerful; she wondered that Edmund should forget her, and felt a pang. She could not turn her eyes from the meadow, she could not help watching all that passed. At first Miss Crawford and her companion made the circuit of the field, which was not small, at a foot's pace; then, at *her* apparent suggestion, they rose into a canter; and to Fanny's timid nature it was most astonishing to see how well she sat. After a few minutes, they stopt entirely, Edmund was close to her, he was speaking to her, he was evidently directing her management of the bridle, he had hold of her hand; she saw it, or the imagination supplied what the eye could not reach. She must not wonder at all this; what could be more natural than that Edmund should be making himself useful, and proving his good nature by any one? (67)

This is a famous scene, and sufficient in itself to refute those critics who claim without qualification that Fanny is a 'detached observer'.[6] Perception is not a passive but an active process, including not only the consciousness but responses of the subject which are out of awareness. The sentence that describes Edmund and Mary's physical proximity is also describing Fanny's increasingly aroused jealousy. Edmund and Mary are hardly visible in their own right. 'After a few minutes, they stopt entirely, Edmund was close to her...' Fanny's excitement does not 'stop entirely', there is a comma where one might expect a period: the five observations included in the sentence progressively build up, as it accelerates with the increasing intimacy of the gestures she strains to catch sight of. 'She saw it': the sentence's climax encloses Fanny's excitement at the same time as it mimics the gesture – Edmund enclosing Mary's hand – that is its provocation. Consciousness is simply observing a scene of riding instruction: the unconscious, registered in the rhythm, presents an episode in which Fanny is both aroused and disturbed.

Fanny recognises that there is something untoward in the emotion she feels and attempts to put down the claims it implicitly discloses before they emerge into consciousness. In a typical example of what Nabokov called the 'knight's move' on the chequerboard of her thoughts,[7] she swerves sideways, to an ostensibly 'rational' and self-condemning reflection. 'What could be more natural than that Edmund should be making himself useful, and proving his good nature by any one?': what indeed? This is a sensible thought which typifies Fanny's conscientious ability to check and question her own emotions, but its function here is to cover over the jealousy and to enable the discharge of accumulated emotion in altered form, as anger at Mr Crawford (displacing on to him the unadmittable jealousy of his sister) and finally, in a comically desperate last resort, into pity for the 'poor mare'. The result of this inner soliloquy is thence to communicate the nature and intensity of Fanny's desire, as well as the energy consumed in repressing it. 'Her fond attachment' to Edmund, as well as her aversion to Mary, can shortly be assumed by the narrator, be taken as read, because so much to substantiate them has been deposited in this passage.

'Her feelings for one and the other were soon a little tranquillized', now remarks the narrator dryly, and Fanny's agitation is replaced by fear that she might appear rude and impatient. She walks towards Edmund and Mary 'with a great anxiety to avoid the suspicion'. Fanny is now committed to the presentation of a false self in compliancy to the wishes of others, of acting a calm and graciousness very far from what she feels. A very fine line separates Fanny's 'extreme civility' here, though, when confronted with Mary's unrepentant half-apology, from 'the politeness which she had been taught to practise as a duty' that makes Julia miserable at being dragged around Sotherton by her aunt and Mrs Rushworth. Julia is said to lack 'that higher species of self-command, that just consideration of others, that knowledge of her own heart, that principle of right which had not formed any essential part of her education' (91) which would make her politeness less burdensome, but whether Fanny feels any less miserable than Julia is unclear, for Fanny's subjectivity disappears in the following dialogue, as if Austen had no clear conceptual hold over what her mimetic transcription of Fanny's agitation has implied.

'Though good health be one of the greatest blessings of life, never make a boast of it, but enjoy it in grateful silence', advised a contemporary moralist for young ladies, Dr John Gregory:

We so naturally associate the idea of female softness and delicacy with a correspondent delicacy of constitution, that when a woman speaks of her great strength, her extraordinary appetite, her ability to bear excessive fatigue, we recoil at the description in a way she is little aware of.[8]

Gregory thus demonstrates how for Austen's contemporaries gender and illness or weakness are linked, and how the propensity to sickness becomes virtually constitutive of a desirable femaleness. Edmund does not exactly value frailty in women (after all he has been instrumental in providing Fanny with the opportunity to ride) but he finds relationships with them easier if he can treat them as the weaker sex, and he suggests that the ride might have tired Mary. She refuses this gambit. '"No part of it fatigues me but getting off this horse, I assure you," said she, as she sprang down with his help; "I am very strong. Nothing ever fatigues me, but doing what I do not like"'. (68) In the Sotherton scene, which soon follows, Fanny is walking with Mary and Edmund in the wood, and has to ask if they may soon sit down. Edmund immediately draws her arm within his. 'Perhaps', he does not fail to add, 'my other companion may do me the honour of taking an arm' (94). Fanny's presence is soon forgotten, and the text is occupied by Mary and Edmund's engaging in something very like a lovers' quarrel, whilst the three of them are still, presumably, linked arm-in-arm together. It is hardly surprising then, that Edmund should soon observe Fanny looking exhausted. Mary declares 'That she should be tired now, however, gives me no surprise; for there is nothing in the course of one's duties so fatiguing as what we have been doing this morning' (95), leaving the reader to reflect on the other sorts of duties that may wear out a person's spirits.

These early chapters of *Mansfield Park*, besides dramatising Edmund's growing feeling for Mary Crawford, are taken up with establishing the ethos of the well-bred, well-fed Bertrams and the actual moral and ethical values that reign in the household of the high-minded, but now absent, Sir Thomas Bertram. Mary's horseriding is 'celebrated' in the drawing room:

> 'I was sure she would ride well,' said Julia; 'she has the make for it. Her figure is as neat as her brother's.'
> 'Yes,' added Maria, ' and her spirits are as good, and she has the same energy of character. I cannot but think that good horsemanship has a great deal to do with the mind.' (69)

By implication Fanny's weak frame disqualifies her from power and privilege. Inferiority of body is for the Bertrams inferiority

of being. The narrator warns us against this solecism by rather
crude ironies against Mary Crawford. 'Her merit in being gifted
by nature with strength and courage was fully appreciated by
the Miss Bertrams', the reader is told and, just in case the point
is missed, that Edmund looks after her 'in an ecstacy of
admiration of all her many virtues, from her obliging manners
down to her light and graceful tread' (112).

As Edmund's infatuation with Mary develops the mare is
borrowed for four successive days. Fanny, whose position in the
social hierarchy is indeterminate, half-way between family and
servant, is left in this interval to savour her marginal status.
Treated as a servant, made to cut roses and then carry them
over the park to Mrs Norris' house (her aunt's excuse is that she
is too busy looking after the real servants) Fanny has to go back
again because she has forgotten to lock the door of the room.
(The use both aunts make of Fanny, 'standing and stooping in
a hot sun' might call to mind the use Sir Thomas, now in
Antigua, makes of his slaves.) When Edmund gets back from his
excursion with Mary and the others on this blazing August day,
he finds Fanny in the background of the family party, silently
nursing a headache. When the way Fanny has been treated is
brought out by Edmund's questioning of his mother and aunt,
he thinks he understands the reason for the malaise that has
driven Fanny to retire upon the sofa. He apparently perceives
only physical debility, to be remedied by a cordial, but the
circumstances have been constructed so as to make it clear that
it is not the heat, nor the servitude, but neglect and envy that
generate her indisposition. Mrs Norris of course thinks she is
malingering.

The figure is now capable of a psychologising exposition.
Fanny Price's stressors include alienation from a (minimally)
supportive family background, inferior social status, her consciousness of which is repeatedly re-enforced, and an affection
which is socially impermissible. The external disconfirming
experience is replicated by her internal self-criticism. These
stresses are driven back into and played out in her body. Thus
Fanny's demeanour – that shrinking and creeping which is so
frequently and perhaps tactlessly noted as typifying her

movements – is a result not only of the inferiority instilled in her by Mrs Norris, nor only of the timorousness of her nature, but of her sense of guilt. She continually experiences culturally inadmissible emotions – envy, jealousy, even rage: these emotions are then forced back into the self, since they are kept as much as possible out of consciousness, and re-experienced physiologically. This is the process that Kleinman refers to as 'somatization'.

Somatisation is often linked to powerlessness and blocked access to resources, and hence headaches and similar symptoms 'radiate symbolic meanings of frustration and unhappiness'.[9] 'The patient complains of headaches and thereby conveys pain in the temples and a painful mental conflict to whose intensification or amelioration the medical care will contribute', he writes.[10] Edmund's glass of Madeira provokes an unspecified 'variety of feelings' in Fanny, leading to a breakdown in tears. His gift-bearing gesture replicates the situation that begins their relationship, when he found her in despair on the stairs and brought her the materials to write to William. A little later in the novel, surveying her 'nest of comforts' in the East room, Fanny thinks how valuable her possessions are to her: 'though she had known the pains of tyranny, of ridicule, and neglect, yet almost every recurrence of either had led to something consolatory ... .Edmund had been her champion and her friend; – he had supported her cause, or explained her meaning, he had told her not to cry, or *had given her some proof of affection which made her tears delightful*' (152, my italics). Like her tears, Fanny's illness gives her a small but sufficient amount of social leverage, for it brings Edmund's attention back to her. The link with the origins of Fanny's condition is emphasised when, in the final paragraph of the chapter her emotions are described: 'Fanny went to bed with her heart as full as on the first evening of her arrival at the Park'. And in a commonplace phrase which begins to resound with metaphorical implications the chapter ends with the statement that Edmund's kindness 'made her hardly know how to support herself'.

Soon, rehearsals for the play are taking place all over the house and Edmund, compromising his belief that acting a play in his father's absence is all wrong, and that the particular play chosen, *Lovers' Vows*, is especially wrong, has agreed to act the part of Anhalt, a clergyman. (He is due himself to be ordained at Christmas.) Mary and Fanny both perceive that he has given in, not on the rational ground he offers – that this will keep it within the family – but out of the desire to be where Mary is. Everyone recognises that this is a betrayal of his principles, and Mary takes it, rightly, as a sign of her growing influence: 'His sturdy spirit to bend as it did! Oh! it was sweet beyond expression' (358), she exclaims later in the novel, looking back at his capitulation. Mary is herself to play Amelia, the clergyman's pupil. In the third act of Kotzebue's play, Amelia 'announces her affection to her lover' in what his translator, Elizabeth Inchbald, calls a 'forward and unequivocal manner'. In her adaptation to the modesty of English taste, the same negotiation is carried on by 'whimsical insinuations'.[11] Fanny who, though refusing to act, knows the play almost by heart, is interested in this scene 'most particularly'; it is one 'which she was longing and dreading to see how they would perform'. 'She had read, and read the scene again with many painful, many wondering emotions, and looked forward to their representation of it as a circumstance almost too interesting' (167).

First Mary and then Edmund arrive in the East room, to ask Fanny to run through their dialogue with them. Meeting together, and with Fanny's presence to give them courage, they decide to rehearse the scene with each other instead. Fanny is to be their prompter. Anhalt is several years older than Amelia, a 'girl' of seventeen or eighteen, Fanny's age. He is her tutor, she has grown to love him in the course of his teaching, and the idea that he has taught her everything she knows, but is blind to the passion he has inspired is bandied to and fro in the dialogue.[12] 'My father has more than once told me that he who forms my mind I should always consider my greatest benefactor', says Amelia, coyly, and adds '(looking down)', 'My heart tells me the same'. Since he has indeed 'formed her mind and gained her affections', (64) Edmund's true partner in the scene could only be Fanny, not Mary. Fanny's almost obsessive interest in the scene can thus be explained, for it holds up a mirror to her, showing her relationship to Edmund, a mirror all the more fascinating to gaze into because only she can look into it, and because it is so distorted. Not only is the barrier to marriage Anhalt's rather than Amelia's poverty and dependence, but Amelia's coquettish effrontery is an unthinkably shameful reflection of Fanny's unspoken desires. Fanny is not only compelled to be present whilst Mary, under cover of the play, courts Edmund, she is forced to witness her unwitting rival act out her own forbidden secret. No wonder she is overcome.

> To prompt them must be enough for her; and it was sometimes *more* than enough; for she could not always pay attention to the book. In watching them she forgot herself; and agitated by the increasing spirit of Edmund's manner, had once closed the page and turned away exactly as he wanted help. It was imputed to very reasonable weariness, and she was thanked and pitied; but she deserved their pity, more than she hoped they would ever surmise. (170)

Fanny's reaction is once again misread by being construed as merely physiological, but the reader, too, is once again likely to misunderstand, since its true sources and nature lie buried in the intricacies of intertextuality. Readers can only gaze fully into the mirror Fanny sees if they are familiar with *Lovers' Vows* (though perhaps Jane Austen assumed her readers would be, as Chapman asserts[13]). Fanny's intense emotions, as in the riding incident, are indirectly projected, displayed in a scene of which she is the ostensibly passive witness. The very indirection of the presentation, its implications only to be caught by readers as sympathetically disposed to the young heroine as Jane Austen seems to have assumed, makes for a cursory reading that misunderstands and slights the observing figure of Fanny.

Hers, as so many critics have noted, is by and large a non-speaking part. Her true emotions are displayed to the reader less through her words than through the implications of the bodily signs I have been discussing. A rationalist reader will discard this information as useless; for Marilyn Butler, for instance, Fanny's 'feebleness' is 'quite incidental' to Austen's main arguments, a failed 'device' for securing the reader's sympathy.[14] To disregard the communications of the body is a consequence of that Western rationalist tradition which elevates the soul or consciousness, and relegates the body as inferior and unculturated. Such dualism identifies subjectivity and person-hood with the ideational or conceptual side of the opposition (mind/body) while relegating the body to the status of an object, outside of and distinct from consciousness. Culture and education, according to this view, pervasive in early feminists like Mary Wollstonecraft and John Stuart Mill, for example, operate upon the mind, whilst the body occupies a distinct realm, transhistorical and transcultural. When Elizabeth Bennet begs Mr Collins to consider her not 'as an elegant female intending to plague you, but as a rational creature speaking the truth from her heart' (PP 109), she is speaking in this tradition in which both terms 'rational' and (unsexed) 'creature' are of equal weight. Culture in this account operates upon a neutral body, or a body in which sex is indifferent: it is 'gender', the social formation of sexual characteristics which is significant. But it can be argued that the sex/gender distinction is in fact a false one, and that the body and its sexuality are themselves enculturated.[15] Social customs and demands operate not only upon the surface of the body – defining the significance of clothes and gesture for example – but upon what Elizabeth Grosz calls 'the depth body', the body's inner processes.[16] Mary's explanation that the girl 'not out' always wears a bonnet, and looks away when you talk to her, is an example of the style, the manners, through which genteel modesty is signalled to the world, but modesty and gentility may be internalised, and become what the narrator, speaking of Fanny, calls 'the modesty of her nature'. If Fanny is represented as tired (and increasingly as the novel goes on as 'trembling') these are not merely external traits, but deposits laid down by her stresses, and signs of a conception of 'character', of the human person, which exceeds that of rationalist epistemology.

Headaches, weariness, and trembling are not the only bodily manifestations of Fanny's besieged condition in this novel, for Jane Austen repeatedly shows her prone to another symptom conjoining desire and powerlessness – blushing. So frequently does Fanny blush (on over twenty occasions in the course of the novel) that one might argue that rather too much use is made of this device, but since no critic, to my knowledge, has felt the blushing to be overdone, or even noticed it particularly, this danger seems to have been avoided, probably because the same physical sign has multiple significations. Like Fanny's frailty and tiredness, blushing is almost always a communication to the reader which is misconstrued by the characters of the novel, functioning both to remind the reader of this disregarded person's intense emotions, and of those emotions' isolation and secrecy. 'Her pure, and eloquent blood / Spoke in her cheekes, and so distinctly wrought, / That one might almost say, her body thought.' Donne's famous lines from *The Second Anniversary* (ll. 244–7) are quoted by Henry Austen in the biographical notice of his sister which prefaced the posthumous publication of *Northanger Abbey*, and applied to the author herself.[17] Fanny's blood too is eloquent, but what, precisely, her body thinks, and what in turn a reader is to make of these physiological 'thoughts' is less distinct than mysterious. The significance of the blush is latent – and therein lies its power as a narrative device.

Blushing seems a particularly salient example for those writers, including feminists, who wish to demonstrate that the body is not outside culture, or language, but deeply conditioned by them, performing social and sexual requirements within itself, as well as upon its surface. Laughing and crying can be plausibly seen as breakdowns of human communicatory capacity,[18] but blushing seems to be communicative, without being instrumental: one is not in control of one's blushes, which seems to indicate some involuntary, physiological process, and yet blushing is a cultural sign, understood by others as a language, and therefore akin to gesture. John Mullan writes that around Sir Charles Grandison 'the women of the novel, all "full of unmeaning meaningness", blush, tremble and weep. In the presence of male goodness, virtuous femininity is legible most when unable to speak'.[19] Of these physiological displays, the blush is certainly the most overdetermined and complicated product, or perhaps one should say, more guardedly, the one disposed most problematically and multifariously in the novelists who learned from Richardson this mode of communicating sensibility and heightening drama. 'Elizabeth blushed and blushed again with shame and vexation' at her mother (PP 100), but things are not so straightforward in the later novel. 'The distinction between the flush of an improper excitement and the virtuous blush of an entranced sensibility is a difficult and shifting one', as Mullan remarks.[20] The blush of modesty, of embarrassment, inevitably entails the consciousness of sexuality, of eroticism, however veiled or denied; but it is also intermingled (the romantic word 'interfused' might be better) with the flush or blush of indignation, of modesty or pride affronted. One thing is clear though: whatever the intricacies of its internal generation, the blush, the 'confusion' in these novels is a warranty of the genteel.

The body functions in the sentimental novel in lieu, and as a precursor of, those techniques for the rendering of inner consciousness which are developed by Austen through free indirect speech, and writers of all political allegiances find the blush an appropriate and compelling mode of divulging motive to the reader. Only in Fanny Burney does the topos become obsessive – a sign of the intractable dilemmas wrought by her conflicting fantasies of self assertion and self-deprecation.[21] The blush, carrying so much freight, often becomes exorbitant, excessive. In Elizabeth Inchbald's *A Simple Story* (1791) the heroine responds to Dorriforth's casual praise thus:

the powerful glow of joy, and of gratitude, for an opinion so negligently, and yet so sincerely expressed, flew to Miss Milner's face, neck, and even to her hands and fingers; the blood mounted to every part of her skin that was visible, for not a fibre but felt the secret transport, that Dorriforth thought her more beautiful than the beautiful Miss Fenton.[22]

This is certainly, in Freud's phrase, 'a temporary erection of the face': but the blush of pride can equally, it seems, consume the body, at least in the hypersensitive and brittle world of *Camilla* (1796), in which conversations seem to be conducted as contests as to who can blush the more furiously and thus acquire the more prestige:

Edgar, biting his nails, looked down.
  'And indeed, I acknowledge myself, in that affair, a most egregious dupe!...'

She blushed, but her blush was colourless to that of Edgar. Resentment against Sir Sedley beat high in every vein ... [23]

In return, Camilla rallies *her* pride:

'Yes, part,' she said with assumed firmness: 'it would be vain to palliate what I cannot disguise from myself... I am lessened in your esteem.' She could not go on; imperious shame took possession of her voice, crimsoned her very forehead, blushed even in her eyes, demolished her strained energy, and enfeebled her genuine spirit.[24]

It does seem that one function of these phenomena in *Mansfield Park* is to convey a peculiarly female relation to the world. Early in the story Tom's profligacy forces his father to give the living intended for Edmund to Dr Grant. 'I blush for you, Tom', says Sir Thomas Bertram, rebuking his eldest son. 'I blush for the expedient which I am driven on... ' (23). But neither Sir Thomas, speaking 'in his most dignified manner', nor his son actually blush: the phrasing is the empty gesture of a man of professed sensibility, akin to the cruder cant of Mrs Norris. Tom listens with 'some shame and some sorrow' but escapes with aplomb intact. Blushing is the realm of the female, and it seems to register the crisis points of their especial position within this culture. At one level the flow of blood to the cheeks may operate metonymically as the sign of the female's sexual or biological instability. But one can say more confidently that it is the sign in which not femaleness but 'femininity' is produced: it designates the woman's embodiment of modesty and sensitivity – and Fanny's aptitude for this particular form of self-expression therefore seems designed on one level to recommend her as an exemplary feminine presence. Willoughby 'colours' when telling lies in *Sense and Sensibility* (76) but only women blush or flush in this novel: 'Maria blushed in spite of herself' when she admits to taking the part of Agatha in the play (139), and Mrs Norris turns red more than once, from anger, indignation or resentment. On the one occasion on which Mary Crawford is seen to blush, in reaction to Edmund's parting chastisement, the enigmatic nature of the phenomenon is exploited. 'She was astonished', Edmund reports to the silently listening Fanny, 'exceedingly astonished – more than astonished. I saw her change countenance. She turned extremely red. I imagined I saw a mixture of many feelings – a great, though short struggle – half a wish of yielding to truths, half a sense of shame – but habit, habit carried it. She would have laughed if she could' (458). It is a tantalising glimpse. 'Shame', says Edmund, but others just as plausibly have read 'anger'.[25]

Fanny's is a markedly sensitive and scrupulous character, and some of her blushing simply dramatises this. She blushes, for example, when she catches herself speaking of Mansfield as 'home' though neither of her parents even notices it (431). When Mary talks about the brevity of brothers' letters, she colours for William's sake (59). When she is at Portsmouth she learns from Henry that Edmund is in London 'and the words "then by this time it is all settled," passed internally, without more evidence of emotion than a faint blush' (401). Such moments seem designed to suggest that Fanny's is a nature which is particularly susceptible to the dictates of conscience, and that decorum and duty are 'internalised' values, lived within the body, and displayed, however ambiguously, on its surface. When Edmund goes away to be ordained, the tables are temporarily turned, Mary is miserable, agitated, and jealous, and seeks Fanny's reassurances about the 'Miss Owens'. Fanny quietly declares that she does not think Edmund likely to marry soon. 'Her companion looked at her keenly; and gathering greater spirit from the blush soon produced from such a look, only said "He is best off as he is," and turned the subject' (290). Mary presumably thinks that she elicits from Fanny a sign of complicity – Fanny's recognition of Edmund's feelings towards Mary. It is typical of *Mansfield Park* that the tables are turned, that interpersonal power be transacted in the 'look'.

Such encounters are more enigmatic than they appear – shall I say? – at face value. The novel contains many moments of peculiarly intimate psychological interaction, and facial signs in this novel acquire an especial significance because (in Austen's characteristic way) what is latent in the dramatic episodes is also openly discussed. In selecting his partner for the play Henry Crawford explicitly brings up the question of 'looks' and 'countenances' in a context which concerns nature and role-playing. '"I must entreat Miss *Julia* Bertram"', he says, smoothly, '"not to engage in the part of Agatha, or it will be the ruin of all my solemnity. You must not, indeed you must not – (turning to her.) I could not stand your countenance dressed up in woe and paleness"' (133). Henry's 'cold blooded vanity', the capacity to project his desires onto others, is disclosed sharply enough in this episode where he does not of course actually *see* Julia (whose face at this moment displays woe and paleness, if ever in her life). There follows a cross-play of countenances and glances, of assumed and involuntary 'looks' as Henry seeks to mollify Julia, 'turning to her with a look of anxious entreaty', and Julia glances at Maria's face, where the suppressed smile of triumph confirms the slight.

The nuances of intimate power relations are elucidated when Mary persuades Fanny to choose a necklace for the ball. When Fanny has chosen (half freely, half in response to what she intuits as Mary's design) Mary tells Fanny that the necklace was actually Henry's gift to her. Fanny instantly disavows the present:

> Miss Crawford thought she had never seen a prettier consciousness. 'My dear child,' said she laughing, 'what are you afraid of? Do you think Henry will claim the necklace as mine, and fancy you did not come honestly by it? – or are you imagining he would be too much flattered by seeing round your lovely throat an ornament which his money purchased three years ago, before he knew there was such a throat in the world? – or perhaps – looking archly – you suspect a confederacy between us, and that what I am now doing is with his knowledge and at his desire?'
>
> With the deepest blushes Fanny protested against such a thought. (259)

Ruth Yeazell remarks of the initial conversation about 'coming out': 'By presuming that the only alternative to the girl who abruptly alters her behaviour when she comes out is the girl who acts immodestly from the start, Mary unwittingly reveals that she finds a modest consciousness unimaginable. All she can recognise is the difference in manners and appearance, the distinction between acting with or without restraint'.[26] For

Mary, Fanny's 'consciousness' must be the consciousness of desire. But the blush is a more problematic text than this. Certainly, one function of Fanny's blush here is to expose the difference in sophistication between the women, and to imply that the trick Mary performs without compunction would be 'a sin of thought' to the morally scrupulous and delicate Fanny. Later it becomes clear Mary takes Fanny's 'consciousness' to mean her understanding that by accepting, by even choosing, Henry's gift, she is symbolically announcing her willingness to accept him.

Blushing resembles a hysterical symptom in that its communication is ambiguous: it both represents Fanny's desire and rescues it, by preserving the desire undetected, undamaged by interference from others. A small instance of this is the moment when Mary interrogates Fanny in the East room, after Fanny has refused her brother's proposal. Distracted for a moment from her initial purpose, Mary chatters on about the marriages and affairs of her London friends and about Henry's conquests, declaring finally 'were I to attempt to tell you of all the women whom I have known to be in love with him, I should never have done. It is only you, insensible Fanny, who can think of him with any thing like indifference. But are you so insensible as you profess yourself? No, no, I see you are not'. The narrator highlights this moment with a one-sentence paragraph:

> There was indeed so deep a blush over Fanny's face at that moment, as might warrant strong suspicion in a pre-disposed mind. (362)

If one has read Fanny as a figure of inflexible moral purity, it is easy to take this blush as the sign of embarrassment, or even perhaps indignation, at the freedom and levity of Mary's treatment of London sexual entanglements. Mary, of course, assumes that Fanny's colouring means she too is in love with Henry, and that her denial is just a convention, her blush a physiological veil, a version of the bonnet worn by a girl who is not yet 'out'. But the pattern of Fanny's earlier blushings implies something quite different.

The blush that covers Fanny's face when Sir Thomas Bertram comes up to her room to announce Henry's proposal is both the most crucial moment of embodiment and the most critical moment of non-speaking in the text. Fanny's dislike of Henry and her love of Edmund are imbricated, the one intensifying the other, in such a way that her opposition to Sir Thomas (unlike her opposition to the play earlier) is morally ambiguous, an ambiguity which is fully exposed at the moment when her uncle, searching for an explanation of her obduracy, comes close upon the truth:

'This is beyond me', said he. 'This requires explanation. Young as you are, and having seen scarcely any one, it is hardly possible that your affections – '

He paused and eyed her fixedly. He saw her lips formed into a *no*, though the sound was inarticulate, but her face was like scarlet. (316)

Is this the flush of mendacity, or the blush of pride? Is her face speaking the secret that her lips struggle to deny? Or does her face represent the shame of that deception? Fanny's face signals her body's treason, at the same moment as her will, struggling to act in the world, and misrepresent her desires, is frozen in impotence by the force of her conscience. Her blushing manifests her desire to the reader (and her shame) but being confined to a signal on the envelope of the body, desire remains mute, inoperative, passive. And Fanny's effort is to 'harden herself', to form a carapace of acquiescence and decorum. Sir Thomas questions her circuitously, about Tom, and then about Edmund. He asks her whether she thinks Edmund is likely to marry Mary. Carrying out her plan, she is able 'gently' and 'calmly' to agree with him, miming once again the 'modest' girl he thinks her. The effect is to deceive Sir Thomas and, since her resistance now seems to him quite unmotivated, to madden him still further.

For Sir Thomas believes Fanny to be a submissive and docile young woman, and what is more, Henry Crawford has recently proved himself a man of good-will and shown that he has the interests of the family at heart by securing the promotion of William from midshipman to Lieutenant. Fanny has seen the letters which bring the news of William's promotion:

The first was from the Admiral to inform his nephew, in a few words, of his having succeeded in the object he had undertaken, the promotion of young Price, and inclosing two more, one from the Secretary of the First Lord to a friend, whom the Admiral had set to work in the business, the other from that friend to himself, by which it appeared that his Lordship had the very great happiness of attending to the recommendation of Sir Charles, that Sir Charles was much delighted in having such an opportunity of proving his regard for Admiral Crawford, and that the circumstance of Mr William Price's commission as second Lieutenant of H. M. sloop Thrush, being made out, was spreading general joy through a wide circle of great people. (298–9)

There can be no doubt that this lobbying is intended to enclose Fanny within a circuit of homosocial obligations: the promotion is designed not merely to please her, but to persuade Sir Thomas, Edmund and even William himself, that Henry is one of the boys. With such leverage, reaching into the heart of the Establishment, it seems almost incredible that Fanny should reject him. (At the same time one should note how it indicates the drive and energy that Crawford devotes to his courtship). Sir Thomas is reduced by her refusal even to consider Henry as a suitor to a state of baffled rage in which he winds up by accusing her of wilfulness, self-conceit and ingratitude and which leaves her crying bitterly. Her face is in such a state that he rethinks his earlier intention of making her confront Crawford himself. Sir Thomas thus reveals himself as less benevolent and more of a politician than he would like to think himself, but Fanny has preserved her secret, and it is he who has been deceived.

The objections that Fanny later offers when Edmund in his turn seeks, more gently, to persuade her – dislike of Henry's behaviour in the autumn, his flirtation with the two sisters, the suddenness of his proposal – are contaminated by this insincerity. To read the novel as offering Fanny as the model of integrity and principle, the undeviatingly moral mast-head of Mansfield Park, is to forget that her unspoken love – the more powerful for its suppression – is the instigator of her conduct, not her rectitude. 'Indeed I cannot act', she declares when pressed to do so, and this has made vivid that fear of any kind of bodily exposure that is the consequence of her ingrained sense of inferiority. But in a looser, more general sense, Fanny 'acts', presenting herself as other than she feels, throughout the novel: and from now on, she is involved in a more conscious deception. When Edmund, for example, urges her to let Henry persuade her, she bursts out with '"Oh! never, never, never; he never will succeed with me." And she spoke with a warmth which quite astonished Edmund, and which she blushed at the recollection of herself, when she saw his look"' (347). Her cogent and rational arguments against her immediate reception of his proposal, reminiscent of Elizabeth Bennet as they are, show clearly that Fanny has become more self-assertive, more self-respecting. But they function in fact to pull the wool over Edmund's eyes. Looking back over the interview she fears 'she had been doing wrong, saying too much, overacting the caution which she had been fancying necessary' (354). Edmund perceives weariness and distress in her face, but the weariness is, once again, due to the exertion of the false self, to the effort required to disguise and misrepresent her motives.

The narrative devices which render Fanny's conscientiousness simultaneously then render her love for Edmund; they are subversive and provocative, occasionally problematic and inert. Some of them mislead readers as they deceive the characters. This supposition at least may go some way towards explaining the critical tradition under which *Mansfield Park* has struggled. Lionel Trilling's famous preface to the novel, itself now an item of history, creates a Fanny who, in contrast to Whately's 'restless' and 'jealous' heroine, epitomises stillness and withdrawal, whose 'debility' is perversely preferred to Mary Crawford's 'vitality', and whom we can barely understand but by keeping in mind 'the tradition which affirmed the peculiar sanctity of the sick, the weak, and the dying'.[27] Trilling's Fanny Price has on the one hand a weak, debilitated body, and on the other a high-principled, undeviatingly righteous soul. A close relation, even an identity, between the two is never envisaged. *Mansfield Park*, he declared, 'discovers in principle the path to the wholeness of the self which is peace' and thus speaks 'intimately' 'to our secret inadmissible hopes'. The final words of Trilling's essay suggest that unspoken desires are indeed at the core of this text, but instead of being attributed to Fanny they are transferred to the critic, or reader, and instead of being sexual they are sublimated into a secular spirituality, the longing for a lost transcendental ideal. Yet Sandra Gilbert and Susan Gubar, twenty years later, in another celebrated work, share the same distaste for what they call Fanny's 'invalid passivity' and remark that 'A model of domestic virtue – "dependent, helpless, friendless, neglected, forgotten"... she resembles Snow White not only in her passivity but in her invalid deathliness, her immobility, her pale purity'[28] – a reading equally as inattentive to the text's transmission of Fanny's actual bodily states. If you obliterate Fanny's desire, you cannot understand her 'invalidism', which is her desire, thwarted and concealed, expressing itself through her body.

Gilbert and Gubar cite Henry Crawford's sentimental appraisal of Fanny as if it were unquestioned by the text, but in fact he is immediately corrected by Mary (297), and Henry's view of Fanny is an item in his own psychopathology. Having begun by trying to make her fall in love with him, he has found, much to his surprise, and to the delight of his sister, that he is in love with her. The chapter (XII of the second volume) 'where he tells of his devotion to Fanny Price, is as pretty an account of such a confidence as can well be imagined, where the worldliness of each is almost lost in the happiness of disinterested love, which both are feeling.'[29] '"My dearest Henry," cried Mary, stopping short and smiling in his face, "how glad I am to see you so much in love!..."' (297). In a chapter narrated from Mary's position, the warmth and openness accorded the Crawfords' relationship at this juncture is one of the novel's ironic and dramatic triumphs. Henry describes to Mary the object of his love:

'Had you seen her this morning, Mary,' he continued, 'attending with such ineffable sweetness and patience, to all the demands of her aunt's stupidity, working with her, and for her, her colour beautifully heightened as she leant over the work, then returning to her seat to finish a note which she was previously engaged in writing for that stupid woman's service, and all this with such unpretending gentleness, so much as if it were a matter of course that she was not to have a moment at her own command, her hair arranged as neatly as it always is, and one little curl falling forward as she wrote, which she now and then shook back, and in the midst of all this, still speaking at intervals to *me*, or listening, and as if she liked to listen to what I said. Had you seen her so, Mary, you would not have implied the possibility of her power over my heart ever ceasing.' (296–7)

In Henry's view all women are fickle, all female sexuality labile ('I am not such a coxcomb', he says brutally in his next speech, 'as to suppose [Maria's] feelings more lasting than other women's') their emotions not worth a fig, and therefore Fanny, whose devotion and constancy are so apparent, cannot be an ordinary woman and must be – in the familiar division – a divinity. 'You have some touches of the angel in you', he declares, 'beyond what – not merely beyond what one sees, because one never sees any thing like it – but beyond what one fancies might be' (344). 'It would be something to be loved by such a girl, to excite the first ardours of her young, unsophisticated mind!' (235), Henry thinks, seeing how Fanny comes to life in the presence of her brother. For him, she is a pre-Victorian Thackeraian Amelia, bent over her sewing, her sexual attractiveness heightened by her weakness and innocence, and the potential therefore of mastery over it. In Henry's fantasy, as in all male fantasies of this kind, Fanny is a blank, or vacant space in which the desire, once aroused, will be wholly directed to him. 'He knew not', the narrator comments, 'that he had a pre-engaged heart to attack. Of *that*, he had no suspicion ... He considered her rather as one who had never thought on the subject enough to be in danger; who had been guarded by youth, a youth of mind as lovely as of person' (326). How wrong he is both in his worldliness and his fantasy, for Maria loves tenaciously and suffers deeply, and Fanny's 'beautifully heightened' colour is a more ambivalent sign than he supposes.

It is Henry's position towards Fanny, though, that has been adopted, too, all unconsciously, by those critics (mostly American, male) who envision a Fanny who is a secular saint or saviour. Overstressing Fanny's dedication to that great good place Mansfield Park, they have tended to elide her conflicts and almost to ignore her passion. 'Fanny as a will struggling only to be itself becomes at last the spiritual centre of Mansfield Park', writes Harold Bloom, echoing Trilling, 'The quietest and most mundane of visionaries, she remains also one of the firmest: her dedication is to the future of Mansfield Park as the idea of order it once seemed to her.'[30] 'An image of the values of thoughtful rest', this Fanny is the female object of a male gaze investing her with a spirituality that is undivided, a 'still centre', whole. 'Pure' and elevated moral motives are substituted for libidinal ones, and the female desiring subject at the very centre of this text is denied. 'In the debilitated but undeviating figure of Fanny Price', writes Tony Tanner, 'we should perceive the pain and labour involved in maintaining true values in a corrosive world of dangerous energies and selfish power-play. She suffers in her stillness. For Righteousness' sake'.[31]

But if Henry's fantasy of Fanny speaks through these critics, one can hardly help noticing that another character's hatred of Fanny speaks through some female commentators on the novel. In many ways she is set to be a feminist heroine: she refuses the assembled might of the patriarchy, she vindicates steadfastly the female desire however subversive it appears to her, and the writing in which she is made palpable employs bodily signs, rhythm and silence as modes of subversion. But at the same time, perversely and maddeningly, she opts to support the very patriarchal values that oppress her. This quiet, seemingly passive girl might be adopted as a heroine, but she turns out to be a traitor. Nina Auerbach, forced to recognise the compelling power of the writing which defines Fanny's position, can hardly contain her rage. 'There is something horrible about her, something that deprives the imagination of its appetite for ordinary life and compels it toward the deformed, the dispossessed', she writes. Fanny, it seems, is a witch, who throws a 'countercharm' over natural joys, with 'her silent withering power', 'feasting on the activities of others', she resembles a 'vampire', a 'monster'.[32] It was Mrs Norris, remember, who 'in the blindness of her anger' saw Fanny 'as the daemon of the piece' (448). More sympathetic critics, though, have passed over Fanny's love for Edmund in silence, distressed, perhaps disgusted, by her choice of object.

There is an analogy between the problems for feminism represented by Fanny and by 'Dora', the famous analysand. To some feminists this figure, as she emerges in Freud's case presentation, is a heroine – 'the one who resists the system'. 'The source of Dora's strength is, in spite of everything, her desire', declared Hélène Cixous.[33] 'The hysteric is not just someone who has her words cut off, someone for whom the body speaks. It all starts with her anguish as it relates to desire and to the immensity of her desire – therefore from her demanding quality', Cixous claims. Catherine Clément disagrees: 'It is metaphoric, yes, a metaphor of the impossible, of the ideal and dreamed of totality, yes, but when you say "that bursts the family into pieces", no. It mimics, it metaphorises destruction, but the family reconstitutes itself around it'. Like Dora, Fanny resists the system, but like Dora, Fanny, as I suggest, is pathologically inscribed by the very patriarchy whose invitations she refuses.

Whilst Sir Thomas Bertram is away, attending to the crisis on his estates in Antigua, Mrs Norris is occupied with another errand, busily prosecuting on his behalf the business of forming a connection with a nearby family of importance and marrying his daughter Maria off to the wealthy, but doltish, Mr Rushworth. It was not an easy task, she eagerly reminds him on his return, to get Lady Bertram to pay the necessary visit:

> 'My dear Sir Thomas, if you had seen the state of the roads *that* day!
> I thought we should never have got through them, though we had the
> four horses of course; and poor old coachman would attend us, out of
> his great love and kindness, though he was hardly able to sit the box
> on account of the rheumatism which I had been doctoring him for,
> ever since Michaelmas, I cured him at last; but he was very bad all the
> winter – and this was such a day, I could not help going to him up in
> his room before we set off to advise him not to venture: he was putting
> on his wig – so I said, 'Coachman, you had much better not go, your
> Lady and I shall be very safe; you know how steady Stephen is, and
> Charles has been upon the leaders so often now, that I am sure there

is no fear.' But, however, I soon found it would not do; he was bent upon going, and as I hate to be worrying and officious, I said no more; but my heart quite ached for him at every jolt, and when we got into the rough lanes about Stoke, where what with frost and snow upon beds of stones, it was worse than any thing you can imagine, I was quite in an agony about him. And then the poor horses too! – to see them straining away! You know how I always feel for the horses. And when we got to the bottom of Sandcroft Hill, what do you think I did? You will laugh at me – but I got out and walked up. I did indeed. It might not be saving them much, but it was something, and I could not bear to sit at my ease, and be dragged up at the expense of those noble animals. I caught a dreadful cold, but *that* I did not regard. My object was accomplished in the visit.' (189–90)

There could hardly be a clearer illustration of the Foucauldian proposition that power functions not through the mediation of ideology, but directly upon the body of the subject. Carole Pateman, discussing the idea of property in the person in her *The Sexual Contract*, comments:

Civil mastery, like the mastery of the slave-owner, is not exercised over mere biological entities that can be used like material (animal) property, nor exercised over purely rational entities. Masters are not interested in the disembodied fiction of labour power or services. They contract for the use of human embodied selves. Precisely because subordinates are embodied selves they can perform the required labour, be subject to discipline, give the recognition and offer the faithful service that makes a man a master.[34]

Mrs Norris' relationship to the coachman reproduces her own relation to Sir Thomas, or rather, to 'the family'. She sacrifices to Sir Thomas the old coachman – and the horses – as a reflection and amplification of her own loyalty, a loyalty which, as the last extraordinary detail in her speech makes clear, even requires self-punishment. Faithful service in the name of the family but also and primarily engaging various libidinal satisfactions – in deprivation, in economy – is the mode of Mrs Norris' life. Among her literary forebears are Samuel Johnson's Tetrica and Eriphile. 'When female minds are imbittered by age or solitude', Johnson wrote, 'their malignity is generally exerted in a rigorous and spiteful superintendance of domestic trifles'[35] and Eriphile, accordingly, makes her nieces' and servants' lives miserable. 'It is her business every morning to visit all the rooms, in hopes of finding a chair without its cover, a window shut or open contrary to her orders, a spot on the hearth, or a feather on the floor, that the rest of the day may be justifiably spent in taunts of contempt, and vociferations of anger.' Mrs Norris, 'spunging' off the housekeeper at Sotherton, triumphing in saving a whole yard of baize, also keeps the servants, like young Dick Jackson (141–2), in line, and devotes much of her energy to their affairs, sometimes successfully combining both satisfactions, as when she takes off 'all the supernumerary jellies to nurse a sick maid' (283). One of her successors is George Eliot's aging gentlewoman Mrs Transome, 'who liked every sign of power her lot had left her' and one of whose meagre pleasures is 'to change a labourer's medicines fetched from the doctor and substitute a prescription of her own' (*Felix Holt*, chapter 1).[36] Nursing the servants and the working classes is a traditional role for the genteel but otherwise disempowered woman, and as these examples illustrate, this benevolence has a Janus face. In her own sphere the doctoring gentlewoman replicates the social relations that characterise the social system in which she lives, benevolence intricated with (and sometimes masking) coercion being the typical form in which relations between inferiors and superiors define themselves. Mrs Norris punishes others for her own dependency and frustration, whilst being able to hide this from herself in the guise of generosity to the recipients and loyal service to the system.

It is likewise with the adoption of the poor niece Fanny Price into the household. Everyone has basked in the pleasure of benevolence, but the project – the procurement – has fed other, less creditable, impulses. Fanny Price is the victim of Mrs Norris for more complicated reasons than is the old coachman. Like Mrs Norris herself, Fanny is a fringe dweller, a single, defenceless female who is not part of the family except by courtesy. The one lives in the small White House, on the edge of the estate, the other in the little white attic at the top of the house. Mrs Norris' attitudes to Fanny reveal aspects of herself that are concealed from overt consciousness. 'The lessons she prescribes all project onto her little niece the worthlessness, inferiority and indebtedness she is so anxious to deny in herself.'[37] Fanny becomes the scapegoat upon whom Mrs Norris can exercise her frustrations and baffled energies: Fanny is humiliated and punished, made to fetch and carry, scolded and victimised, deprived of heat in the East room, so that Mrs Norris can momentarily appease her own sense of functionless dependence, and reaffirm the strictness of the social hierarchy which gives meaning to her life. More importantly, Mrs Norris' pathological response to her dependent status, which forces her to both conscious and unconscious exactions upon her body, is used to suggest affinities between the two figures. Behind Mrs Norris' 'reddening' on such occasions as Dr Grant's slighting of the Moor Park apricot, or the coach being sent round for Fanny, is a rage for which propriety and social arrangements allow but a bodily and passive outlet. There is a hidden demand within her shows of outward loyalty, analogous to the inadmissible feelings that Fanny communicates by blushing: and Mrs Norris perceives correctly (as if unconscious were speaking to unconscious) that Fanny has 'a little spirit of secrecy, and independence, and nonsense, about her' (323) which as it happens has just been demonstrated in the scene in the East room.

The shape of *Mansfield Park* gives increasing importance to the self-communings and meditations of Fanny Price. Moving further and further away from the ensemble scenes of the first volume the essential drama in the second and third comes to reside in the isolated anxieties of its heroine. Just before the ball, in the second volume, when Edmund, leaving her the chain, intimates that he has decided to ask Mary to marry him, and retires with the protest that (nevertheless) she is one of his 'two dearest', Fanny's struggle with her desires receives its fullest expression in the novel. It is clear to the reader, long before this, that Edmund, though solicitous of Fanny, is not attracted to her as he is to Mary, so that Fanny's devastated reception of the news is ironically conditioned. 'She was one of his two dearest – that must support her. But the other! – the first! She had never heard him speak so openly before, and though it told her no more than what she had long perceived, it was a stab; – for it told of his own convictions and views' (264). Once more jealousy is the instigator of the fullest display of Fanny's feelings: the passage repeats the phrase 'it was a stab' so as to mime Fanny's attempt to incorporate the newly acquired certainty that Edmund intends to marry Mary into herself. 'It was a stab, in spite of every long-standing expectation; and she was obliged to repeat that she was one of his two dearest, before the words gave her any sensation' (264). 'A disembodied human emotion is a nonentity', wrote William James,[38] and this language seems designed to make his point dramatically: Fanny experiences her reaction as a corporal sensation, and the calmer, more 'rationalising' thoughts which follow still continue to manifest, as an undercurrent, the wake of the paroxysm that has convulsed her:

> It was her intention, as she felt it to be her duty, to try to overcome all that was excessive, all that bordered on selfishness in her affection for Edmund. To call or to fancy it a loss, a disappointment, would be a presumption; for which she had not words strong enough to satisfy her own humility. To think of him as Miss Crawford might be justified in thinking, would in her be insanity. To her, he could be nothing under any circumstances – nothing dearer than a friend. Why did such an idea occur to her even enough to be reprobated and forbidden? It ought not to have touched on the confines of her imagination. She would endeavour to be rational, and to deserve the right of judging of Miss Crawford's character and the privilege of true solicitude for him by a sound intellect and an honest heart. (264)

'It ought not to have touched on the confines of her imagination' is a particularly arresting phrase. Here the imagination is a guarded space, surrounded by railings, perhaps a Park, a space cleared from other rampant and untamed, uncivilised, impulses. Freud once compared consciousness to a drawing room, adjoining which is a 'large entrance hall, in which the mental impulses jostle over one another like separate individuals'.[39] On the threshold between these rooms stands a watchman, who 'examines the different mental impulses, acts as a censor, and will not admit them into the drawing room if they displease him'. But even impulses which have got into the drawing room of the conscious need to 'catch the eye of consciousness' to become fully known to the subject, and it is at this moment that Fanny's eye catches sight of her own, in Trilling's phrase, 'secret inadmissible hopes'. She has become, in the very strenuousness of her denial, aware of those hopes, and they are now, manifestly, on the agenda of the novel. Her feelings manage to infiltrate the thoughts that are designed to put them down. 'She had not words strong enough to satisfy her own humility'; Fanny belabours herself with those words – 'nothing', 'presumption', 'insanity' - of which the intensity is but a witness to the power of the desires they combat. Fanny has learned from the patriarchy (there seems an exact use for this term in this novel, where Sir Thomas both acts the family patriarch and is part of the governing class of his country) that the object of her desires is taboo: as soon as the desire emerges into consciousness it is regarded with dismay. It is as if Fanny's childhood and physiology, the political ideology of conservativism, and Fanny's loyalty have all collaborated to invest Sir Thomas' restrictions with sacerdotal force, or as if the conservative social ideal of the eighteenth century moralists has met its perfect inhabitant. Fanny's subjectivity as it is laid out here thus replicates the structure of the social hierarchy which she inhabits.

Fanny wishes not only to behave, to act, but to feel, and even to imagine, as she has been directed. Indeed, her thoughts do perform as she has been tutored; what she says, to herself, is a replication of what Sir Thomas and Edmund, were they privy to her desires, might say. But that is not all that this dramatic representation of Fanny's thoughts divulges. Fanny is telling herself and telling herself vehemently what her social position is, and what she may or may not think and desire: but the vehemence itself is the rebellious or libidinal element seeking its displaced expression. Fanny is more completely a product of her culture (or rather she is exposed as more completely a product) than any other character, but the narrator adds a crucial rider when she declares, in so many words, that 'feelings of youth and nature' (instinctual and unculturated elements of the subject) play the determinative part. She intervenes to plead for sympathy and understanding for the figure:

She had all the heroism of principle, and was determined to do her duty; but having also many of the feelings of youth and nature, let her not be much wondered at if, after making all these good resolutions on the side of self-government, she seized the scrap of paper on which Edmund had begun to writing to her ... and ... locked it up with the chain, as the dearest part of the gift. (265)

Fanny is not, it is hence suggested, emotionally or psychologically crippled by her feelings for Edmund, even though on many occasions they exact a physiological cost: just as she locks up his letter in her desk, she keeps her love safe in one part of her consciousness. Fanny's loyalty to the family, and especially to Sir Thomas, may then be analogous to Mrs Norris', but it does not result in total repression of her desire, in neurotic acting-out, (like catching a cold to save the horses) or projection of that punishment onto others. Fanny is saved from that fate by the strength of her early love for William, and his for her, which, rescuing her from her mother's indifference, forms, so to speak, a core of self-worth, and flows uninterruptedly into her love for Edmund. Much as she is ashamed of her feelings, they make up henceforth part of her conscience, and their location (not beyond the pale) is revealed, and kept before the reader in those occasions, continually contrived by the author, when she blushes. What Fanny's conscience is committed to, for the rest of the novel, is a moral 'holding operation': to keep herself aware of, and therefore in a sense loyal to her feelings, but not to let these be enacted in false or perverted ways. In a sense then, Fanny's inhibitions, however unattractive as social demeanour, and however unproductive of action, are the central constituents of her psychological and moral self, and therefore critics who speak of Fanny's 'passivity' misconceive the nature of the drama which the novel's second half unfolds. One must be wary, too, of confusing what one might call this psychological conservation with the political or ethical conservativism with which it overlaps and which is occasionally explicitly expounded or articulated.

Such passages of Fanny's conscientious meditations do have to be brought into some sort of relation, though, with Sir Thomas' famous reflections on his daughters' education: 'He

feared that principle, active principle, had been wanting, that
they had never been properly taught to govern their inclinations
and tempers, by that sense of duty which can alone suffice'
(463) for this emphasis (reiterated at intervals throughout the
novel) seems to be proposing Fanny within the moral scheme as
an exemplary instance of someone who is principled and dutiful.
Yet since her conception of her duty is fundamentally understood, at the psychological level, as the product of the pathology
of her special nature and upbringing, here the psychological
and political-moral arguments of the novel are in collision.[40]
The value that is set upon Fanny's modesty (so frequently
displayed) is at odds with the presentation of it as, in one light,
shrinking, indoctrinated, self-abasement, the value that is set
upon conscientiousness is compromised because Fanny's is
excessive and unprofitable, and in some ways incapacitating.
Fanny more generally seems to be offered as a model of right
behaviour, whilst simultaneously she is explored as a misguided,
though well-intentioned and scrupulous product of a specific
social and personal history. There is something pathetic and
comic in this still young woman's private intensities (a pathos
and comedy that are – unobtrusively – noted by the narrator)
that makes it difficult not to inflect the phrase 'all the heroism
of principle' with irony. And – to complicate matters even
further – the novel is, as I have been suggesting, actually
running a narrative line which vindicates not conscience, or
duty, or self-sacrifice, but desire. Despite appearances, Fanny is
not a weak or depressive personality: she certainly is ashamed of
her derelictions from what Sir Thomas might wish for her, but
she does not repudiate her inconvenient feelings: the continuity
between the confirming love of William and her love for
Edmund ensures that neither are kept out of consciousness or
repressed.

The problem is that the ethical and libidinal narratives of
Mansfield Park are inextricably plaited together. Fanny, for
example, dislikes Mary for several sorts of reasons, good as well
as bad, but how to tell one class apart from the other? The 'bad'
reasons (one might say, determined to tease them apart) are the
jealous ones – Mary's physical grace, her winning charm, her

tact and diplomacy, her wit – everything about her that entices Edmund, and draws him away from Fanny. The 'good' reasons (within the novel's ethical framework) are the ideological ones – Mary's defective sense of propriety, her impudence, her lack of Christian dutifulness, her mercenary motives: but to hold these separate from the perceptions of Fanny's jealousy for long is impossible. Any analysis of Mary's conversation will produce precipitates of both worldliness and kindness, warmth and cynicism, ambition and wit. To say that Fanny's 'good' reasons are masks for, rationalisations of, the 'bad', would simply be to ascribe everything to the libidinal motive, and there are very strong reasons against doing this, not least the volume of critical readings which determine to read the novel as a political or ethico-political text. The resulting readerly unease can be illustrated by the scene in volume II, chapter IV where Fanny and Mary sit in the shrubbery one November day:

> 'Yes', replied Miss Crawford carelessly, 'it does very well for a place of this sort. One does not think of extent *here* – and between ourselves till I came to Mansfield, I had not imagined a country parson ever aspired to a shrubbery or any thing of the kind.'
> 'I am so glad to see the evergreens thrive!' said Fanny in reply. (209)

An example of Mary's flippancy, lack of response to nature, worldly ambition, disregard of Fanny's feelings? Her tactlessness is considerably mitigated when one considers how little Fanny has given her, how little chance she has of knowing the other's feelings. Fanny's turning the conversation registers the narrator's disapproval of Mary, but at the cost of underlining her own failures. Fanny can risk openness with Mary least of all: what is left for her but to talk of the evergreens? Her silence, when Mary runs on and talks in her most worldly manner of Mrs Rushworth's marriage being a 'public blessing', unlike the silence of Elinor Dashwood, who does not think Robert Ferrars deserves 'the compliment of rational opposition' (SS 252), is not a calm rationalism: by this stage of the novel it swarms with unstated and conflicting motives. Plausible as are the dynamics of the relationship, the ethical valuations are inexactly mapped onto it. The reader questions the implied validity of Fanny's condemnation, for though Mary is flippant and careless, Fanny's silence is constructed not simply out of disapproval, but out of inhibition. This is a microcosm of the novel – the interpersonal relations are entirely cogent, but the distribution of moral or ethical values seems undermined by what they reveal.

Mansfield Park is obviously in one sense a *bildungsroman*, the story of Fanny Price's growing up, education and maturing into a woman able to play an adult role in society.[41] But it is a question whether her coming out is ever actually accomplished. The social ceremony that marks her maturity and her social acceptance is a minor theme in the novel which only serves to indicate that if Fanny Price does 'come out' it must be in other senses. Certainly the occasion does not inaugurate a speaking Fanny Price able to engage on any more free or equal terms with her social world; instead it issues in a phase of the novel in which Fanny is still more the beleaguered and isolated consciousness. 'Coming out' in its society sense is a gendering ritual that designates the girl's maturing into a woman, a ceremony that presents her upon the stage of the patriarchy as marriageable, and marriageable within the network of family and political alliances ('connections') that makes up 'society'. It's characteristic of *Mansfield Park* that the ball, heralded by many touches as a significant occasion, is in fact extrinsic to the main drama, and that much of Fanny's actual activity is designed to subvert it, to strip from it the symbolic significance it might have. Nothing could be less relevant to the inner purposes of Fanny Price than this ceremony which bestows upon her the accolades of society and foretells her marriage to Crawford.

When, at an earlier moment in the novel, Fanny was pressed to take another stage, and stand-in for Mrs Grant as Cottager's wife, she was brutally reminded by Mrs Norris that her dependent position ought to control her behaviour and motives. 'I shall think her a very obstinate, ungrateful girl', she says 'sharply', 'if she does not do what her aunt and cousins wish her

– very ungrateful indeed, considering who and what she is' (147). In indignation at this insult (obscene, shocking, literally, because it brings to the surface the imperatives and relationships decency keeps hidden) Mary moves her chair closer to Fanny and attempts to comfort and console her companion by talking of her future 'coming out'. By 'supposing Fanny was now preparing for her *appearance*, as of course she would come out when her cousin was married', she kindly but misguidedly attempts to compensate for Mrs Norris' degradation by ministering to the young lady's vanity, including Fanny within the family, and suggesting, too, in effect, the triumphs and rewards there might be in identifying one's destiny wholly with the social, throwing oneself into the family's life and purposes. By association, then, coming out is already designated as a mode of capitulation to the requirements of 'the family' as a political institution.

But there is evidently no thought of Fanny's coming out at Maria's wedding – the novel's salient example of 'proper' behaviour, a public alliance that is a transgression of the libidinal self – even though Sir Thomas gives her a gown on the occasion, a gown that she wears on her first individual invitation to dine out at the Grants', which is where Henry first notices and takes an interest in her. It is only when the signs of Henry Crawford's courtship come to Sir Thomas' notice that he decides upon the ball, which will, indeed, mark the family's formal adoption of Fanny, and her incorporation into the system of alliances and connections which makes up ruling society.

This *rite de passage*, though, is conducted with its principal participant unconscious, or at best, unwillingly aware of its significance. For the ball, Fanny has still only the same gown that she wore to Maria's wedding, the gift of her uncle, and on this occasion the dress, she feels, needs ornaments. In choosing these Fanny is, in fact, symbolically guarding herself against appropriation by the larger social world. It is only when 'having, with delightful feelings, joined the chain and the cross, those memorials of the two most beloved of her heart, those dearest tokens so formed for each other by every thing real and imaginary – and put them round her neck, and seen and felt how full of William and Edmund they were' (271) that she allows herself to wear Mary's (in fact Henry's) necklace. Irwin Ihrenpreis compares Austen's symbolism with Scott's in *Waverley*, writing that 'When the hero dresses himself in the tartan, he takes on its associations; it does not reflect his; for Scott uses the tartan as a metaphor for Jacobinism'. But 'in Austen's stories, a thing, a gesture, an occupation seldom has moral significance or general meaning apart from the individual to whom it belongs. Austen can transform all the circumstances of common life into implicit moral comment: space, time, landscape, architecture, furniture. What she will not do is attribute independent symbolic meaning to those circumstances.'[42] It might be that the lack of fit between Henry's chain and the cross indicates symbolically Henry's disregard of Christian standards, or predicts their final incompatible destinies: much more likely, though, what it indicates is the difference between Edmund's thoughtfulness, attuned to her needs, and the gesture of possession which Henry's 'gift' actually is. The cross and the chain must obviously have some symbolic significance, though of a generalised kind, but their primary reference is to Fanny's own private history: it is the feeling that the ornaments are 'full' of Edmund and William that makes Fanny delight to wear them next to her flesh. In other words Fanny constructs an alternative patriarchal route of possession of herself, but it is a possession which is not constructed around her but by her, a route through her own love and desires; it alludes to a private and continuous emotional history (and source of strength) which enables her to safeguard herself, and simultaneously to avert and to perform that act of appropriation which is the ceremony of 'coming out'.

The narrator makes plain her feminist distaste for the ritual. 'Miss Price, known only by name to half the people invited, was now to make her first appearance, and must be regarded as the Queen of the evening. Who could be happier than Miss Price? But Miss Price had not been brought up to the trade of *coming out* ... ' (266–7). Austen's tone recalls Mary Wollstonecraft: 'What can be more indelicate than a girl's *coming out* in the fashionable world? Which, in other words, is to bring to market a marriageable miss, whose person is taken from one public place to another, richly caparisoned ... '[43] It is clear that the novelist sees that this ceremony simply clinches the patriarchal conception of its women as commodities, and of which Fanny's romanticism cannot prevent her from being a victim. This paradox is captured in the novel's shifts of tone, between the tender sympathy with which Fanny's consciousness is represented, and the surrounding narrative's worldly and astringent irony, which enacts the fact that Fanny is enclosed within a society whose harsher imperatives cannot indefinitely be refused.

Fanny's entry into 'the world', in fact, though, is deferred. After the ball, after the proposal, Fanny's demeanour – the shyness, the averted face, the few, reluctantly spoken, words – is still that of a girl not 'out'. How could it be otherwise? Her purposes and ends have nothing to do with her social promotion, and hers is a pre-engaged heart. She does, of course, speak sharply to Crawford on one or two occasions, but 'coming out' in the largest sense – in the sense of Fanny becoming an adult speaking subject – is also deferred, a shelving of issues and postponing of crisis brought about by shifting the scene to Portsmouth, for by this means the narrative is located almost entirely within Fanny's isolated, receptive, consciousness.

Sir Thomas' purpose in sending Fanny home for a while is rendered in a series of sadistically-toned metaphors:

> He certainly wished her to go willingly, but he as certainly wished her to be heartily sick of home before her visit ended; and that a little abstinence from the elegancies and luxuries of Mansfield Park, would bring her mind into a sober state, ...
>
> It was a medicinal project upon his niece's understanding, which he must consider as at present diseased. A residence of eight or nine years in the abode of wealth and plenty had a little disordered her powers of comparing and judging ... (369).

The medical metaphors suggest how coercion disguises itself in the mask of kindness. With an effect which is recurrent in *Mansfield Park* (where the incompatibility between people's private feelings towards the same subject is a repeated irony)

Fanny receives the proposal with something close to rapture and sees it also, but in a very different fashion, as a restoration to health. 'The remembrance of all her earliest pleasures, and of what she had suffered in being torn from them, came over her with renewed strength, and it seemed as if to be at home again, would heal every pain that had since grown out of the separation' (370). Fanny imagines that at Portsmouth she will 'feel affection without fear or restraint', be 'unassailed' there, 'safe from the perpetual irritation of knowing [Edmund's] heart'. She dreams of a mature self-possession, of being at last comfortable, 'at peace'.

Of course Sir Thomas' assessment is the more shrewd. Portsmouth is the abode of 'closeness and noise ... confinement, bad air, bad smells' (432) – a place of incessant hullabaloo, frayed carpets, dirty crockery, and bad manners, and much more importantly, of neglect and emotional isolation. Fanny is here still more the receptor of others' acts, responding non-verbally, but through her body, to the various assaults of her surroundings. She quickly 'loses ground as to health', as Henry perceives from her face on his visit after scarcely a month's stay: and the narrator adds 'could he have suspected how many privations, besides that of exercise, she endured in her father's house, he would have wondered that her looks were not much more affected than he found them'. Sir Thomas is now answered with a correspondingly dour irony:

After being nursed up at Mansfield, it was too late in the day to be hardened at Portsmouth; and though Sir Thomas, had he known all, might have thought his niece in the most promising way of being starved, both mind and body, into a much juster value for Mr Crawford's good company and good fortune, he would probably have feared to push his experiment farther, lest she might die under the cure. (413)

One might imagine that, in this setting of grim urban verismo, Fanny Price is set on the pathway of prolonged endurance, physical debility, collapse, delirium and madness that is the fate of Fanny Burney's heroines Cecilia and Camilla – and that is Burney's attempted resolution of the intractable and confounding imperatives of these novels – were it not for the assurance, partly conveyed in this narrational style, of a grasp of realistic contingencies able to outface such melodramatic outcomes.

Fanny certainly is in a liminal state, 'betwixt and between'[44] neither in nor out, neither fully accredited adult, nor fully protected dependent, cut off from society, isolated in a place which is neither, it turns out, home nor holiday. She is marooned for seemingly endless weeks whilst events that affect her decisively take place elsewhere, in London, Bath, Norfolk and Newmarket, and only filter through to her, if at all, in anxiously awaited, eagerly read, but unsatisfactory letters. The main narrative is now shifted into these letters, and this means that the other characters, apart from Henry, who also seems different in a new setting, voice themselves in another, and less flexible mode. Uninterrupted and unnuanced by the presence, however quiet, of another person, and by her reactions, the personas represented by the letters of Mary, Edmund and Lady Bertram are simpler, or perhaps one should rather say, more continuously self-displaying and self-exposing. Because there is none of the automatic self-checking that the interplay of feeling between the characters is shown to induce, Mary can be plausibly degraded in her letters to the mercenary London flirt that Fanny's jealous fancy has always imagined her 'really' to be. Thus the stance of the narrator, or of the novel, now assumes an identity with Fanny's – the distinction between the two tones and views (kept open with some difficulty throughout the novel and still maintained with regard to Henry) is gradually closed. Alone, dependent, her anxieties exacerbated by her suspense and isolation, Fanny naturally puts the worst of constructions on Mary's tone and reported conduct, but there is no prompting from the narration now, to give her lack of independence its due weight. The reader is given Fanny's prejudiced reactions, but because technically there can be no corrective material, no 'very, very, warm embrace' on Mary's part either to mitigate her speech or to disarm Fanny's hostility, Fanny's censorious readings, however plausibly given as reactions under the pressure of her own increasingly insistent tensions, tend to carry the day. After the denouement and her return to Mansfield, it is possible for the narrator to say that Fanny is happy because 'Edmund was no longer the dupe of Mary Crawford' (461) finally adopting Fanny's tone and opinions as her own, or rather sacrificing that space between the narrator and the character which allows ironic leverage.

'A friendly Letter is a calm and deliberate performance in the cool of leisure, in the stillness of solitude, and surely no man sits down to depreciate by design his own character'[45] Samuel Johnson had declared, but in Edmund's long letter, in chapter XIII of the third volume, Austen adopts, or rather adapts, the convention of the sentimental novel and Edmund, under pressure, does expose his heart, his bleeding heart, to his correspondent. The painful intensity of Edmund's feelings towards Mary struggles here with his recognition of her inaccessibility. The resulting medley of shifting resolves and self-abasements renders the vacillations of his thought in a deictic mode that anticipates the stream of consciousness and that, of course, by revealing with such naked sincerity the helplessness of his passion for Mary, makes his letter especially painful for Fanny to receive. 'How shall I bear it?' she exclaims on reading this letter, and a variety of turbulent emotions succeed. 'She was almost vexed into displeasure, and anger, against Edmund' (424), declares her narrator, but the dramatic presentation of Fanny's thoughts makes that 'almost' seem a defensive, protective move, an authorial intervention to preserve a notion of the heroine as morally stable, admirably uninvaded by the rage which simultaneously the text shows she does experience:

'He is blinded, and nothing will open his eyes, nothing can, after having had truths before him so long in vain. – He will marry her, and be poor and miserable. God grant that her influence do not make him cease to be respectable!' She looked over the letter again. '"So very fond of me!"' 'tis nonsense all. She loves nobody but herself and her brother. Her friends leading her astray for years! She is quite as likely to have led *them* astray ... '(424)

'Such sensations', writes the narrator, recognising that it is rage rather than thought that is displayed here (and the text, as in earlier passages, conveys the disarray of Fanny's responses as much as in anything else by its rhythms) 'were too near a kin to resentment to be long guiding Fanny's soliloquies' and they soon subside into an emotion more habitual with her, gratitude. The narrator seems, indulgently, to approve.

Tom Bertram's illness is brought into the story with that curt and perhaps defensive irony that is Austen's accustomed note in the face of serious sickness, but the device of introducing the topic at first through the conventionally empty phrases of Lady Bertram's 'epistolary intercourse' and then showing how her actual encounter with her son transforms her style ('I am so shocked to see him, that I do not know what to do. I am sure he has been very ill') has the effect of bestowing plausibility and naturalness on Tom's illness itself. Lady Bertram's letter-writing style is a surrogate for the character, and persuades the reader that he is recreated, thus masking the pat convenience of this reformative event.

When Fanny is first introduced into the family, Tom 'was just entering into life, full of spirits, and with all the liberal dispositions of an eldest son, who feels born only for expense and enjoyment' (17). Among the cousins, he, the heir, is at the opposite extreme to Fanny. A sportsman, he is vigorous, confident, untroubled, uninhibited. After the debacle with the theatricals, he is absent from the novel and the Park, throughout the second volume, enjoying himself with his numerous 'friends.' But with Fanny at Portsmouth, the fates of the cousins become counterpointed and interrelated. Tom, too, is away from home, at Newmarket. A selfish but amiable wastrel, his debaucheries have eventually brought on a hectic fever, in which he is neglected by his good-time companions. Lying on his sick bed, alone, belatedly discovering the value of 'home and family which had been little thought of in uninterrupted health' (427), Tom longs to come back to Mansfield, where the seriousness of his condition, exacerbated by distress at Maria's conduct, makes the family 'apprehensive for his lungs'. The two figures thus move close together: Fanny brought so low by anxiety and loneliness at Portsmouth, Tom by illness and the desertion of his friends at Newmarket. The pair are linked too by the way Fanny's response to the news of Maria's adultery replicates the symptoms of his fever. Fanny's body once again registers the impact of the news, as if moral shock and physical illness were now indistinguishable in her: 'There was no possibility of rest. The evening passed, without a pause of misery, the night was totally sleepless. She passed only from feelings of sickness to shudderings of horror; and from hot fits of fever to cold' (441). Fanny remains in redoubled suspense, this news being only the climax of a succession of strains and anxieties, and is brought tragically close to collapse. 'She had, indeed, scarcely the shadow of a hope to soothe her mind, and was reduced to so low and wan and trembling a condition as no mother – not unkind, except Mrs Price, could have overlooked.' (442) When Edmund's letter finally arrives with its proposal for her return to the Park, it is just the 'cordial', the medicine, she needs. In a reversal of Sir Thomas' and her own projects three months earlier, it is at the Park that she is now to be cured. Return to Mansfield is the precondition for Fanny's recovery of health and spirits, a recuperation beautifully hinted at by the description of the burgeoning spring landscape as she enters the Park. Mrs Norris, on the other hand, whose loyalty to the family and estate is more compulsive, more urgent, perhaps even more genuine than Fanny's, and who has doted on Maria, as Fanny has on her brother, has invested everything in her, takes over the role of invalid, reduced by events to a catatonic state, 'an altered creature, quieted, stupified, indifferent to all that passed' (448).

The resolution of the novel and the ultimate instauration of Fanny on the estate as Edmund's wife is predicated upon the true heir's prior renunciation of his errant ways. Illness is for Tom, as for Marianne Dashwood, a corrective experience: he and Mrs Norris are the only characters in this novel who finally undergo substantial change. 'He had suffered, and he had learnt to think, two advantages that he had never known before' (462), and we are to believe that a conscience has been implanted in him by this experience of the vulnerabilities of the flesh. Reformed and domesticated, he is thus able to assume his inheritance. Sketchy and conventional as this history is, it clearly places Tom, not Fanny, at the centre of any moral continuity bound up with the estate, and his reform occurs quite independently of Fanny's story. Tom Bertram still remains in the background, and is forgotten in the novel's last chapter, but it is only because the Prodigal Son has come home, has understood and now subscribes to the conservative values of the family, that the assured continuity exists within which she herself can contribute. At Mansfield, Fanny becomes 'indeed the daughter that [Sir Thomas] wanted' (472) but she is not literally the 'inheritor' of Mansfield Park, as so many critics allow themselves to say, nor 'the guardian of a debased heritage'.[46] The relationship of Sir Thomas's social and political beliefs to hers remains problematic, and her 'determination to do her duty' (if that is what it has been) does not actively bear upon the estate's actual reform, prosperity or improvement. She comes back, less as victor than as convalescent, for the novel's conservativism is found, I suggest, not in its adherence to Burkean political ideals, and certainly not in endorsement of the patriarchy, but in its being willing to settle, with Fanny, for 'comfort' and 'peace' within an admittedly imperfect social world. To give the latter part of the novel a therapeutic stress is difficult in fact to reconcile with that more orthodox reading which sees Fanny return in triumph, her conduct and endurance vindicated.

In another sense though it is certainly true that Fanny is a bearer of the novel's key values. Tom's sickness leads him to renounce his earlier hedonism, and the negligent behaviour of his friends leads him to recognise the worth of blood-ties. Fanny's conscientiousness, and her mistrust of relationships outside the boundaries of the family (however idiosyncratic, dictated by her own history) thus gets this implicit vindication. Fanny's love for Edmund is eventually reciprocated and consummated, but its problematic nature – its immaturity or otherwise – is an issue that is shelved. If at Portsmouth Fanny's physical condition regresses, she also shows some signs of emotional independence and self-possession, but these, on her return, come to nothing either. Fanny is brought back to Mansfield, sits and listens while Edmund unburdens his soul, still remains the unspeaking subject, and the narrator-mother of *Mansfield Park* (famously – 'My Fanny' (461)) does not allow her daughter, even at the close when she is vindicated by events, fully to express her love or speak her mind. When Fanny is 'now at liberty to speak openly' her words are unheard, reported at cursory third hand, absorbed into the narrator's style.

> Fanny, now at liberty to speak openly, felt more than justified in adding to his knowledge of [Mary's] real character, by some hint of what share his brother's state of health might be supposed to have in her wish for a complete reconciliation. Nature resisted it for a while. It would have been a vast deal pleasanter to have had her more disinterested in her attachment; but his vanity was not of a strength to fight long against reason. (459)

The slip into the vulgarism 'a vast deal' in the sketch of Edmund's reception of Fanny's news betrays the patent implausibility of this further attempt to twist her spite into an ethically defensible, because independent, position. Perhaps the psychological dynamics of the writing require that when this mother-less heroine no longer needs the attention and protection of her author (when, as is inevitably entailed by the plot, she becomes taken into the male-centred world) she is to be abandoned, for in no other of Austen's novels is the cynicism or flippancy of the treatment of outcomes, in the last chapter, so apparent as in this.

'Fanny Price is physically frail … but she is emotionally sound … Fanny demonstrates emotional strength and health', concludes a recent critic, Kenneth L. Moler.[47] I have wished to demonstrate that neither aspect of Fanny is unproblematic and that the physical and emotional aspects of her being are seen as inextricably interrelated. It is on this basis that many of the novel's most dramatic occasions are constructed, but Jane Austen's representation of Fanny's psychology is so full and intricate that it causes conflict within the novel's ethical, and ultimately conventional, structure. As Moler's remark suggests, too, the issues of 'health' cannot be kept separate from questions of moral valuation (as *Emma* is to demonstrate vigorously), which in this novel are also problematic. I argue that Fanny's is a narrative of female destiny in opposition to but also caught within patriarchal structures, like Dora, and that what is true of the character is also true of the text, like Freud's.

Fanny Price's famous invalidism, her deplorable weakness, is thus not just a tiresome plea for the reader's special attention, or a version of that romanticism which invests the young woman with a frail and ailing body as confirmation of and tribute to male power, but, in effect, a radical, and subversive – and irresolvable – critique. The critique is so discomforting in fact that many critics have wanted either to demonise or to sanctify the character, or to sentimentally (as it seems to me) revision the novel as a coherent political or ethical narrative, and to bury its libidinal, erotic, motifs. Of course this is another selective reading: I have made the heroine 'my Fanny' too. One might wonder, in turn, about the motives of this (male) critic in reconstructing the figure, and the novel, in these apparently nonpolitical, neo-romantic terms. What reply shall he give – but to blush?

CHAPTER 3

Emma: the picture of health

Educators, naturally enough, have read *Emma* as a novel about education. More sophisticated, or more self-conscious, latter-day authors and readers have thought it to be about authorship, or about reading. Many accounts exist which see it as a novel about perception, or understand it in epistemological terms, or interpret it as a novel of hermeneutics. Some have even fancied *Emma* to be about its heroine's imagination.[1] There is hardly a critic who, once having entered the close and intricate world the novel constructs, has not found it hospitable to a coherent and plausible reading, or who has not found something new and interesting to observe in Highbury. But with very few exceptions, no one has yet diagnosed *Emma* to be a novel concerned with health.

One exception is J. R. Watson's article 'Mr Perry's patients: a view of *Emma*' (1970)[2] and, taking his hint, I will begin this exploration of matters of health in the novel by noting the predominance of this figure, the country apothecary or local doctor, who historically is the precursor of the general practitioner.[3] Except that predominance is hardly the word, for Mr Perry, though very well known to all the novel's readers, never actually appears on its pages. He is omnipresent and very active, but scarcely seen, cloistered with Mr Woodhouse whilst the drama goes on elsewhere, or glimpsed occasionally as he rides about the village, or when Emma catches sight of him 'walking hastily by' as she is waiting for Harriet outside Ford's, referred to (every twenty or thirty pages): implied, but not presented. Most often he is reported on indirectly, through two or even three intermediaries, as when Harriet tells Emma how

Miss Nash has told her, that Mr Perry told *her*, that he saw Mr Elton on the road carrying the famous portrait, and teased him that 'He was very sure there must be a lady in the case'. Or he appears by proxy, through Mr Woodhouse attributing to him his own opinions about the healthiness of Cromer, or when he is appealed to about the digestive merits of wedding cake. When his speech is most fully conveyed to the reader (and his accents are briefly captured) it is still indirect speech. He makes his most confused, most blurred appearance, of course, in Frank Churchill's blunder about his setting up his carriage (344) as an item of Highbury gossip that provides Frank and the reader with a good deal of amusement, but leaves Mr Perry and his concerns still strangely indeterminate.

This effect of Mr Perry is one consequence of the narrational choice made by the author of this novel. Emma's is the salient, and the controlling point of view. Mr Perry is only one of a number of examples of figures who inhabit the middle distance of the text, access to whose conversation or thoughts is not given us, as a consequence of this restriction of narrative perspective. Yet this feature of Mr Perry is not, one might argue, an accidental or unfortunate result of this procedure. Many of the allusions to him, such as Emma's reminding her father how he nursed her through the measles (or indeed, his setting up, or not setting up, his carriage) are designed to suggest his part in the social establishment of the village. Though a professional, he is, like Mr Cole or Mr Weston, also an entrepreneur, rising in prosperity with the rise in his reputation, and if he is able to think of a carriage, and set up as a gentleman, that is presumably because he is in constant attendance on the community's richest patient.[4] When called to the genteel poor, like the Bates, he does not, we understand, charge a fee, and thus, in another mode, makes clear his claim to gentlemanly status. All this contributes to the *effet du réel* – to the novel's careful construction of the social verisimilitudes of village life – but the mode of his presentation also plays its part in the sense of depth that is one of its more remarkable achievements.

Mr Perry is a nodal point, not only as a relay-station of gossip, but as a key reference in the distinctive sociolect of Highbury, a speech idiom which, taking its cue from Mr Woodhouse, is much concerned with discussion of and enquiries about sickness and health. Highbury gossip interprets his purchase of the carriage, not as a sign of his prosperity, or of his social prestige, but in terms of his own ill health. 'It was owing to [Mrs Perry's] persuasion, as she thought his being out in bad weather did him a great deal of harm' is Frank's recital of the gossip (344–5). Economic relations and social determinants are thus displaced or partially concealed by their redefinition as matters of health. By redefining social (and gender) relations wholly as a language of the body, of seemingly self-produced, autonomous conditions, here and as we shall see, in more important instances, Highbury remains oblivious to the political and social structures that are actually organising its world. Highbury knows people, becomes familiar with them, comes to own them, in the mode of patienthood. All these inferences are tucked away in the midst of a narrative whose apparent enticement is to give a crucial clue about the romantic relation of Frank and Jane. Yet Mr Perry's plural and eccentric position within the text helps at the same time to problematise the very questions of health and illness on which he is the deferred and obscured authority.

In *Emma*, both the high and the low, both the rich and powerful Mrs Churchill of Enscombe, and the poor cottager whom Emma and Harriet go to visit, are noticed as sufferers from ill health. The novel is littered too with para-medical paraphernalia and talk, from Isabella's claims about the favourable air of Brunswick Square, to Harriet's treasured court-plaister, to the Hartfield arrowroot dispatched for Jane, to Emma's speculations about that special 'constitution' of Frank Churchill's which makes him cross when he is hot. It could be argued that Jane Austen uses these matters of health merely as a pretext, as incidental topics of conversation or concern in the novel, whilst really focusing on the more crucial matters her critics have so thoroughly elucidated – those matters of motive and perception, of imagination and self-knowledge, the life of consciousness, that can plausibly be made the central stuff of this psychologically adroit novel. After all, health is used as a pretext in the novel itself by its characters.

Jane Fairfax arrives in Highbury supposedly to try the effect of her native air on a long-standing cold (caught early in November, as it happens, in the first phase, the first strain, of her secret engagement). Frank uses his fixing of the spectacles of the deaf, sleepy – and presumably now also blinded – Mrs Bates as a cover for dallying with Jane by the piano, or rushes out with umbrellas on the excuse that 'Miss Bates must not be forgotten' to welcome Jane to the ball. Emma, finding Harriet's disappointed presence too uncomfortable after accepting Mr Knightley's proposal, remembers that she has a bad tooth, and has long wanted to see a dentist – a convenient excuse for shipping her off to Isabella in London. Jane Austen thereby avoids her encroaching on Emma's happiness as the novel draws to a close (and Harriet's reproachful letter is reported on, but not given, for the same reason) but at the risk of (or even with the purpose of?) our making comparisons between the rights of a Harriet Smith and the constant medical attention deemed the perquisite of the more powerful.

The author can thus be caught up to the same trick as her characters, as when, to give another example, she contrives to bestow a sore throat on Harriet, getting her out of the Christmas eve visit to the Westons, so that Emma and Mr Elton may reach a confrontation alone. But is it merely incidental – a bit of narrative scenery – that on returning back from Mrs Goddard's, where she has found that Harriet was 'very feverish and had a bad sore throat', Emma and Mr Elton, walking 'in conversation about the invalid', should be 'overtaken by Mr John Knightley, returning from the daily visit to Donwell, with his two eldest boys, whose healthy, glowing faces shewed all the benefit of a country run, and seemed to ensure a quick dispatch of the roast mutton and rice pudding they were hastening home for'? (109) Or is this an example of a stringent narrative economy, working in terms other than plot, the inscription of tensions, here to do with health, gender and appetite, that will later need to be resolved? When the information that Frank Churchill has gone back to Richmond on the very evening of Box Hill, and therefore broken with Jane, needs to be conveyed, Miss Bates is the ventriloquist:

'It was before tea – stay – no, it could not be before tea, because we were just going to cards – and yet it was before tea, because I remember thinking – Oh! no, now I recollect, now I have it; something happened before tea, but not that. Mr Elton was called out of the room before tea, old John Abdy's son wanted to speak with him. Poor old John, I have a great regard for him; he was clerk to my poor father twenty-seven years; and now, poor old man, he is bed-ridden, and very poorly with the rheumatic gout in his joints – I must go and see him today; and so will Jane, I am sure, if she gets out at all. And poor John's son came to talk to Mr Elton about relief from the parish: he is very well to do himself, you know, being head man at the Crown, ostler, and every thing of that sort, but still he cannot keep his father without some help; and so, when Mr Elton came back, he told us what John ostler had been telling him, and then it came out about the chaise having been sent to Randall's to take Mr Frank Churchill to Richmond. That was what happened before tea. It was after tea that Jane spoke to Mrs Elton.' (382–3)

Hidden in Miss Bates' loosely-knit chatter is the information which explains why Jane has suddenly decided to take the job as a governess. The reader, invited to read from the point of view of Emma, for whom there is 'nothing in all this either to astonish or interest' skims over poor John Abdy as an irrelevance, and, even when he or she is wise to the plot, dismisses John as a cunning decoy. But is he merely a decoy, or is the reference to him planted to further an interest of the text less overt still than the romance plot of Frank and Jane Fairfax?[5] One thing his mention does reveal (but we are too preoccupied to notice) is that Miss Bates has a moral life and exercises the sort of charity and attention towards inferiors and dependents that the reader and Emma find it still so hard, even at this moment, to give to her.

Plot contrivance and the opportunity for some mild and traditional comedy at the expense of the hypochondriac: these are certainly ways of accounting for the plethora of medical talk and incident in *Emma*. Yet Watson was able to take this further. 'The comedy about health is able to illuminate character in a significant way' he suggests. 'One of the ways in which the nature of certain characters in *Emma* is established is by observing the ways in which they react to illness in others, the degree of forbearance and kindness which they show; behind such trivial actions as mending Mrs Bates's spectacles and reassuring Mr Woodhouse there lies a necessary human law, the duty to comfort the fatherless, and the widows in their affliction'.[6] The theme of health enables Jane Austen to bring out serious issues in a comic mode, he argues, particularly in revealing Emma's continuous self-abnegation in the face of her father's relentless demands. How suggestive this is as a general claim can be illustrated by the scene at the Woodhouse dinner for the Eltons where Jane Fairfax's daily walk to the post office becomes the focus of discussion.

The chapter is one in which, for a while, Emma's distinctive point of view is in abeyance. Mr John Knightley and Jane, old acquaintances, for both of whom Highbury was home, but who have both moved in a wider, more sophisticated and harsher world than the one that presently encloses them, have met in the rain that morning, and John Knightley cross-questions (since he is in the law) Jane about her habit of walking to the post office in all weathers. For the first time in the novel we hear conversation between two intelligent equals other than Emma and John Knightley's brother. What Jane says is sensitive, wise – and downright misleading. 'You have every body dearest to you always at hand, I, probably, never shall again; and therefore till I have outlived all my affections, a post-office, I think, must always have power to draw me out, in worse weather than to-day' (294). The reader is likely to assume that Jane is alluding to the prospect of a future as a governess, especially as this shortly becomes the explicit topic of conversation, but the narrational pretext would be, of course, that she may only be thinking of separation from the Campbells and Dixons. She has, as it happens, received a letter from Frank only that morning, just as Mrs Weston has, announcing his impending visit, or at least this is the implication of the 'air of greater happiness than usual – a glow both of complexion and spirits' which Emma shortly detects in her.

Concern that Jane might have damaged her health by her foolhardiness is expressed in a brief spectrum of responses. John Knightley's interrogation is followed by Mr Woodhouse, whose old-fashioned gallantry and courtesy, as well as his vapidity, are expressed in his concerned inquiry 'My dear, did you change your stockings?' His placid assumption 'My dear Miss Fairfax, young ladies are very sure to be cared for', is, in Jane's circumstances, both pathetic and ludicrous, nor as ideologically innocent as it might seem. Mrs Elton's bullying interference is contrasted with Mrs Weston's maternal solicitude – 'Better wait an hour or two, or even half a day for your letters, than run the risk of bringing on your cough again'. All this concern, all this kindness (who, despite Mrs Elton, can doubt that it *is* kindness?) would actually prevent Jane from doing what she most wants and needs to do. Not only would Mrs Elton's scheme of getting 'one of our men' to fetch Jane's letters inevitably result in Frank being known as her correspondent, Jane would be denied an excuse for escape from her aunt and grandmother, and the suffocating atmosphere of their rooms. The kindness – even Mrs Weston's – has an element of aggression in it, an unconscious wish to keep Jane within known bounds, and in its misdirected concern replicates the claustrophobia of her family life. The scene is a text for Arthur Kleinman's observation that the stress/support model is a woefully incomplete notion of the social reception of crisis and illness, for what is stress at one moment may be support the next, and kindness itself can also be a burden.[7] That supportive community of Highbury is also, at times, almost insupportable (though, fortified by the prospect of Frank's visit here, Jane stands up for herself).

Highbury's medicalised sociolect installs the body as the key to understanding – or at least communicating with – the person. Care for others is expressed, in a limited and sometimes damaging mode, as concern for the minor stresses and strains of their physical living. Though superficially supportive, such a mode of transacting relationships is not an enhancing or enabling one, for it positions persons too readily as patients and depends too completely upon obliviousness to or naiveté about their inner psychological and instinctive life. It is because Jane's motives are, deliberately, hidden from this community (and initially from the reader) that her body necessarily becomes the site for the construction of meanings, and that her instance thus replicates, in an amplified mode, the novel's representation of Mrs Churchill.

Through its comfortable concern with its denizens' well-being, the novel poses a series of important questions, I suggest, about the nature of health, which are put more insistently through its gallery of sufferers from so-called 'nervous' disorders. Not only does Isabella Knightley, as might be expected, complain of 'those little nervous head-aches and palpitations which I am never entirely free from any where', but even placid Harriet, even Mrs Weston, let alone Jane Fairfax, suffer from, or complain of these symptoms called 'nerves'. But the two grand embodiments of the nervous constitution in *Emma* are Mr Woodhouse and Mrs Churchill and they preside, one way or another, over the novel's action.

Nervous disorder was a common diagnosis at this period, in other places than Highbury. The King himself was a sufferer, as Fanny Burney reports in her court journal for 1788. '"I am nervous" he cried; "I am not ill, but I am nervous; if you would know what is the matter with me, I am nervous."'[8] 'It was... only in the eighteenth century', writes the medical historian W. F. Bynum, 'that it became possible to suffer from the "nerves"'.[9] George Cheyne's *The English Malady or a Treatise of Nervous Disease of all Kinds* (1733), a very popular textbook of the early part of the century, was chiefly responsible, he suggests, for putting the notion of the nerves and the nervous system as a source of human suffering into general circulation. Cheyne described the nervous patient, Bynum reports, as 'a personality type found in those with "weak, loose, and feeble, or relaxed nerves", the result of which was extreme sensitivity to hot and cold, weak digestion, a tendency to alternative diarrhoea and costiveness, and other signs of valetudinarianism'.[10] 'Nervous disorders are the Diseases of the Wealthy, the Voluptuous and the Lazy', Cheyne wrote in a censorious moment, in which he none the less makes a significant point.[11] The argument of his book is that this new (and very widespread) disease entity was the product of increasing wealth and leisure among the middle classes, and this association of the nervous temperament or constitution with affluence continues through the century as 'nervous' disorders make their appearance in an increasing number of textbooks. The work on irritability, sensibility and the nervous system undertaken most notably in Britain by Robert Whytt at the mid-century[12] would have grafted a new 'scientific' understanding onto this already current conception, and confirmed its association with amplified or exacerbated sensibility (which was also a preserve of the leisured classes).

The typical symptoms of the nervous patient are described, for instance, in the Introduction to a book called *A View of the Nervous Temperament* published by Dr Thomas Trotter in 1807:

An inaptitude to muscular action, or some pain in exerting it; an irksomeness, or dislike to attend to business and the common affairs of life; a selfish desire of engrossing the sympathy and attention of others to the narration of their own sufferings; with fickleness and unsteadiness of temper, even to irascibility: and accompanied more or less with dyspeptic symptoms, are the leading characteristics of *nervous disorders*; to be referred in general, to debility, increased sensibility, or torpor of the alimentary canal.[13]

Some behavioural features distributed between Mr Woodhouse and Mrs Churchill are obviously predicated here. Trotter's social profile of the typical patient is equally apposite, since he suggests that 'torpid habits of living' are the consequence of patients with money in the public funds having no need to work for their livelihood, 'without any of those urgent motives which preserve energy of mind, so condusive to health'. When he later warns that nervous patients may become dependent upon a 'gossiping physician' who becomes 'a kind of appendage to their establishment', Trotter could well be describing Mr Woodhouse and Mr Perry.

Being singular in the selection of friends, they seldom mix in company; sedentary from habit, they go little abroad; their amusements and recreation are thus limited, and such as possess the talent of bringing news, and telling a story, are at all times welcome guests. But as the tale of their own complaints engrosses so much of their conversation, a medical gossip, before all others, is the most acceptable.[14]

As one might expect, Cheyne, Trotter, and other physicians recommended a frugal diet, exercise and fresh air to relieve the condition. Walking and gardening are recommended, for instance, to young ladies: 'And while her nervous aunts are moping their evenings over the card table, she will gather health by her cheerful excursions; and preserve her bloom of countenance by the only means that can give it an additional charm'.[15] It's in a similar vein that the narrator recommends Mrs Goddard's school in Highbury, 'reckoned a particularly healthy spot' where young ladies were certainly not (as in, presumably, more affluent and prestigious establishments) 'screwed out of health and into vanity'. Instead, Mrs Goddard lets them 'run about a great deal in the summer, and in winter dressed their chilblains with her own hands' (21–2).

Thomas Trotter also strikes a Woodhouse-like note of solicitude about young ladies getting wet feet:

The lady of weak health, who may wish to display an ancle, should be very guarded how she throws off her warm socks. Many evils befal the sex from cold feet: such as follow on walking abroad with thin shoes on damp roads ... I have known some serious nervous ailments brought on by a young lady evading the orders of a judicious parent; and after being dressed, retiring privately to put off the additional petticoat and understockings, that she might dance the more lightly.[16]

This is 'medical' advice which is actually focusing or activating ideology and gender politics: the young woman is defined equally by her propensity to sickness as by her coquetry and the two are seen to be linked as essential properties of the female.[17] 'My dear, young ladies are very sure to be cared for', as Mr Woodhouse tells Jane, but this means in effect that young women, as a given of their gender, are positioned as patients, or potential patients, at a lower level of bodily capacity and resourcefulness than young men, and, while entitled to 'care', have initiative taken from them. This element in its attitude to Jane is hidden from Highbury, but not from the novel.

Various doctors suggested various organic pathologies as the substratum of nervous disorders, but increasingly they were understood as 'functional' conditions, a term which is sometimes used in modern discussion, as in psychoanalysis, to designate disorders which have behavioural, and therefore 'real' symptoms, but for which no organic cause can be discovered. Such conditions – akin to hysteria – are, as Bynum writes, particularly intriguing to historians (he might have added, literary critics) because 'they seem to show most clearly the cultural, social, and ideological factors which influence definitions and perceptions of disease and constrain the behaviour of both patients and their doctors'.[18] Though perceived as 'disease' by both parties to the medical transaction, disorders of the nervous system, 'temperament' or 'constitution' are best, in fact, characterised as illness, whose meaning inscribed the social and cultural circumstances of the patient – as was implicitly recognised through the emphasis in doctors' accounts on the social class of sufferers.

Mr Woodhouse is described as 'a nervous man, easily depressed' and his needs influence and perhaps dictate the life of his daughter, but the other chief sufferer from 'nerves' in *Emma* exerts an even more powerful hold on events in Highbury. Mrs Churchill, of the great Yorkshire family, is known only by report as 'a very odd-tempered woman' (according to the mild, forgiving Mrs Weston). Her name alludes to Sarah Churchill, Duchess of Marlborough, Pope's Atossa, the type of the captious great lady ('Last night, her Lord was all that's good and great / A Knave this morning, and his Will a Cheat'[19]). Emma's idea of her is that 'while she makes no sacrifice for the comfort of the husband, to whom she owes every thing... she exercises incessant caprice towards *him*' (123). 'The evil of the distance from Enscombe', a disgruntled and disbelieving Mr Weston tells Mrs Elton,

'is, that Mrs Churchill, *as we understand*, has not been able to leave the sopha for a week together. In Frank's last letter, she complained, he said, of being too weak to get into her conservatory without having both his arm and his uncle's! This, you know, speaks a great deal of weakness – but now she is so impatient to be in town, that she means to sleep only two nights on the road'. (306)

The lady's nerves being soon 'under continual irritation and suffering' from the noise of London, she removes once again to Richmond.

The adopted son, Frank Churchill, is evidently her favourite. His engagement to Jane Fairfax (like Mr Churchill's sister's marriage to Captain Weston an unsuitably low connection) needs must be kept secret or presumably he would be 'thrown off with due decorum' like his predecessor. 'His importance at Enscombe was very evident', as Emma perceives. 'He did not boast, but it naturally betrayed itself, that he had persuaded his aunt where his uncle could do nothing, and on her laughing and noticing it, he owned that he believed (excepting one or two points) he could *with time* persuade her to any thing' (221). Emma can only partly understand his meaning, of course. Frank has now, in February, been almost six months engaged to Jane, and it is this 'time' that he is presumably playing for. To persuade his aunt he must keep in her good books; thus, though he wants to be with Jane, and preparations for the ball are in full train, when she summons, he must go.

A letter arrived from Mr Churchill to urge his nephew's instant return. Mrs Churchill was unwell – far too unwell to do without him; she had been in a very suffering state (so said her husband) when writing to her nephew two days before, though from her usual unwillingness to give pain, and constant habit of never thinking of herself, she had not mentioned it; but now she was too ill to trifle, and must entreat him to set off for Enscombe without delay. (258)

If in Highbury Frank plays the part of intending suitor to Emma, at Enscombe he plays the role of solicitous son. He departs, grumbling 'He knew her illnesses: they never occurred but for her own convenience'. He has himself, of course, acquired his step-mother's talent for manipulation.

Is Mrs Churchill 'really ill' (316) or not? Frank offers conflicting readings of her condition, perhaps depending on the degree of inconvenience she causes him. Knowledge of this figure on the distant horizons of *Emma* is filtered through Frank's reports, and obscured by the supervening questions of his motivation, and these reports are then refracted in the light of the desires of those who receive them. When the Churchills are in London, he finds it no more easy, apparently, to come to Highbury. 'His aunt could not bear to have him leave her. Such was his own account at Randall's. If he were quite sincere, if he really tried to come, it was to be inferred that Mrs Churchill's removal to London had been of no service to the wilful or nervous part of her disorder' (316). On this occasion Frank 'could not be prevailed on by all his father's doubts, to say that her complaints were merely imaginary, or that she was as strong as ever' (317). The mystery, or undecidability, of Mrs Churchill's illness is not resolved, either, by her death. 'Mrs Churchill, after being disliked at least twenty-five years, was now spoken of with compassionate allowances. In one point she was fully justified. She had never been admitted before to be seriously ill. The event acquitted her of all the fancifulness and all the selfishness of imaginary complaints' (387). She is now admitted into Highbury discourse on its own terms as 'Poor Mrs Churchill!' But Highbury is obtuse and the ambiguity persists, since she is carried off, as the narrator makes occasion to say, 'by a sudden seizure of a different nature from any thing foreboded by her general state'.[20] How one reads Mrs Churchill's illness depends then upon one's own interests, position and point of view – perhaps one's own state of health. The phrase 'the wilful or nervous part of her disorder' is interesting, especially considering Mr Woodhouse. Are 'nerves' then an aspect of the will, referable to the self as moral agent? When Elton flatteringly insinuates that Emma's visit must have been a 'cordial' to Harriet, Emma puts him neatly in his place by replying 'My visit was of use to the nervous part of her complaint, I hope: but not even I can charm away a sore throat' (114). Does Jane Austen, as George III apparently did, oppose 'nervous' to genuine disorder?

Whatever its 'real' nature, Mrs Churchill's ill health functions well enough to keep Frank running back to her. He is prevented from making the strawberry party, too, as he says, by 'a temporary increase of illness in her; a nervous seizure, which had lasted some hours' (363). Mrs Churchill then, has great – in fact, very precise and crucial – influence upon the action of the novel. Without her, there would be no need to keep the engagement so long a secret; without her illnesses Frank would be free to come and go, and enjoy himself as he pleases. Without her caprices he could himself be less 'self-willed' and have no need to flirt with Emma. Her demand for attention originates a cascade of incidents, for his late arrival at Donwell provokes the crisis in Frank and Jane's relationship, generating the tense and unhappy Box Hill party, which in turn impacts upon Emma and her relationship with Mr Knightley. She is thus the always absent origin of the novel's events.[21] High in the social hierarchy, she is high in the hierarchy of causes. Her power – based, of course, on her status as an elder and her affluence – infiltrates the smallest events of provincial Highbury.

Mrs Churchill, the sufferer from 'nerves', operates in the novel as the covert double of Mr Woodhouse, the 'nervous man' whom Emma spends so much of her time and energy attending to and comforting. If one reads the novel to emphasise the 'wilful' side of their disorders, the parallels are striking. She is elderly and rich, Frank is her adopted son, she uses her illnesses to keep him at home and to prevent him from marrying, by fear that he will displease her and lose his inheritance. Mr Woodhouse is elderly and rich, Emma is his unmarried daughter; he uses his ill health to keep her at home and to discourage the journeys abroad, the social contacts, that might lead to marriage. Her distant power over Highbury is paralleled by his local one: he is consulted in everything, in every arrangement his welfare and whims are of first concern. The parallel is disguised because Mr Woodhouse is presented as kindly and generally liked, while Mrs Churchill is thought to be cantankerous and generally disliked. The reader's knowledge of Mrs Churchill is gathered from hostile witnesses – principally Mr Weston: Mr Woodhouse is seen only through friendly and benevolent eyes. No one in the novel would think of comparing the two. She is a minor character in far-off Yorkshire whereas he is the unconsciously presiding genius whose words open the novel and whose welfare determines its close. But the parallels generate – or so it might be argued – what Jane Austen, having chosen to construct her narrative from Emma's position, choosing Emma's as the salient point of view, can of necessity render only by subversive means. She foregrounds the sweetness of Mr Woodhouse's character, his kindness and his courtesy, whilst the hidden Churchill homology indicates the power-relations that an impartial analysis would display as the organising dynamic. The relation is clothed in love and dutifulness, but the skeleton of its structure is Mr Woodhouse's inevitable authority as the patriarchal elder, and his power over Emma's life.

Such a Foucauldian emphasising of power-relations can doubtless be challenged by those readers and critics who would see Mrs Churchill's treatment of Frank rather as a contrast to Mr Woodhouse's dependence on Emma, understanding it to work similarly to the way Mrs Elton's bullying and patronising function as an extension or parody of Emma's own faults, a parallel which casts some light no doubt, but which turns out in the end to be specious. (And certainly Emma's sentiments towards her father are quite different from Frank's towards his aunt.) Mr Woodhouse's fussing never actually stands in the way of Emma's activities – she manages to go to the Westons', the Coles', to take part in the ball at the Crown, despite his fears and inhibitions.[22] Yet to restrict one's notion of power to this behavioural level is certainly to limit the possibilities of the novel. Mr Woodhouse's influence over Emma's thoughts and feelings, it could well be argued, is less direct, and more tenacious than his simple objections to rich food or late nights. All neurotic symptoms have the potential to ensnare others in their toils. And one might be inclined to disbelieve in Mr Woodhouse's illness to precisely the same extent that one disbelieves in Mrs Churchill's. For most parts of the novel the comedy that attends Mr Woodhouse's foibles is certainly an encouragement to believe that his complaints are greatly exaggerated. What, apart from sensitivity to noise, fear of danger, dislike of travel and change, not to speak of 'torpor of the alimentary canal' – are his symptoms? 'His habits of gentle selfishness' are selfishness nonetheless; and though he is well-meaning and charitably disposed, it is scarcely possible not to notice that all the real good, all the active charity in the novel, is Emma's and Knightley's, and that a good deal of Emma's involves overriding her father's wishes. Left to himself, his benevolence has a self-cancelling quality that renders it dubious – witness Mrs Bates' Tantalus torture with the sweetbread and asparagus. On the other hand (and here the analogy with Mrs Churchill again appears) when after she has accepted Knightley Emma thinks about her father's future welfare, she seems to take for granted that his physical condition is declining, and that his demands upon her cannot be refused. Mr Woodhouse's illness, however intangible, has the pressure of a social, and emotional, fact.

The reader who opens *Emma* stands, with its heroine, on the margins of a community. The narrative of the novel requires that the reader share the idiom and valuations of that community, whilst being aware, of course, that these values are far from absolute, and that, moreover, their relation to 'Jane Austen's' own is obscure. One can repudiate the idiom, read with the eye of a stranger, substitute different standards and another form of speech and describe the community around Henry Woodhouse, for example, as 'Emma's idiot father and his circle of ossified friends'[23] but this will not help to understand the dynamics of that community, nor to make Austen's presentation of it explicable in the new terms. One is left with no standpoint except outside a novel whose narrative technique invites precisely that one enter the ways of its world. How then to make sense of the relationships around him, to understand not only Mr Woodhouse himself, but those (some of them evidently meant as authorial deputies) who treat Mr Woodhouse, not merely with deference, but with kindness and affection – even love? Imagining a psychoanalytic case-study of Emma, Avrom Fleishman posits a latter-day diagnosis of her father. 'It's often assumed by the layman that people with evident *hypochondria* are really well, but [Emma's] father, though not organically, is clearly mentally ill. The diagnosis of his illness is probably *premature senility*, featuring acute anxiety.'[24] Dangers attend any attempt to understand Mr Woodhouse in modern medicalised terms, such as the one I have just used, 'neurotic'. All the same, the text gives signs that Mr Woodhouse's nervous inhibitions do have far reaching influence on Emma, and that they are potentially destructive, even though their presence is chiefly displayed in the process of Emma's triumphing over them. (Not always – she doesn't succeed in preventing Mr Woodhouse's comments about doctors and bathing places from maddening John Knightley.) In fact, her management of her father's domestic life is used to throw light on his ill health at the same time as it illustrates the nature of the capabilities she brings to the task. Consider the little comic episode that ends chapter II:

> What was unwholesome to him, he regarded as unfit for any body; and he had, therefore, earnestly tried to dissuade them from having any wedding cake at all, and when that proved vain, as earnestly tried to prevent any body's eating it. He had been at the pains of consulting Mr Perry, the apothecary, on the subject. Mr Perry was an intelligent, gentlemanlike man, whose frequent visits were one of the comforts of Mr Woodhouse's life; and, upon being applied to, he could not but acknowledge, (though it seemed rather against the bias of inclination,) that wedding-cake might certainly disagree with many – perhaps with most people, unless taken moderately. With such an opinion, in confirmation of his own, Mr Woodhouse hoped to influence every visitor of the new-married pair; but still the cake was eaten; and there was no rest for his benevolent nerves till it was all gone.
>
> There was a strange rumour in Highbury of all the little Perrys being seen with a slice of Mrs Weston's wedding cake in their hands: but Mr. Woodhouse would never believe it. (19)

No doubt the cake is an overt symbol of celebration and festivity – the wedding itself. But because it is to be eaten, and eaten with relish, it symbolises, in a more amplified fashion, the bodily enjoyments that Mr Woodhouse's mode of life is devoted to reducing. He resists all walks, outings, late nights, dances, trips, expeditions, excursions, engagements, marriages on the pretext that these activities endanger health. His programme is the denial of almost all bodily activity and almost all bodily enjoyment – as amusingly illustrated in the loin of pork which he suggests should be 'boiled with a little carrot' but which the Bates, not having in this case the benefit of his advice, have, unprompted, roasted with apples. He does not like to be reminded of the body's demands and appetites. The cake's richness, so irrationally distressful to him, can be read as a sign that Miss Taylor has escaped from Hartfield and is no longer a spectator at life's feast. What it symbolises can be amplified further, for by a simple substitution of one appetite by another, a simple displacement of the genital or sexual to the oral or gustatory, it can imply that the comic manifestations of his valetudinarianism originate in a disturbed sexuality.[25] When Mrs Elton talks of him as her 'beau', and of his gallantry, and of her 'caro sposo' being jealous, the sexualised banter is glaringly inappropriate, but given such hints readers have a right to wonder whether, as John Düssinger suggests, some malformation of sexual life may not be at the root of Henry Woodhouse's condition: or rather, whether his condition (which is to say, of course, his role in the novel) cannot appropriately be understood in an holistic mode which would include sexuality as an aspect of his illness. Certainly Emma's health is contrasted with his hypochondria, and in Emma health and sexual appetency are linked.

For Emma is not defeated by her father's neurotic proscriptions. She is able to get around him (for his own good) by a stratagem of her own. Her outwitting her father here is part of a series of effects which demonstrate that Emma's qualities – of independence, initiative, resourcefulness – can be relied upon for everyone's and her own good, as when, faced with his recommendation to Miss Bates of 'a *little* bit of tart, a *very* little bit' Emma 'allowed her father to talk, but supplied her visitors in a much more satisfactory style'. Her stratagem here aligns her with Frank Churchill's 'young person' who (as he tells the appalled Mr Woodhouse) will sometimes slip behind a curtain and throw up a window, at a ball, a moment when Frank himself is practising tricks on the old gentleman. 'I am sure it was a source of high entertainment to you, to feel that you were taking us all in', as Emma tells Frank concerning the engagement, 'I think there is a little likeness between us'. Her resourcefulness involves co-opting Mr Perry, the very man Mr Woodhouse thinks is his friend and ally, and Mr Perry's giving the cake to his children – the sign of his own marriage and sexual fecundity. The sly joke that rounds the chapter off works by suppressing and condensing the connecting information (which would be something like this: 'Dear Mr Perry, as long as this wedding cake remains in the house it will make my father miserable. Do take it home to Mrs Perry and give a slice each to your children'). The text as read thus enables the pleasurable saving of psychological energy that, as Freud claimed, all jokes make. Does the joke not also communicate a hostility to – at least a derision of – Mr Woodhouse that the text nowhere explicitly admits? The laugh against him is therapeutic; it expresses – at several different levels – health triumphing in the face of a mild but stubborn perversity. And by handing the last word to him, it demonstrates the largesse of its own comic vitality.

The incident fulfils Mrs Weston's just-expressed hopes. 'Dear Emma was of no feeble character; she was more equal to her situation than most girls would have been, and had sense and energy and spirits that might be hoped would bear her well and happily through its little difficulties and privations' (18). In fact 'spirit' is the quality in Emma that is the most reliable antagonist of her father's pathology. 'Spirit' or 'spirits' are, in themselves, morally neutral, but in relation to him, they reveal their value. 'Her father's spirits required support' and it is Emma's own spirit which can be relied upon, it seems, to surmount the impediments placed in her way by his nerves, and that make her, in so far as she is so, a free or autonomous being. The word or term is used very frequently in the novel. 'With an alacrity beyond the common impulse of a spirit which yet was never indifferent to the credit of doing every thing well and attentively', she is 'inspirited' by the opportunity to interfere in Harriet's love-life, just as she is 'animated' by suspicions of Jane's. When she is told that Frank is to arrive soon 'Emma's spirits were mounted quite up to happiness' (189). Emma's partner in spirits and mischief in fact is Frank, who has 'the constitution of the Weston' and 'seemed to have all the life and spirit, cheerful feelings and social inclinations of his father' and whose talk is 'the effusion of lively spirits' (198). Much later Jane Fairfax herself speaks of 'his temper and spirits – his delightful spirits'.

'Spirit' is at least as important a quality of Emma as her imagination, though it has remained largely invisible to (or perhaps, taken for granted by) her commentators. As I have suggested, for Jane Austen the property is in itself morally neutral: to possess 'spirit' (like Mary Crawford – or even Selina Hawkins), verve, courage, or perhaps merely a strong ego, is not necessarily to have 'merit'. But it is at least – in the context of *Emma* – to have potential value, and in certain conditions, to become 'delightful'. Intricate in its history, the word overlaps, of course, with a sense of 'spirit', as in 'spiritual', contradistinguished from the bodily or earthly. The novel includes one exchange which obviously uses 'spirit' in the derived sense of 'guide' or 'monitor', when Emma asks cheekily of Mr Knightley 'Does my vain spirit ever tell me I am wrong?', and he replies 'Not your vain spirit, but your serious spirit. If the one leads you wrong, I am sure the other tells you of it' (330), though here, of course, Emma's very question demonstrates her spirit in the other sense.

In the cluster of meanings most germane to Austen's use in *Emma* (though other overtones are not excluded), the word seems to suggest a bridging or holistic conflation of the physical and the mental, for the mental alacrity it sometimes celebrates runs quickly into physical energy and activity, and 'good spirits' can hardly be thought of except against a background of bodily well-being. Definition 14 in Johnson's *Dictionary* is illuminating about what Jane Austen's usage frequently implies: 'That which gives vigour or cheerfulness to the mind; the purest part of the body, bordering, says Sydenham, on immateriality. In this meaning it is commonly written with the plural termination.' As Johnson's citation of Dr Thomas Sydenham (1624–89) suggests, 'spirits', in the plural, carries a medical history. Often 'spirits' (or 'pneuma') were imagined, as in Johnson's definition, as being situated within the body, where they designated partly a physical agent and partly a force.[26] The usage derived ultimately from the animal, natural and vital spirits of Galenic physiology, conceived as highly rarefied liquids, which coursed through the veins, vessels, and ultimately the nervous system of the patient. The conception was thoroughly outmoded in medicine, but still vestigially current in other forms of writing during the later eighteenth and early nineteenth centuries. Lydia Bennet, for instance, is described as having 'high animal spirits' (PP 45). Cowper in a poem first published in 1803 could write 'To Mary': 'Thy spirits have a fainter flow /I see thee daily weaker grow /'Tis my distress that brought thee low'. Maria Edgeworth's Flora Campbell, an exact contemporary of Emma, similarly has 'a constant flow of good spirits and the charming domestic talent of making every trifle a source of amusement to herself and others'.[27] The OED gives an interesting instance from 1790 which connects spirits in this residual medical sense with appearance: 'her spirits retired inward, her cheeks grew pale, and down she sank'. Animated or good spirits and 'bloom' were thus connected: the attractive appearance of the female being the outward sign of her physiological and sexual well-being.

In this period, then, 'spirits' are ceasing to evoke a medical context and are in the process of being naturalised as an essential given of the emotional self. And it is this process of naturalisation and diffusion of meaning (previously also undergone by the medieval 'humours') which tends to make them unproblematic and hence invisible to analysis. Their representation, too, though a crucial tactic of the novel, can pass without comment. The reason why Jane Austen's commentators remain silent on certain aspects of the text may be that whilst imagination and perception, as mental faculties or aspects of consciousness, have been the central subject of Western philosophical enquiry, 'spirits', which enters our vocabulary from another, a (proto)scientific, tradition, has been naturalised, as a fact of being, understood as a constituent part of bodily nature. Of course people in our culture – the culture we still share with Austen – have, or are in, 'high' and 'low' spirits, just as they may be good or bad humoured – how else to describe them? But people in China or Mali would not necessarily recognise themselves in these terms. As for us, we hardly notice how 'spirits' conflates psychological and physical being. Austen's critics, following Knightley, examine Emma's 'errors of imagination', and stress the novel's understanding of the creative nature of perception, because through that discourse the novelist could be inserted into the mainstream epistemological tradition and given an honourable place there, but there has been no equivalently sophisticated philosophic treatment of the body. Virginia Woolf famously declared that 'English has no words for the shiver and the headache',[28] but it is possible to amplify her comment, and generalise as truly that the language has no developed discourse for translating the responses of all kinds of bodily human-being into conceptual discussion. Moreover 'spirits', eagerness and activity, as demonstrated in the novel, are less easy to theorise since they essentially consist in praxis: one can therefore discourse at will about Emma's 'mistakes' or misconceptions, without taking account of the animation and energy transmitted in the prose, which is equally a part of that construction in language which we identify as Emma Woodhouse. A reading aloud is needed, and is often all that is needed, to mark the rhythmic vitality with which her life is transcribed. But to enlarge in discourse on the way that Emma's spirits are represented as a factor of her (moral) life runs the risk of seeming banal to some and inconsequential to others. It would be equally a mistake to erect 'spirit' into a stiffly moral value, to stand with, say, 'reason', 'perception' or 'self-knowledge', an abstract quality to be pitted against these in a gladiatorial contest of abstractions, when the presence of Emma's spirits in the text is as hidden, is as internal, fluid and intricate as their supposed antecedent physical nature. The question certainly is closely bound up with Jane Austen's invention of free indirect speech and her utilisation of the novel form as the legitimation of female desire.

A favourite passage of writers wishing to display Austen's control of her medium, the irony that simultaneously represents Emma's thoughts, and reveals their dubiousness, the exposure of 'how precisely Emma's judgment is going astray'[29] is her initial response to Harriet:

> She was not struck by any thing remarkably clever in Miss Smith's conversation, but she found her altogether very engaging – not inconveniently shy, not unwilling to talk – and yet so far from pushing, shewing so proper and becoming a deference, seeming so pleasantly grateful for being admitted to Hartfield, and so artlessly impressed by the appearance of every thing in so superior a style to what she had been used to, that she must have good sense and deserve encouragement. Encouragement should be given. Those soft blue eyes and all

those natural graces should not be wasted on the inferior society of Highbury and its connections. The acquaintance she had already formed were unworthy of her. The friends from whom she had just parted, though very good sort of people, must be doing her harm. They were a family of the name of Martin, whom Emma well knew by character, as renting a large farm of Mr Knightley and residing in the parish of Donwell – very creditably she believed – she knew Mr Knightley thought highly of them – but they must be coarse and unpolished, and very unfit to be the intimates of a girl who wanted only a little more knowledge and elegance to be quite perfect. *She* would notice her; she would improve her; she would detach her from her bad acquaintance and introduce her into good society; she would form her opinions and her manners. It would be an interesting and certainly a very kind undertaking; highly becoming her own situation in life, her leisure, and powers. (23–4)

The reader certainly notices, and delights in, the subterfuges of Emma's thinking here – in the agility of the transition from 'very good sort of people' to 'bad acquaintance' and hence to 'good society', for example, and the whisking away of the internal monitor Mr Knightley's opinions between two parentheses. The point is not that one does not remark the self-deception and snobbery, even arrogance, that these manoeuvres manifest, but that one picks up, at the same time, contrapuntally, and as a part of that very same self-deception and arrogance, the warmth, the eagerness, the panache and brio that enable these feats of psychological legerdemain to pass off successfully as if what were taking place were a process of reasonable thought. Emma's activity here is delightful to behold. Wayne Booth, the critic I have quoted, writes that Emma concludes 'with a beautiful burst of egotism', that pulsing and emphatic series of final good resolutions, but in common with most of Austen's critics he is more comfortable in talking about the egoism ('Emma's unconscious catalogue of her egotistical uses for Harriet'[30]) than about the beauty. Not to reckon with what the narrator shortly conceptualises as 'alacrity' and 'real good-will', though, is not to read half the information conveyed in this prose.

It is not long before Mr Knightley is pointing out the dangers to Harriet and to Emma in this friendship. His fears are dismissed or at least deflected by Mrs Weston, who (mistakenly, as it turns out) thinks well of the friendship and, in Knightley's words, 'would rather talk of her person than her mind':

'Very well; I shall not attempt to deny Emma's being pretty.'

'Pretty! say beautiful rather. Can you imagine any thing nearer perfect beauty than Emma altogether – face and figure?'

'I do not know what I could imagine, but I confess that I have seldom seen a face or figure more pleasing to me than hers. But I am a partial old friend.'

'Such an eye! – the true hazle eye – and so brilliant! regular features, open countenance, with a complexion! oh! what a bloom of full health, and such a pretty height and size; such a firm and upright figure. There is health, not merely in her bloom, but in her air, her head, her glance. One hears sometimes of a child being "the picture of health;" now Emma always gives me the idea of being the complete picture of grown-up health. She is loveliness itself. Mr Knightley, is not she?' (39)

To which Knightley agrees, adding, 'I love to look at her'. Mrs Weston's point seems to be that any account of Emma's faults, or any analysis of her merely as a moral agent, like Knightley's here, cannot do justice to her and even seems by the way. She is in good company in pointing to other than moral properties as sources of Emma's attraction. David Hume concluded his section on 'the qualities immediately agreeable to others' in *An Inquiry Concerning the Principles of Morals* (1751) with the concession that there are attractions about which ethical analysis finds nothing to say:

But besides all the *agreeable* qualities, the origin of whose beauty we can in some degree explain and account for, there still remains something mysterious and inexplicable, which conveys an immediate satisfaction to the spectator, but how, or why, or for what reason, he cannot pretend to determine. There is a *Manner*, a grace, an ease, a gentleness, an I-know-not-what, which some men possess above others, which is very different from external beauty and comeliness, and which, however, catches our affection almost as suddenly and powerfully ... This class of accomplishments, therefore, must be trusted entirely to the blind, but sure testimony of taste and sentiment; and must be considered as a part of ethics, left by nature to baffle all the pride of philosophy, and make her sensible of her narrow boundaries and slender acquisitions.[31]

A reading of Emma as a moral agent, confronting or manipu-
lating a world (or a person) external to herself, misses this 'part
of nature'. Mrs Weston does not mean that Emma instantiates
some general quality 'Health', but that the quality, 'health',
cannot be better known than by Emma's embodiment of it. As
far as Mrs Weston is concerned, she *is* health, and health is
realised in her beauty. What – in the largest sense – health is, is
to be known in the activity of the life that is Emma's, in what I
have called her spirit: not a moral quality in itself, and certainly
not guaranteeing laudable or ethically admirable conduct, but
appealing to an understanding of another's life on a larger
ground than that of the moral philosopher and ethicist whom
Knightley here represents. Mrs Weston is not, as Mr Knightley,
separating the two in Cartesian fashion, accuses her, talking
merely of Emma's person rather than of her mind: when she
goes on to say that Emma 'has qualities that may be trusted', it
is not just her love of Emma that speaks, but her recognition
that something like what Samuel Johnson called 'the exuber-
ance of content' underwrites Emma's ultimate moral victory.

Towards the end of *Emma* there is a conversation that is
designed to be compared with this one. Throughout the novel
Frank Churchill has commented on Jane's pale looks to Emma,
often in a snide and critical fashion, but when their engagement
is public and Jane has recovered, he is free to enthuse. 'Did you
ever see such a skin?' he exclaims ' – such smoothness! such
delicacy! – and yet without being actually fair. – One cannot
call her fair. It is a most uncommon complexion, with her dark
eye-lashes and hair – a most distinguishing complexion! – So
peculiarly the lady in it. – Just colour enough for beauty' (478).
Henry Crawford and Frank Churchill, though often aligned in
a certain brand of Austen criticism, are to be distinguished: the
one cool, calculating, and selfish, the other warm-hearted,
impulsive, and selfish. But here Frank's drooling over his 'prize'
(Knightley's term, unfortunately) brings him close to Henry's
appraising survey of Fanny. 'She is a complete angel', he
resumes:

'Look at her. Is not she an angel in every gesture? Observe the turn of her throat. Observe her eyes, as she is looking up at my father. – You will be glad to hear (inclining his head, and whispering seriously) that my uncle means to give her all my aunt's jewels. They are to be new set. I am resolved to have some in an ornament for the head. Will not it be beautiful in her dark hair?' (479).

'The head'! For the moment Frank seems to be thinking of Jane as an artefact to be decorated and enjoyed as a prestigious possession. Mrs Weston, despite the term 'picture', is not thinking of Emma as a specular object. 'Bloom' is a suspicious term, as de Beauvoir pointed out,[32] but here Mrs Weston does not connect it, as male observers do, as a rule, with the promise of sexual responsiveness. Instead, she connects Emma's attractiveness with a child's. Austen's novels usually dismiss children and their doting parents with some acerbity, but in *Emma* Mr Perry's children, John Knightley's boys, and, to a lesser extent, Mrs Weston's own pregnancy are all important signifiers of vitality and 'normal' healthy growth, and here the idea is that the child evades or renders null and void moral categories, living the prehistory of a properly ethical life. Emma's complexion is not to be admired, either, because it is aesthetically 'beautiful'. Most importantly, 'the blind but sure testimony' of Mrs Weston's 'sentiment' reproduces in her praise the very inflections of Emma herself, the repetition, the emphasis, ('complete', 'loveliness itself') – reproduces that emphatic and spirited rhythm which is the textual manifestation of Emma's vital subjectivity.

Jane Fairfax is the shadowy background, the obscured antithesis to the heroine, and her story contributes much to the chiaroscuro of this picture of health. Jane's health is frail, and her beauty, unlike Emma's, is no assurance of vitality. Her presentation takes up the issues present more sketchily in the references to Mrs Churchill. Although she acts and speaks directly in the text, her position within it, her reserve and her secret forbid access to her inner life. What is therefore understood of her is constructed on the site of her body, her 'look', which depending on the observer, can signify either propensity to ill-health or beauty and distinction. In the absence of open speech, Emma, like her neighbours, is perpetually reading Jane's body. Her prejudice against Jane (and her own abundant health) make her unresponsive to certain aspects of the sensitive and cultivated woman whom she ought to have made her friend, but the proneness to illness, the precariousness of Jane's condition, is discernible, even though, after her introduction by the narrator in the second volume, Jane is perceived – glimpsed would be a better word – largely through Emma's eyes. The narrator introduces Jane as an orphan, whose mother died 'overcome with consumption and grief' and it is the fear of TB, 'the standing apprehension of the family' that apparently motivates her aunt's continual fussing ('Did you remember your tippet?'), Highbury's neighbourly concern over her walks in the rain, as well as Knightley's urgent action to prevent her overtaxing herself by singing. Tuberculosis, as Susan Sontag writes, was thought a disease particularly 'apt to strike the hypersensitive, the talented, the passionate',[33] and a multitude of literary and musical heroines and heroes of the nineteenth century illustrate her observation. Consumption was conceptualised as a peculiarly romantic disease, one in which artistic talent fed off and in turn fed, the exorbitancies of feeling, the sudden and irrational changes of mood, characteristic (or so it was thought) of the consumptive's condition. So early in the century, Jane Austen makes this triad of talent, passion, and illness the substance of this minor theme counterpointing the major of Emma – musical metaphors, because of all the arts music is the one most intertwined with and expressive of conditions such as Jane's.

The strained and unhappy course of Jane Fairfax's re-lationship with Frank Churchill over the months she spends in Highbury is obscured from Emma Woodhouse. What is centrally occluded from her, of course, is the part that she herself plays in generating and exacerbating these strains. We know little about Jane's inner life – except that music is evidently important to her, that the piano sent to her is made by Broadwood's (who also made a piano for Beethoven), that she sings, unlike Emma, in Italian – and it is as tempting for literary critics, as for Emma, to construct a romance out of such hints. Yet there is evidence that behind the heroine's story, a story of expanding horizons, is another of increasing isolation, tension and pain. Only intermittent signs of Jane's gradual collapse under the various stresses of her situation are disclosed to the reader. At the Coles', Emma is preoccupied with Mrs Weston's idea that Mr Knightley might be romantically interested in Jane, and so Frank and Jane's singing together is only the background of her thought, to which (a poignant, poetic hint of romance beyond her ken) 'the sweet sounds of the united voices gave only momentary interruptions', until at the end of her second song, Jane's voice grows thick and Knightley feels called upon to intervene. Frank wants to press on, but Knightley, solicitous as always, urges Miss Bates to put a stop to the singing – 'Miss Bates, are you mad, to let your niece sing herself hoarse in this manner?' Next day, surprising Frank and Jane at the Bates' 'at least ten minutes earlier than [Frank] had calculated' Emma finds 'Jane Fairfax standing with her back to them, intent upon her pianoforte':

That she was not immediately ready, Emma did suspect to arise from the state of her nerves; she had not yet possessed the instrument long enough to touch it without emotion; she must reason herself into the power of performance; and Emma could not but pity such feelings, whatever their origin, and could not but resolve never to expose them to her neighbour again. (240)

Emma is not altogether mistaken in that this 'offering of love', the piano, heightens Jane's emotions and increases her difficulties in about the same proportion: it is very characteristic of Frank that this expression of his passion simultaneously destroys the peace of his object.

What further glimpses we have of Jane reinforce this intuition of gradually multiplying strains that could lead to collapse. At Donwell Jane momentarily comes to the forefront of the picture as, escaping from her aunt and Mrs Elton, she turns – desperately, it must be – to Emma for help. Over Emma's protests that she is fatigued already and must not walk home, she declares 'I am ... I am fatigued; but it is not the sort of

fatigue – quick walking will refresh me. – Miss Woodhouse, we
all know at times what it is to be wearied in spirits. Mine, I
confess, are exhausted. The greatest kindness you can show me,
will be to let me have my own way, and only say that I am gone
when it is necessary' (363). There are many instances in the
novel when Emma's imagination (as distinguished from her
fantasies or fancies) enables her to respond quickly and
accurately to the feelings of another person, and this is one of
them:[34]

> Emma had not another word to oppose. She saw it all; and entering
> into her feelings, promoted her quitting the house immediately, and
> watched her safely off with the zeal of a friend. Her parting look was
> grateful – and her parting words, "Oh Miss Woodhouse, the comfort
> of being sometimes alone!" – seemed to burst from an overcharged
> heart, and to describe somewhat of the continual endurance to be
> practised by her, even towards some of those who loved her best. (363)

Emma's perception might just be born out of her own family
circumstances, but this is more perception than transference,
and more acuity of response than perception, for it is the
continual endurance Jane must practise towards Frank
Churchill which the narrative ultimately implies here.[35] That,
even so, Emma's response is temporary and incomplete is
quickly made plain in the recessive comment she makes to herself on Jane's exclamation, revealing as she does so, her own un-
reconstructed hostilities to Miss Bates. '"Such a home indeed!
Such an aunt!" said Emma as she turned back into the hall
again' (having just been reminded of the splendour of the estate
with which she is connected), 'I do pity you. And the more
sensibility you betray of their just horrors, the more I shall like
you'.

What exactly occurs in the lane when Jane meets Frank on
this walk home is unknown, and while he and Emma flirt
outrageously the next day at Box Hill, Jane has no presence in
the text. She is understood as an auditor of Frank and Emma's
exchanges though, and Frank speaks indirectly to her when he
declares bad-temperedly (*a propos* the Eltons) that engagements
based merely on a brief stay at a watering place are folly. 'How
many a man has committed himself on a short acquaintance,

and rued it all the rest of his life!' The strain which Jane is under now reveals itself in her intervention, and in a tiny but telling (since signs are so scarce) psychosomatic symptom, which suggests how close Jane is to breaking point:

> Miss Fairfax, who had seldom spoken before, except among her own confederates, spoke now.
> 'Such things do occur, undoubtedly.' She was stopped by a cough. Frank Churchill turned towards her to listen.
> 'You were speaking,' said he, gravely. She recovered her voice.
> 'I was only going to observe, that though such unfortunate circumstances do sometimes occur both to men and women, I cannot imagine them to be very frequent. A hasty and imprudent attachment may arise – but there is generally time to recover from it afterwards. I would be understood to mean, that it can be only weak, irresolute characters, (whose happiness must be always at the mercy of chance,) who will suffer an unfortunate acquaintance to be an inconvenience, an oppression for ever.' (372–73)

Mary Lascelles called this 'a guarded reply',[36] but it seems to me, in the circumstances, tantamount to a public retraction of the engagement (Jane is to formalise the break in a letter). That Frank understands Jane's words in this decisive sense is discernible in the abrupt shift of the conversation to the topic of going abroad which immediately follows. Emma, too, retrospectively perceives that this was a moment of crisis: 'On Box Hill, perhaps, it had been the agony of a mind that could bear no more'.

In these climactic chapters, the lives of the heroine and the shadow-heroine are inter-related with great skill. The attack on defenceless Miss Bates which brings to a head the immaturities and hostilities latent in Emma is not allowed to be forgotten and passed over by Mr Knightley. He forces her to confront it, and once confronting it, she is filled with contrition. The crisis in Frank and Jane's relation, on the other hand, remains unresolved. Frank abruptly leaves for Richmond, though no message from his aunt has called him back, and Jane is left to endure: her difficulties, unable to be explored openly, can only double back into the self, and – in Jane's case – the now mounting stresses precipitate illness. Emma, courageously making what reparation she can, calls on the Bates the next day, and learns of Jane's decision to take the governess job, so remorselessly pressed upon her by Mrs Elton. 'Jane she had a distinct glimpse of, looking extremely ill' (378). That is all she sees of Jane, but Miss Bates' artless talk allows a more complete presentation of the breakdown through which Jane is passing. 'Do not think us ungrateful, Miss Woodhouse,' says Miss Bates,

'for such surprising good fortune (again dispersing her tears) – but, poor dear soul! if you were to see what a headach she has. When one is in great pain, you know one cannot feel any blessing quite so much as it may deserve. She is as low as possible. To look at her, nobody would think how delighted and happy she is to have secured such a situation. You will excuse her not coming to you – she is not able -'.
(379)

Jane Fairfax's position at this moment is illuminated, I think, by the work that Arthur Kleinman has undertaken among contemporary Chinese patients suffering from the condition known as 'neurasthenia'.[37] The symptoms of this clinical entity, first defined by an American, George M. Beard, in the later part of the nineteenth century, are, among others, prolonged and extreme exhaustion, headaches, dizziness and insomnia, and the condition was attributed to 'impoverishment of nervous force'. 'Neurasthenia', conceptualised as a physical disease, is now discredited in the West, and no longer diagnosed. The widespread phenomenon of neurasthenia in Chinese society is related, Kleinman argues, to that culture's traditional reserve or repression of the display of emotion outside the family, to the prevalence of ideologies of collective experience and expression. Psychological illness has long been stigmatised in China, where, especially in the cultural revolution, it was construed as anti-social. Kleinman in fact suggests that depression was, and is, recognised as politically subversive, a dangerous emotion because it points to sources of individual human misery and need that social manipulation cannot explain or control. Thus, social custom and political forces combined to repress, and to deprive of articulation, such emotions as grief, rage, despair or loneliness. When, on the other hand, these were expressed as physical symptoms, they were legitimised and respected. 'Neurasthenia' thus 'takes on the blame for misfortune and misery'.[38] Miss Bates, by regarding Jane's illness as physical, only incidentally related to her acceptance of the governess job, and by separating the symptom from its cause, manages to preserve her view of Mrs Elton and her neighbours undamaged, just as the notion of neurasthenia enables the Chinese to believe that their complaints do not entail any criticism of the culture, the social system, in which they occur, or are unrelated to their personal history. Miss Bates' pathetic strategy of dividing Jane's symptoms from her social plight exposes, of course, Austen's perception of the reality of somatisation, and thus of the social and gender relations which it serves to obscure.

Kleinman gives many case histories of patients. Frequently separated from their spouses by state directives that require them to work many hundreds of miles apart, or condemned to jobs that involve constant harassment by ignorant and un-educated superiors, these, often intelligent, people experience what in the West we would call depression, even despair. Jane Fairfax, an orphan, living in cramped quarters with her impoverished elderly aunt and grandmother, entangled in a socially unacceptable arrangement with a man who lives a long way off, without access to major institutions, pressured by a dominating and ignorant social superior to accept employment abhorrent to her – is her situation so very different? Emma wishes 'to show attention to Jane Fairfax, whose prospects were closing' but Jane refuses her overtures. What she does learn is relayed by Mr Perry:

when Mr Perry called at Hartfield, the same morning, it appeared that she was so much indisposed as to have been visited, though against her own consent, by himself, and that she was suffering under severe headachs, and a nervous fever to a degree, which made him doubt the possibility of her going to Mrs Smallridge's at the time proposed. Her health seemed for the moment completely deranged – appetite quite gone – and though there were no absolutely alarming symptoms, nothing touching the pulmonary complaint, which was the standing apprehension of the family, Mr Perry was uneasy about her. He thought she had undertaken more than she was equal to, and that she felt it so herself, though she would not own it. Her spirits seemed overcome. Her present home, he could not but observe, was

unfavourable to a nervous disorder: – confined always to one room;
– he could have wished it otherwise – and her good aunt, though his
very old friend, he must acknowledge to be not the best companion for
an invalid of that description. (389)

Here is depicted, in the anthropologist's terms, an idiom of
bodily distress which expresses and communicates mental
suffering in a mode produced by and acceptable in, a specific
social situation. In Jane Fairfax's position, the direct and overt
expression of her distressed emotion is forbidden. Her symptoms
express not only her immediate situation, but focus, too, the
larger social condition of the single disempowered woman. Mr
Perry seems to perceive that Jane's illness is the manifestation of
social stress – indeed his address and tact here help to substantiate his status in the community.[39] Emma, willing to read
Jane's condition as a physical illness, in the Highbury style,
sends Hartfield arrowroot (presumably for her digestion), which
is returned, naturally enough. But hearing later of Jane 'seen
wandering about the meadows at some distance from Highbury' (a telling glimpse of a desperate extremity) her heart is
grieved 'for a state which seemed but the more pitiable from this
sort of irritation of spirits, inconsistency of action and inequality
of powers' (391), and she sees, or intuits, that Jane's breakdown
has something to do with her own failures of perception.

Intercepting these accounts of Jane is news of Mrs Churchill,
an apparently quite different, but also restless female sufferer
from 'nerves', whose death soon leads to the revelation of the
secret engagement. (Jane is returned to health, as Mrs Elton
coyly puts it, 'by a certain young physician from Windsor'). As
an immediate result Emma discovers that Harriet has set her
hopes not on Frank Churchill but on George Knightley, and
realises, as a consequence, her own feelings for him. But
Knightley is away in London, driven there by the conviction
that Emma loves Frank, and there is, for a while, no means for
Emma to verify Harriet's belief that her feelings for Mr
Knightley are reciprocated. Emma is isolated and powerless,
cut off from contact with he who might reassure and support
her, and for a brief, but intensely wretched passage of time, her
condition is made to replicate the powerlessness Jane has long

endured. Dependent now entirely upon the desires and behaviour of others, she suffers her remorse and wretchedness alone, secretly, without speech, since both what she repents of and what she now knows about her feelings, must be concealed from her only remaining companions, Mrs Weston and her father. But her unusual mood, her sighs and abstraction, do, despite her efforts, impart her condition to Mrs Weston, chatting on about Frank and Jane. '"Are you well, my Emma?" was Mrs Weston's parting question', and Emma replies bravely 'Oh! perfectly. I am always well, you know' (420). 'I did not quite like your looks on Tuesday', Mrs Weston says a few days later, 'though you will never own being affected by weather, I think every body feels a north-east wind' (436) – a perfect example of the miscomprehension that is Highbury's kindness. Between these two meetings, though, Emma's health has passed through its own crisis.

Emma is confined to the house, in the novel's most sombre episode, with her father, on a long wet July evening, condemned now to think over the past, and its things ill done, and done to others' harm.

The evening of this day was very long, and melancholy, at Hartfield ...

The weather affected Mr Woodhouse, and he could only be kept tolerably comfortable by almost ceaseless attention on his daughter's side, and by exertions which had never cost her half so much before. It reminded her of their first forlorn tête-à-tête, on the evening of Mrs Weston's wedding day; but Mr Knightley had walked in then, soon after tea, and dissipated every melancholy fancy. (421)

'How was she to bear the change?' Emma had asked herself at the very opening of the novel, foreseeing a life stretching before her of lonely evenings with her father, and now she asks again, even more gravely, 'How was it to be endured?' Emma's miserable confinement recalls not only that first evening, but the day when, kept in by snow and ice, she brooded over her mistakes about Harriet and Mr Elton. The future that she faces is frightening enough, but the language is moderate, carefully unemphatic, as if not to give way to the panic that, none the less, begins to pervade her thoughts. 'The prospect before her now,

was threatening to a degree that could not be entirely dispelled ',
' in great measure ', ' it was reasonable to suppose ', ' Her present
forebodings she feared would experience no similar contradiction ': these measured phrases are actually conveying the
passion they control, and it is this reserve, this sense that she is
surveying her condition with unusual responsibility, that is
behind the force of the bitter oxymoron with which Emma's
initial survey of her plight climaxes: ' If all took place that might
take place among the circle of her friends, Hartfield must be
comparatively deserted; and she left to cheer her father with the
spirits only of ruined happiness '.

This sequence is a kind of nocturnal, and as her thoughts
review and carefully close down each possibility of future escape
or relief, the emphases and repetitions that once defined Emma's
bounding spiritedness now mount near to hysteria. Her
thoughts finally confront what is most hurtful, the possibility
that it might be Harriet who draws Mr Knightley away from
' them ':

Mr Knightley to be no longer coming there for his evening comfort!
– No longer walking in at all hours, as if ever willing to change his own
home for their's! – How was it to be endured? And if he were to be lost
to them for Harriet's sake; if he were to be thought of hereafter, as
finding in Harriet's society all that he wanted; if Harriet were to be the
chosen, the first, the dearest, the friend, the wife to whom he looked for
all the best blessings of existence; what could be increasing Emma's
wretchedness but the reflection never far distant from her mind, that
it had been all her own work?

When it came to such a pitch as this, she was not able to refrain from
a start, or a heavy sigh, or even from walking about the room for a few
seconds – . (422–3)

Extraordinary as it is, this spirited young woman now begins to
display the symptoms of 'nerves'. The blockage of energies
denied their natural outlet is defined metaphorically by her
incarceration within the comfortable prison of her father's home
and Emma now tastes that aspect of the nineteenth-century
lady's destiny which is to live perversely or aberrantly through
the body the energies and powers denied other fulfillments in
her world.[40]

Nothing of the sort, of course, happens. Next day the weather clears, Emma steps into the garden, and there follows that proposal scene which Chapman rightly called the 'consummation' of Jane Austen's art:[41]

> With all the eagerness which such a transition gives, Emma resolved to be out of doors as soon as possible. Never had the exquisite sight, smell, sensation of nature, tranquil, warm, and brilliant after a storm, been more attractive to her. She longed for the serenity they might gradually introduce; and on Mr Perry's coming in soon after dinner, with a disengaged hour to give her father, she lost no time in hurrying into the shrubbery. – There, with spirits freshened, and thoughts a little relieved, she had taken a few turns, when she saw Mr Knightley passing through the garden door, and coming towards her. (424)

Disregarding mud and rain, he has ridden from London to console her. The subsequent scene in the garden, in which, beginning almost as strangers, they come, at first haltingly, to understand each other and are reconciled, a scene which 'cleared from each the same degree of ignorance, jealousy and distrust', is made possible only because another conference is taking place inside the house, and Emma's role as nurse to her father has been temporarily assumed by Mr Perry.

> 'You are going in, I suppose,' said he.
> 'No' – replied Emma – quite confirmed by the depressed manner in which he spoke – 'I should like to take another turn. Mr Perry is not gone.' (429)

It is a very light touch, but the moment is loaded with accumulated implications. Mr Perry, cloistered indoors with his 'friend' and patient, in a social relationship construed as a medical one, Mr Knightley and Emma walking out in the garden, eventually making and accepting a proposal of marriage, a triumph over that repression or denial that has organised Mr Woodhouse and his daughter's life so far: counterpointing the indoors and the outdoors, the confinement to habit and the capacity for growth, the chapter picks up the crucial polarities around which this novel is constructed.

Yet that scene, though it resolves Emma's and George Knightley's misunderstandings, is not the consummation of the tale. One remarkable feature of *Emma*'s structure is that over fifty pages and ten more chapters follow the event that forms the usual climax and resolution of the romantic novel (about twenty pages are all that is needed after the reconciliation and acceptance in *Pride and Prejudice*, for instance; a brief chapter in *Persuasion*.) The length of this coda in *Emma* is partly due, no doubt, to the need to disentangle the plot of Frank and Jane, and to give adequate time for Harriet to fall in love again, but the illusion of the passing of time needed for these events is used to serve another purpose, which, in meeting the problem that Mr Woodhouse inevitably poses to the possibility of marriage, brings to a head the characters' most fundamental conflicts, and with it, the novel's interest in the nature of health.

The marriage that concludes all of Austen's novels is seen by several contemporary critics as a regrettable capitulation to convention, both artistically and morally, an evitable sacrifice of the energies of the once bravely independent heroine to the confines of an established institution.[42] But marriage is effectively problematised in this novel, and its eventual accomplishment involves such surmounting of difficulties, and triumphs of both gender and social politics, as make the reader's desire for the narrative's closure the accomplice of an achievement in Emma which unites the fulfillment of her desire, the assumption of a social role, and the resolution or cure of her father's influence.

In the ideology of 'Hartfield', of course, marriage has been proscribed. All the micro-initiatives of Emma (like introducing the new round table into the drawing room, like giving the cake to Mr Perry) serve an overriding purpose that is conservative, for they are premised upon the continuity of Hartfield as a stable, unaltered, domestic system. It is a crypto-marriage itself, in which if, as Emma sees, she has certain privileges, these are paid for by certain collusions. But if Emma has caught from her father the notion that marriage is not for her, as well as (more importantly) a good deal of complacency about the advantages of Hartfield over every other situation, these ideas in themselves are not necessarily dangerous ones nor inimical to her happiness. She has even imagined, sketching her future to Harriet Smith in chapter X of the novel, a life of spinsterhood, of domestic confinement (she calls it 'comfort' here) of refused opportunities, analogous to and perpetuating her father's. But her pronouncements are absurd because of the transparent incompatibility between their dogmatism and what is simultaneously disclosed, as she speaks, of her bodily and sexual nature. As Nancy Armstrong puts it, Austen here makes 'Emma's speech reveal as writing the very truth it denies as speech'.[43] 'She always declares she will never marry, which, of course, means just nothing at all' remarks Knightley to Mrs Weston, and he is right. Emma is prevented from thinking of Knightley himself as a possible sexual partner, too, by the role that he is constantly placing himself in, of adviser, critic, father-figure, mentor (though nothing of course prevented eighteenth-century heroines from being in love with mentors): but once alerted by her jealousy of Harriet, at the first touch of reality, the ideology collapses.

A more fundamental consequence of her father's influence on Emma, though, is displayed as a kind of perversion and the source of the novel's dynamics. The two early chapters in which Isabella and Mr Woodhouse discuss their symptoms, their doctors, and argue the rival merits of Cromer and South End as health resorts, which interrupt the plot, the progress of Emma's schemes for Harriet and Elton, display his valetudinarianism in a comic light but demonstrate too how much effort, how much ceaseless attentiveness and adroitness Emma needs to maintain family harmony and her father's 'comfort'. Emma, of course, rarely tries directly, as Isabella does here, to combat her father's opinions and prejudices: instead she seems untroubled by his mild but dogged aggressions. Except for the brief acknowledgement of 'efforts which had never cost her half so much before', which falls from her under stress at the crisis, she never repines at her father's demands. 'As a daughter, she hoped she was not without a heart', Emma thinks fervently after the catastrophe at Box Hill (377). But though not made explicit, it might well be argued that the relationship's toll is displayed in the very contrast between her kind 'heart' at home and her intolerance abroad. Just as her moment of service to Jane Fairfax seems to prompt a moment or spasm of spite, so the tax of Emma's devotion to her father shows in the transferences and hostilities that generate most of the novel's crises.

Emma's imagination – her projections onto and fantasies about both Harriet and Jane – is certainly misunderstood, though, if it is thought of as malign or mischievous in itself and as needing always to be corrected by Knightley's perception or reason. It is rather an avenue by which her health expresses itself, the exercise of that capacity for exploration and innovation intrinsic to any healthy and growing organism. Emma's mistakes and unintended cruelties exemplify the spirit, a physiological as well as psychological given, with which she is enabled to circumvent and surmount her father's, and her community's, notions of female capacity. One recognises as typical of Emma that 'eager laughing warmth' (348) which accompanies her conspiracies with Frank, (here the card-game, which is at Jane's expense) a risk-taking eagerness which is the principle of her development even while it lays her open to disaster and reproach. As D. A Miller puts it, 'Emma's abundance of good health seems less a guarantor of good conduct than a Nietzchean bounty ... a spontaneous energy of will that doesn't bother to count the cost of its blissful assertion, whether that cost be defrayed by others, who may be hurt (Miss Bates) or virtually annihilated ("Harriet was nothing, she was everything herself") or by Emma herself, whose desire is overbearing enough to welcome a self-inflicted wound ("it darted through her, with the speed of an arrow, that Mr Knightley must marry no one but herself")'.[44]

The breakthrough of self-knowledge is almost as formal in *Emma* as it is in *Pride and Prejudice* ('Till this moment I never knew myself') but its precise articulation is certainly astonishing for a writer still supposed to be a proper lady. Emma does not tell herself – or not at least in so many words – that she 'loves' Knightley. Instead, her moment of revelation is depicted as a moment of ownership, of property, of reaching out to take what is rightfully one's own. 'Why was it so much worse that Harriet should be in love with Mr Knightley, than with Frank Churchill? Why was the evil so dreadfully increased by Harriet's having some hope of a return? It darted through her, with the speed of an arrow, that Mr Knightley must marry no one but herself!' (408) This is an instant physiological occurrence which is simultaneously the experience and recognition of sexual passion, as well as the assertion of a right of possession – a climax, perhaps, of true *jouissance*.[45]

It takes so long after this moment, after the proposal, for the novel to work itself out because though Emma wants Mr Knightley, and wants marriage to him, too, hers is *not* wholly a Nietzschean bounty, and the consummation of her desire must not annihilate her father. 'She hardly knew yet what Mr Knightley would ask; but a very short parley with her own heart produced the solemn resolution of never quitting her father. – She even wept over the idea of it, as a sin of thought' (435). Mr Woodhouse's condition is ultimately as undecidable as Mrs Churchill's, but its social effects, like hers, are undeniable. Knightley perceives that 'a transplantation would be a risk of her father's comfort, perhaps even of his life, which must not be hazarded' (448–9) and decides to move in. Even with this dazzlingly progressive initiative, how to assuage Henry Woodhouse's inevitable distress at the news involves a good deal of anxiety and the novel's last few chapters are given up to a strategic management of this elderly patient which demonstrates to the full the nature of Emma's health.

Mr Woodhouse is never so clearly a nursling in the novel as he becomes now when his whole family concerts its efforts to break to him the news of the impending event which will make him finally an impotent and superannuated figure. Interweaving, not without irony, the lengthy process which persuades him to accept the 'evil' of the forthcoming marriage is Mrs Weston's nursing of her newly born child. The communal or family nursing involves the strategic co-option of Isabella and Mrs Weston, but even so, Emma needs 'all the spirits she could command' in breaking the news to him. Still, however, Mr Woodhouse's 'nervous system' dictates postponement of the wedding day. The impasse is resolved by recourse to new reserves of spirit on the narrator's part: 'In this state of suspense they were befriended, not by any sudden illumination of Mr

Woodhouse's mind, or by any wonderful change of his nervous system, but by the operation of the same system in another way. – Mrs Weston's poultry house was robbed one night of all her turkey – evidently by the ingenuity of man – Other poultry-yards in the neighbourhood also suffered. Pilfering was *house-breaking* to Mr Woodhouse's fears … ' (484). The ingenuity of Austen here matches the ingenuity of her heroine. Making the appeasement of nerves and conservative fears the occasion for their *bouleversement*: replicating Emma's little stratagem with Mrs Weston's wedding cake, this is a joke which artfully unites consideration for the sickly with satisfaction and triumph for the well.

If we were to follow Mr Perry on his rounds in Highbury, then, we would learn a good deal about the social politics of illness, about the power-relations of illness behaviour, and about the attribution of meanings to bodies and faces. But the novel in which he so elusively features goes beyond an anthropology or political analysis of illness, to a larger concern – a metaphysics or epistemology of health. Enclosing her heroine within a community preoccupied with, and talking constantly about, ill health, Jane Austen conducts an investigation, though not of course in abstract terms, into the meaning – moral, spiritual, psychological, physical – of health. Working through and beneath the novel's amused depiction of bodily events as the focus and currency of power-relations is an larger and more urgent enterprise, which is something to do with manifesting, displaying, declaring the condition of good health.

But 'health' is notoriously difficult to speak about, and the work of Georges Canguilhem, himself the 'hidden' master of Foucault, is needed here to throw light on the novel's dynamism. Canguilhem's *On the Normal and the Pathological*[46] is an important argument that the concept of health cannot be understood as an intrinsic condition or capacity of the human organism, but must be understood as a response to demands, as a relationship between the organism and the environment. Pathological changes are not merely quantitative, as Claude Bernard, Comte and earlier pathologists had suggested, but qualitative, and involve a whole reorganisation within, or mode of adjustment of, the diseased organ, the institution of a new 'norm' at another level. Hence, 'normal' must give way to 'normative' as a description of the healthy state, for as Canguilhem writes, 'The sick living being is normalized in well-defined conditions of existence, and has lost his normative capacity, the capacity to establish other norms in other conditions'.[47] Citing Goldstein's clinical observations made upon men with neurological lesions in the First World War, he notes that what these patients revealed is 'the establishment of new norms of life by a reduction in the level of their activity as related to a new but *narrowed* environment'[48] (Canguilhem's italics).

Being healthy means being not only normal in a given situation, but also normative in this and other eventual situations. What characterizes health is the possibility of transcending the norm, which defines the momentary normal, the possibility of tolerating infractions of the habitual norm and instituting new norms in new situations ... Health is a margin of tolerance for the inconstancies of the environment ... As there is a psychological assurance which is not presumption, there is a biological assurance which is not excess, and which is health.

In a striking phrase, he writes 'good health means being able to fall sick and recover, it is biological luxury'.[49] Importantly, too, Canguilhem's conception of health includes pathological propensity. 'We think', he declares, 'that the power and temptation to fall sick are an essential characteristic of human physiology. To paraphrase a saying of Valéry, we have said that the possible abuse of health is a part of health.'[50]

Canguilhem's philosophy is worked out in relation to detailed physiological evidence, but its emphasis on health as the capacity to respond to changes – 'life understood as activity of opposition to inertia and indifference'[51] – has obviously broader and more general applications and can illuminatingly be transferred to *Emma*. Emma's 'abuse' of her gifts is reprimanded by Mr Knightley, but now one sees that this is beside the point: Emma would not be Emma without her capacity for mistakes, her capacity to transgress and recover, and it is this which makes her embody that health which is the keystone of the novel's structure. In this light, too, the novel's series of enclosed environments reveals its metaphoric nature: enclosure is used to mark limited or narrowed possibility, and limited possibility is coterminous with diminished vitality. Beginning in a drawing room, it is nine chapters before the scene of *Emma* widens beyond Hartfield, and even then, the only excursion beyond the boundaries of the parishes of Highbury and Donwell (a disastrous one, of course) is to Box Hill. Highbury is a (literally) narrowed environment and within it, at intervals, a series of other enclosed or confined spaces metonymically suggests the relation between freedom, or opportunity, and health, both spiritual and physical. Not only the drawing room at Hartfield, in which Emma in her melancholy vigil feels imprisoned for life, but the crowded rooms at the Crown, whose windows Mr Woodhouse fears might be thrown open by thoughtless young persons, the narrow stairs and confined accommodation of Mrs and Miss Bates, which is so much to the detriment of their niece's welfare: all these imply how readily confinement and sickness reciprocally reinforce each other. In all sorts of ways – the evening at the Westons', when the party may be marooned by snow, the carriage in which, coming home from this outing, Emma is confined with Mr Elton – the novel calls the reader's attention to the limits of the spaces within which its personages enact their lives and its crises unfold. On the other hand, outdoor life and action (John Knightley's racing boys, Robert Martin going three miles round to get Harriet walnuts, George Knightley's walking in at all hours) is obviously associated with opportunity and freedom and, in turn, with health, and it is normally the prerogative of the males. Exercise, like open windows, is anathema to a notion of health that conceptualises it as conservative, the guarded maintenance of a narrowed norm of stability, and that links it to a fixed conception of feminine capacity. As Anne Elliot is to remark in *Persuasion*, 'We live at home, quiet, confined, and our feelings prey upon us': the enforced confinement of women's (or ladies') lives, makes psychological as well as physical health more precarious.

Whether his sickness is 'real' or not, in the metaphysics of the novel, Mr Woodhouse thus *represents* ill health. He is solely concerned with the preservation of that limited environment within which he can function adequately. The sick adult and the child, remarks Canguilhem, may show superficial similarities, but to compare one to the other is an absurdity 'because it ignores that eagerness which pushes the child to raise itself constantly to new norms, which is profoundly at variance with the care to conserve which directs the sick person in his obsessive and often exhausting maintenance of the only norms of life in which he feels almost normal, that is, in a position to use and dominate his own environment'.[52] At Donwell, in a room 'especially prepared for him with a fire all the morning', entertained with collections and picture-books, tended by the pregnant Mrs Weston, Mr Woodhouse has 'no other resemblance to a child', as the narrator dryly remarks, than his lack of taste. Because of his family and social position, Mr Woodhouse can co-opt others to carry out on his behalf those strategies of enclosure and defence typical of the sick person; he creates around him a social space which normalises his invalidism. As the richest patient in Highbury, his influence ensures that his refusals become perceived as necessary, even as natural, within Highbury's behavioural world.

It is Emma's capacity to break out and through the invisible network of his sickness, a network diffused through the sociolect of Highbury, that typifies her triumph and the note of genuine satisfaction and celebration that attends the final wedding. The issue of health then is not only the focus of social and gender politics. What Canguilhem allows this discussion to suggest is that to think about health is necessarily to think morally, and thus that focusing on Emma's health, her father's hypochondria, and Jane's illness (as centres round which this novel is organised) brings into play thereby a discourse of the moral life more inclusive and amplified than that one of the ethical virtues within which the novel has often been thought. 'Spirits' and 'nerves' are culturally determined modes of understanding and representing the body which the text makes use of, but as it dramatises their presence, and their conflict, Austen, as I have argued in this reading, vindicates the validity of that overriding term or notion, 'health'. The author herself is expressing an Emma-like spirit in the inventiveness, wit and cleverness of this novel, too, and it is this which makes *Emma* an enactment or articulation, a celebration, a triumph – not just a picture – of health.

CHAPTER 4

Persuasion: *the pathology of everyday life*

That future of confinement to an unvarying, limited neighbourhood, supported with the spirits only of ruined happiness, sighted for a moment by Emma Woodhouse from the Hartfield windows on a miserable evening in July, becomes the actual condition of the gradually disclosed heroine of *Persuasion*, Austen's last completed novel. If *Emma* is a picture of health, the first volume of *Persuasion*, one can say with only a small exaggeration, is a portrait of suffering. Anne Elliot is a woman oppressed and insignificant, a 'nobody', discouraged by a burden of grief and regret that she has borne alone for the seven years prior to the novel's inception.

> Her attachment and regrets had, for a long time, clouded every enjoyment of youth; and an early loss of bloom and spirits had been their lasting effect... No second attachment, the only thoroughly natural, happy, and sufficient cure, at her time of life, had been possible to the nice tone of her mind, the fastidiousness of her taste, in the small limits of the society around them. (28)

Having been persuaded to break off an engagement with a man whom she still loves, she wears her sadness and deprivation in her prematurely aging body and face. 'A few years before, Anne Elliot had been a very pretty girl, but her bloom had vanished early', now 'faded and thin', 'her spirits were not high', as her only friend Lady Russell admits, and this lack of resilience and of energy is evidenced in her first act in the novel, her intervention to persuade her sister Elizabeth about the ambitions of the hanger-on, Mrs Clay. Elizabeth arrogantly repudiates her advice, as she has foreseen. After a mild intercession from Anne, Elizabeth responds with renewed rudeness. 'Anne had done – glad that it was over, and not absolutely hopeless of doing good' (35). Anne's oppressed and marginal state – she has no energy to persist, and not being absolutely hopeless is her accustomed condition – is represented by her marginal position in the dialogue; her initiative is suppressed by the narrative, and Elizabeth's bullying instead allowed to dominate the page.

Anne's condition has been a prolonged, and private, mourning. Her loss and her grief are set by the novel within a continuum of other mourners who freely display their grief. Anne compares herself explicitly with Captain Benwick, the sailor who has suffered the unexpected loss of his fiancée, Fanny Harville, while at sea six months before. Everyone feels sympathy for him, '"And yet," said Anne to herself, as they now moved forward to meet the party, "he has not, perhaps, a more sorrowing heart than I have. I cannot believe his prospects so blighted for ever. He is younger than I am; younger in feeling, if not in fact; younger as a man. He will rally again, and be happy with another"'(97). This is Anne Elliot's lowest point in the novel, and it is characteristic of its mode of narration that she speaks only to herself, in a mood that marks her dissension, mild, but latently bitter, from the mood of those about her. Anne's authority in the narrative is promoted by the self-reflection that distinguishes the character's thoughts – by the perception that her own position as a woman is a determinant of her suffering – and here, additionally, by the accuracy of her prediction. Benwick, of course, does rally, and forgets Fanny Harville, but her brother, Captain Harville, though less the object of public attention, grieves for her longer and more poignantly. He cannot speak to Anne of his sister without 'a quivering lip' near the novel's close (232). The uncertain relationship of bereavement to its social signs is considered too in the extended presentation of Mrs Musgrove's demonstrative grief over the loss of her son, Dick, a grief that is 'real' as well as exaggerated and absurd, and by the mockery of woe carried about by William Walter Elliot, in his funereal livery and crape-banded hat, mourning for a wife he evidently does not grieve over.

These are not the only deaths which cast their shadows across the events of *Persuasion*. It is commonly agreed, in fact, that loss, and the human adjustment to loss, is a major theme of the novel.[1] There are losses of many kinds: of health, of hopes, of career, of one's home, of husbands and wives: perhaps, or so some critics argue, of a sense of stable value, even, some might claim, of the whole system of values that underpinned Jane Austen's other novels. 'By the time she wrote *Persuasion*,' argues David Monaghan, for example, 'Jane Austen seems to have lost faith in the gentry'.[2] Monaghan is one of many critics who read the Elliots' abdication of their country estate and their removal to Bath as symptomatic of a crucial transformation in English society, one indicative of a new hollowness in the code of polite manners, and the loss of the old order representing 'an ideal of civilised existence far beyond anything the Musgroves or the sailors could hope to achieve'.[3] 'In *Persuasion*', writes Mary Poovey, 'the fact that the social and ethical hierarchy super-intended by the landed gentry is in a state of total collapse is clear not only from the fiscal and moral bankruptcy of Sir Walter Elliot but also from the epistemological relativity that is emphasised both thematically and formally'.[4] 'Just about all the previous stabilities of Jane Austen's world are called into question in this novel',[5] declares Tony Tanner, arguing that Austen in *Persuasion* demonstrates a 'crisis' or even 'chaos' in the gentry's values, and that this is in turn reflected in or signified by a shift in Austen's own priorities and narrative techniques. The novel is seen as Austen's farewell to a way of life. 'She is clearly undertaking a radical reassessment and revision of her system of values', claims Tanner.[6]

To read *Persuasion* as 'shaking the foundations of Austen's conservativism'[7] is to make Austen into a social historian of percipience indeed, discovering between the end of March 1815, when *Emma* was finished, and the beginning of August the same year, when *Persuasion* was begun, that the rural gentry were spiritually and financially bankrupt, foreseeing the modern condition, turning to newly discovered romantic values, and even more, it seems, anticipating the modern, or even postmodern, conviction of the relativity of all value and perception. David Spring has shown how unfounded are the historical assumptions upon which the view of *Persuasion* as depicting a social transformation rests: Sir Walter Elliot is not abandoning his estate in removing to Bath, and renting his property, he is simply repairing his fortunes in a time-honoured way. At the end of seven years he will return to Kellynch.[8] The navy men are not an alternative class, taking over power, their entrepreneurial initiative poised to take over the leading role in society vacated by the hollow gentry: they are gentry themselves, integrated and absorbed into the existing social order, as Benwick's eventual marriage to Louisa Musgrove exemplifies. The Musgrove family is ironised, but it is not a destructive irony: in all essential respects, they are a very good sort of people, uneducated and provincial perhaps, but the backbone of rural society. Mary Musgrove (née Elliot) has not come down in the world, and Charles Hayter, the educated young clergyman, is rising in it. There is no suggestion that such a society is either despicable, or in decline. Charles Musgrove is a representative and undistinguished country gentleman, but he does well for himself on the family's appearance in Bath, explicitly voicing opinions which the novelist's one cursorily contemptuous venture into Elizabeth's consciousness, when she decides not to invite the Musgroves to dinner, implicitly vindicates: 'It was a struggle between propriety and vanity; but vanity got the better, and then Elizabeth was happy again' (219). 'What's an evening party?' says Musgrove. 'Never worth remembering. Your father might have asked us to dinner, if he had wanted to see us' (223). When Mary protests that they have been invited to meet Mr Elliot – 'the future representative of the family' – he replies roughly, 'Don't talk to me about heirs and representatives ... I am not one of those who neglect the reigning power to bow to the rising sun. If I would not go for the sake of your father, I should think it scandalous to go for the sake of his heir. What is Mr Elliot to me?' There is still vigour and conviction in the country gentry's code of values and in this speech they are seen to be congruent with the hospitality and independence celebrated in the naval figures. There are additional reasons of course why 'The careless expression was life to Anne, who saw that Captain Wentworth was all attention, looking and listening with his whole soul' (224) and certainly these things are seen from a point of view less implicated, less able to partake fully in the way of life they evoke than in earlier novels.

The view that *Persuasion* is a novel diagnosing radical shifts in social power, and that this vision corresponds to a radical recension in Austen's techniques and values seems to be motivated by the still-lingering embarrassment that a novel should be, to use the ironic phrase she used in defence of her art in *Northanger Abbey*, 'only a novel'. It is as if to vindicate or explain Jane Austen's status as a canonical or classic author it was necessary to make her into a social theorist, to make Austen prophesy the downfall of the class to which she belonged, or attribute to her, if not a radical politics, at least a 'radical' rethinking of her techniques. It is the easier, perhaps, to think of Sir Walter Elliot as a representative figure (rather than as a patent eccentric) because Bath, a real place, seems to function in this novel as the symbol – the structural embodiment and institutionalisation – of his own vanity and snobbery. One could easily suppose that Bath is presented in *Persuasion* as a specific micro-culture, a place in which traditional values have been replaced by commodity values, a built environment which seems to give concrete expression to a culture of narcissistic self-involvement. One could point, for instance, to the antithesis set up between Anne's thoughts of the autumn months in the country 'so sweet and so sad' and her dread of 'the possible heats of September in all the white glare of Bath' (33), and suggest that this is a hint at the false surface, the exclusion of the natural world and the inward turning that could be said to be characteristic of Bath's architecture. Eighteenth-century Bath is a city of enclosure, Squares and Circuses of geometric design explicitly sequestering the gentry who were to inhabit them from any natural wildness or irregularity. Describing John Wood's early eighteenth-century proposals for Queen's Square, the social historian R. S. Neale writes that 'Nature, except in the shape of a green turf and formal shrubs, was expressly excluded. There were to be no forest trees in the square, only low stone walls and espaliers of elm and lime'.[9] Later in the century the lease of the Royal Crescent (1767–74) prevented the adjacent landowner from growing any tree more than eight feet high. The typical architecture of eighteenth-century Bath followed Wood's liking for 'enclosed spaces, designed to provide some isolation from the economic bustle of civil society and free from the intrusion of the labouring population who built and serviced the city'.[10] Separation of the gentry sections of the city both from the natural world and from the lower classes who were necessary to its existence was designed into its structure.

In Bath itself, in the novel, this social distribution of space is conveyed in the fact that addresses have a precisely calibrated economic and hence social value. Laura Place, for example, leased by the Elliots' cousin, Lady Dalrymple, a member of the (Irish, and therefore fringe) aristocracy, was an especially prestigious address, with one house built by John Eveleigh in 1792 advertised for letting at £120 per annum, with 'the special attraction of two water closets'.[11] The addresses are disposed in the novel as signifiers of social status – Camden-place, Gay Street, Lansdown Crescent, Marlborough Buildings – to be quickly, immediately, read as locating the addressee in a precise position on the social scale.[12] 'Westgate-buildings!' exclaims Sir Walter Elliot, 'and who is Miss Anne Elliot to be visiting in Westgate-buildings? – A Mrs. Smith ... And what is her attraction? That she is old and sickly' (157). Addresses are thus related to surnames and, as well, to fit and comely bodies, as markers of social rank.

Bath's *raison d'être* and subsequent prosperity was based upon its hot springs and medicinal waters. By Jane Austen's time it had become a resort which combined facilities for the renovation of health, and venues for the pursuit of social and sexual liaisons, a place in which the medicinal and the erotic were intertwined – an eighteenth-century Magic Fountain. 'Where the waters do agree, it is quite wonderful the relief they give', Mrs Elton tells Emma, and compounds the impertinence by adding 'And as to its recommendations to *you*, I fancy I need not take much pains to dwell on them. The advantages of Bath to the young are pretty generally understood' (E 275). Mrs Smith is one of those among its visitors who is lodging there for the purpose of health; she has come on the – arguably rational – grounds that the hot baths will relieve, if not cure, her rheumatism. But Bath had been for many years, as Defoe declared, 'the resort of the sound rather than the sick',[13] and its culture as an elegant watering place treats the body in another mode. The body is perceived as an object; it's to be prized or appraised, like handsome furniture, as a commodity. Thus when Elizabeth Elliot bestows a card upon Wentworth, her gesture is not a sign of forgiveness or reconciliation, a prompting of the inner moral life: 'The truth was, that Elizabeth had been long enough in Bath, to understand the importance of a man of such an air and appearance as his. The past was nothing. The present was that Captain Wentworth would move about well in her drawing-room' (226). The male body becomes an item of social circulation here as much as the female has always been, as for example at Netherfield. It is thus easy to elide Sir Walter Elliot's narcissism and vanity into representative status, as he stands 'in a shop in Bond-street' counting handsome faces as they go by (141–42). In its drawing rooms and evening parties the values he articulates can be seen to be reified, and he commodifies people on the streets as Lady Russell appraises handsome curtains.

Like all of Austen's novels, *Persuasion* is a study in the moral atmosphere of place. Obviously the novel contrasts, as does Anne Elliot herself, the warmth and hospitality of the Harvilles at Lyme, generous with their limited accommodation, with the cold formality of her father and sister in their two drawing rooms at Bath. The 'elegant stupidity' of their evening parties is evidently intended as typical of Bath society: on the other hand, as a resort, the city is atypical of the life of the gentry, and / many aspects of the novel confirm this. *Persuasion* is certainly constructed in a more polarised mode than any other of Jane Austen's novels (even *Sense and Sensibility*): warmth, hospitality, enterprise, initiative, exertion and the future belonging – by and large – to the sailors, chill formality, snobbish self-regard, inertia and the past belonging – by and large – to the Elliots, their cronies and relations. But this simple polarity is actually

greatly complicated by a number of features, not least of them
the overlap, as I have already suggested, between the Musgroves
and the Harvilles. The Musgroves are as hospitable as the
Harvilles (one of the novel's subtle touches is the way the two
families form an unobtrusive alliance as soon as events introduce
them). Lady Russell is misguided and imperceptive, shares
many of the dubious priorities of Sir Walter Elliot, but her value
for rank does not prevent her from taking Anne to visit in
Westgate Buildings, 'on the contrary, she approves it' (157).
Bath is as hospitable to the Crofts and their naval acquaintances
as it is to the Elliots and their circle. Moreover it is a condition
of the novel's plot that Anne Elliot's life be unusually confined
and restricted so that opportunities for the depiction of
representatives of the gentry other than the Elliots are necessarily curtailed.

Nevertheless, Bath and the Elliots are linked in a metonymic
relationship, and the rest of the novel has a contrastive and
interrogative function towards the corpus of values they
represent. Bath excludes nature, excludes the labouring and
serving classes, and attempts to repress the knowledge of growth
and change, of decay and death. Sir Walter lives out an infantile
fantasy of narcissistic omnipotence.[14] Bath society represses
that knowledge of the body as an unstable and imperfect
subjective condition upon which its economy initially wholly,
and still in part, depends, just as the labouring classes and
wilderness are expunged from its spaces. But the novel discloses
a 'real world' both inside and outside Bath in which the reader's
attention is constantly being drawn to these necessary conditions
of human life, to what Lady Russell calls 'the uncertainty of all
human events and calculations' (159) and especially to thoughts
about the human body very different from his simple equation
of handsomeness and value.

Not being a great reader, Sir Walter Elliot is unlikely to have
come across the quarto volumes of John Caspar Lavater's *Essays
on Physiognomy*, widely as these circulated in the last decade of
the eighteenth and the first of the nineteenth centuries, but if he
had, he would have found there a notion of human nature not
entirely at odds with his own. These heavy, profusely illustrated

volumes outlined a theory of correspondence between features and moral character, between physical appearance and inner life. The many engravings of the faces of famous and unknown men and women with supplementary and elucidatory commentaries attempted to enforce the proposition that character can be read off from appearance, that, in Lavater's own words, 'virtue and vice, with all their shades, and in their most remote consequences, are beauty and deformity'.[15] Deviations from an ideal model of beauty were interpreted as 'symptomatic of analogous anomalies in the hidden psyche'.[16] 'Physiognomy', he wrote, 'is the science or knowledge of the correspondence between the external and the internal man, the visible superficial and the invisible contents'.[17]

But of course Sir Walter has no theory, and for him there is no correspondence: the 'invisible contents' might as well not exist: value exists only in appearance, and his moral world consists only of a hierarchy of assessments based exclusively on physical harmony and comeliness. Lavater is relevant to the novel he inhabits, none the less, because of the germ of truth, or of plausibility his new 'science' drew upon: the instinct, at its basis erotic or libidinal, to read health and vigour as virtue, to see handsomeness as integrity, an instinct in whose trap, for instance, Elizabeth Bennet is caught when she takes Wickham's presentation of himself as the injured but generous victim of Darcy's undeserved enmity on trust: 'Till I can forget his father, I never can defy or expose *him*', he asserts, piously enough. 'Elizabeth honoured him for such feelings', says the narrator, adding, 'and thought him handsomer than ever as he expressed them' (PP 80). It is an unconscious assumption often made in these novels, and *Persuasion*, which opens so decisively with a figure who equates value only with handsomeness, and who has, to all intents and purposes, no inner life or moral sense, carries the exploration of the problem of the relation between the face, the body, and the inner self further and into new, more disturbing areas. *Persuasion* is disturbed, too, by the collision between the enshrinement of that libidinal fantasy in the conventions of the romantic plot, and the promptings of a strenuous and critical realism.

Sir Walter thinks he and his like are immune from time: the narcissistic fantasy of his vanity expresses itself most powerfully in this delusion, which the novel subsequently underscores by emphasising the changes and vicissitudes wrought by time, and of the human body as an object besieged by its onslaughts. For time and vicissitude, the actions of nature, are more explicitly foregrounded in this novel than in any other of Jane Austen – with that much of the traditional critical readings one can wholeheartedly agree – and it is their action upon the body which makes the most salient contrast with the culture of Bath.

A. Walton Litz once claimed that *Persuasion* represents Jane Austen's most successful effort 'to build this sense of physical life into the language and structure of a novel'.[18] For Litz the 'deeply *physical* impact of *Persuasion*' is to be attributed to the novelist's 'poetic use of nature as a structure of feeling, which not only offers metaphors for our emotions but controls them with its unchanging rhythms and changing moods' and in the novel's development of 'a rapid and nervous syntax designed to imitate the bombardment of impressions upon the mind'.[19] Perceptive though these suggestions are, they fail to detect (perhaps because in one sense it is obvious) the series of occasions or events which refer explicitly to physical life and that are distributed through the novel as if to remind us (*pace* Sir Walter) that physical life is necessarily also physical vulnerability. After the opening Kellynch chapters in which he has been amply seen preening himself on his preservation from the ravages of time, Anne is claimed by Mary and goes to stay at Uppercross. Hardly has Wentworth been heard of in the neighbourhood, than her nephew falls and dislocates his collarbone, and Anne, faced with Mary's hysterics and the general confusion, takes charge of the household, eventually becoming the little boy's nurse, a situation which effectively delays her encounter with her former lover. Several of the scenes which follow depict her, specifically, in the role of nurse, attending to the child. The pretext for the shift of the novel's scene to Lyme is Wentworth's desire to see his old friend Harville, who 'had never been in good health since a severe wound which he received two years before' (94). Harville's lameness has curtailed his career and prospects in the navy, forced him into restricted accommodation, and makes it necessary for him to return home from their ramble in Lyme early, thus leaving only Anne and Wentworth to cope with subsequent events on the Cobb. Fatal injuries occur in civilian life too, and the scene of Louisa's jump, which climaxes events in the first volume of the novel, proves a turning point since it alters her personality and future and, in turn, the futures of Benwick, Wentworth and Anne Elliot. When, early in the second volume, Anne finally arrives in Bath, one of her first acts is to renew the friendship she had formed at school with a woman whom she had previously known 'in all the glow of health and confidence of superiority' and who is now poor and almost friendless, and, among her other misfortunes, is 'afflicted with a severe rheumatic fever, which finally settling in her legs, had made her for the present a cripple' (152). In each of the novel's main locales is found someone who is disabled as a result of injury or disease, or occurs an incident that serves to remind us of the vulnerability or fragility of the body. Pervading it all is Anne Elliot's unspoken sense of her own loss and deprivation, the result of the 'rupture' (28) with Wentworth. *Persuasion* is a novel of trauma: of broken bones, broken heads and broken hearts.

This reading of the novel then centres about the notion of injury, and for the most part, *Persuasion* depicts spiritual or mental pain and physical pain in the same terms, as when Wentworth speaks of Benwick's 'pierced, wounded, almost broken' heart. It's concerned with the ways people adjust to loss, or curtailment of life, and live through, or cope with, its deprivations. Mrs Smith appears now as an important figure, a significant commentary on the position of Anne. *Persuasion* is a short book, scarcely more than half the length of *Emma*. Even within this small compass, Mrs Smith is often considered a puzzlingly predominant flaw or intrusion, for conversations with her and discussions of her friend Nurse Rooke's ingenious ways of procuring advantages occupy two chapters in the second volume of the novel, the fullest just before its climax. The extended treatment the figure is given may be seen, in this light, as a crucial elaboration of the thought of the novel (though it cannot rescue the melodrama of her unmasking of Mr Elliot's 'hollow and black' heart) for the story of Mrs Smith, like the story of Anne Elliot, displays Jane Austen's intense interest in the resources of the human spirit in the face of affliction.[20] Austen's concern is not so much with accidents or misfortune as such, as with the positive human responses to suffering. In particular, she depicts (and critically examines) the isolated individual's attempt to gather the emotional resources to cope with chronic pain of a psychological nature, and the modes of support and nursing that enable others to endure and overcome their suffering and deprivation. And because pain and injury make so much of the material, it is inevitable that coping and nursing will also occupy the novel's attention.

Nurse Rooke's profession is a necessary element in the hidden economy of Bath: and, though essential to the plot of *Persuasion*, she is even more of an obscured figure in the novel she inhabits than Mr Perry is in his. Anne does not even notice her when she opens the door. Like Mr Perry in *Emma*, though, Nurse Rooke opens the door to one of *Persuasion*'s most important thematics. She is only one of a number of professional nursing figures who are momentarily noticed in the text, and who associate in the reader's mind nursing and femaleness, the nurse as the guardian of the small child with the nurse as attendant on the ailing adult. After Louisa Musgrove's fall, for example, Henrietta, her sister, wants to nurse her but 'Charles conveyed back a far more useful person in the old nursery-maid of the family, one who having brought up all the children, and seen the last, the very last, the lingering and long-petted master Harry, sent to school after his brothers, was now living in her deserted nursery to mend stockings, and dress all the blains and bruises she could get near her' (122). Nursing is thus linked not only with femaleness, but with social marginality. Sarah joins Mrs Harville, 'a very experienced nurse; and her nursery-maid, who had lived with her long and gone about with her every where, was just such another' (113). Mary has her favoured nursery maid too, Jemima. Nurse Rooke, besides her other professional duties, is a mid-wife. She attends the fashionable lady Mrs Wallis in her confinement, and as Mrs Smith with characteristic impudence says to Anne, 'She must be allowed to be a favourer of matrimony you know, and (since self will intrude) who can say that she may not have some flying visions of attending the next Lady Elliot, through Mrs Wallis's recommendation?' (208) Finally, as Anne and Wentworth take their reconciliatory stroll round Bath together they pass, unnoticed, 'nursery maids and children'. These glimpsed figures on the peripheries of the novel associate nursing with both mothering, and with social powerlessness: the nurse is a metaphor for both.[21] It is as if there were a necessary relationship between femaleness and nursing, as if true womanliness were expressed in devotion to the well-being of others, whether children or ailing adults.

Such was the view of moralists of this, as of later, periods. Thomas Gisborne's *Duties of the Female Sex* of 1796 proposes that the 'unassuming and virtuous activity' of the female character is especially developed 'in contributing daily and hourly to the comfort of husbands, of parents, of brothers and sisters, and of other relations, connections and friends, in the intercourse of domestic life, under every vicissitude of sickness and health, of joy and affliction'.[22] Alistair Duckworth explains that the incident at Uppercross in which Anne attends her nephew emphasises the 'utility' of her response: 'It suggests that the self, even when deprived of its social inheritance, may still respond affirmatively and in traditionally sanctioned ways, that deprivation need not lead to despair or to disaffection.'[23] This is certainly the view of Charles Musgrove, who announces that his son's dislocated collar-bone is 'quite a female case' and need not prevent him dining out to meet Captain Wentworth, and underlined by Anne Elliot herself, who declares more mildly to Mary, put out that she is left at home, 'Nursing does not belong to a man, it is not his province. A sick child is always the mother's property, her own feelings generally make it so' (56). This conservative generalisation is immediately contradicted by Mary's alacrity at being released from the duty to her child by Anne's offer to stay at home. But the nobility of Anne's sacrifice is also qualified in this instance because of the ulterior motive behind her offer: her apparent dutifulness to the child is a means of protecting herself from the pain of an encounter with Wentworth. The social role, however 'traditionally sanctioned' here, as elsewhere, does not quite fit the emotions and motives of she who adopts it. Later, Anne's care of the child is to serve as a pretext for her not engaging in conversation with her former lover.

Femaleness and nursing are thus ideologically linked, but it is a curiously restricted femaleness. The nurse is a functional substitute for the nurturing and nurturant, supportive, mother – in Alexander Pope's phrase, 'the tender Second to a Mother's care':[24] whilst being quintessentially female, her femaleness is thought of as maternal, not sexual. A true woman will necessarily be a good nurse, but her womanliness will be one in which her own purposes and sexual desires will be subordinated to, and sublimated in, her ministrations to the child or to the patient. Her hands are intimate with the body, and she has therefore a quasi-sexual relation to the subjects whom she attends, but her own sexuality is necessarily screened or suspended. Anne Elliot is assigned, or assigns herself, to a range of ancillary roles in the households at Uppercross and Lyme – listener, confidante, 'umpire' between husband and wife, accompanist on the piano – but her role as nurse subsumes these others, and it is precisely as a nurse that she values herself most and is most valued by those around her. In positioning herself thus as mother-substitute, as she does, for instance, by taking over the care of the injured child from Mary, she expunges herself as a desiring subject. In effect, she is representing to herself, and allowing her circle to assume, that her romantic story is closed, is in the past, that she does not entertain ambitions or desires on her own behalf, but only on behalf of those to whose well-being she attends. The role of nurse is eminently female, not without initiative, and not without strength, but without desire. It is a role in which Anne comes to be valued, but her value is predicated upon the obliteration (or suspension) of her own bodily needs. Whilst she plays, her hands mechanically at work, 'equally without error and without consciousness' (72), others engage in the courtship dance; whilst she attends to Mrs Musgrove or her injured nephew,

Wentworth narrates the history of how he was 'made', regales the admiring Musgroves with his exploits: he re-creates himself as an active, desiring principle, whilst she salvages what identity she can as listener and as confidante of others.

Anne's laborious and demanding attentions to the child (she has Mary to worry about, too, of course) are amusingly juxtaposed with the merely verbal solicitude of the Musgrove sisters for 'dear, good Dr Shirley's being relieved from the duty which he could no longer get through without most injurious fatigue', Dr Shirley being the elderly rector of Uppercross, whose curacy they have their eyes on for Charles Hayter. On the beach at Lyme, Anne listens and encourages once again, amused to detect the motivation of Henrietta's enthusiasm for Dr Shirley's settling by the sea; 'The sea air always does good', that artless young lady exclaims, 'There can be no doubt of its having been of the greatest service to Dr Shirley, after his illness, last spring twelvemonth' (102). Once again, like Mr Perry setting up his carriage, talk about health serves to disguise the economic and, in this case, sexual motives which are actually in operation. That caring for others may afford substitute gratifications is not, I think, a point the novel dwells on, but it is clear that nursing gives Anne a pretext for a semi-permanent adoption of that role of bystander to which she has consigned herself, and in which she takes both comfort and pride.

Yet because *Persuasion* depicts the body as fragile and vulnerable, nursing does emerge as an important value, despite its association with the sexually and socially subordinate. The companionate marriage of the Crofts is a good example. Mrs Croft herself remarks that the only time she has ever been ill was when she was left on shore, separated from her husband. 'I lived in perpetual fright at that time, and had all manner of imaginary complaints from not knowing what to do with myself...' she tells Mrs Musgrove (71). When they come to Bath, the Admiral is 'ordered to walk, to keep off the gout, and Mrs Croft seemed to go shares with him in every thing, and to walk for her life, to do him good. Anne saw them wherever she went' (168). But this turns into genial parody as altruistic female attendance becomes self-injury. A week or so afterwards Anne sees Admiral Croft walking alone. Croft, asking her to take his arm, makes a remark that matches his wife's earlier ones. 'I do not feel comfortable if I have not a woman there', and explains why he is out without her. He may have kept down the gout, but she has become the invalid: 'She, poor soul, is tied by the leg. She has a blister on one of her heels, as large as a three shilling piece' (170).

More importantly, the novel puts nursing in a new light by assigning nursing functions, or something equivalent to them, to the heroic male, Wentworth. The scene where he is first displayed (and displays himself) for example, is intercepted by a passage in which he exchanges places with the listening, attendant, Anne. His bragging of his achievements and prizes, his careless boasts of nonchalance in the face of danger are rendered indirectly, through her listening consciousness. Then when Anne's attention is claimed by Mrs Musgrove, he recedes into silence. In the foreground is Mrs Musgrove and her thoughts about her lost, apparently 'worthless' son, Dick.

> 'Ah! Miss Anne, if it had pleased Heaven to spare my poor son, I dare say he would have been just such another by this time.'
> Anne suppressed a smile, and listened kindly, while Mrs Musgrove relieved her heart a little more; and for a few minutes, therefore, could not keep pace with the conversation of the others. (64)

When Wentworth is in turn appealed to by the grieving mother, his attitude replicates Anne's, and is relayed by her. She detects 'an indulgence of self-amusement' in his face at first, but 'in another moment he was perfectly collected and serious; and almost instantly afterwards coming up to the sofa, on which she and Mrs Musgrove were sitting, took a place by the latter, and entered into conversation with her, in a low voice, about her son, doing it with so much sympathy and natural grace, as shewed the kindest consideration for all that was real and unabsurd in the parent's feelings' (67–8). This is not that showy gallantry towards women which his sister shortly criticises him for, but a quick and intuitive solicitude that precisely matches Anne's. This passage is an example of the flexibility of the point of view in this novel: though the listening consciousness still remains Anne's, the narrative moves seamlessly away from her to inform us of the speech of Wentworth (which she could hardly hear) and even penetrates to the quality of Mrs Musgrove's feelings.

'No summons mocked by chill delay': Wentworth's responses to appeals for help and sympathy are always ready 'instantly'. The word is habitually tagged to his gestures, movements, and actions, an index of that bodily ease and confident physical efficiency which support his enterprise and daring. The most signal example of his humanity is recounted by Captain Harville just prior to the fall on the Cobb. Anne and Harville are talking of Benwick's recent bereavement. Fanny Harville died in June, but the news was not known to him until August, when he came home from the Cape. 'I was at Plymouth', says Harville, but Benwick's ship was due to dock at Portsmouth. 'There the news must follow him, but who was to tell it?':

> 'Nobody could do it, but that good fellow, (pointing to Captain Wentworth.) The Laconia had come into Plymouth the week before; no danger of her being sent to sea again. He stood his chance for the rest – wrote up for leave of absence, but without waiting the return, travelled night and day till he got to Portsmouth, rowed off to the Grappler that instant, and never left the poor fellow for a week; that's what he did, and nobody else could have saved poor James. You may think, Miss Elliot, whether he is dear to us!'
>
> Anne did think on the question with perfect decision, and said as much in reply as her own feelings could accomplish, or as his seemed able to bear. (108)

Wentworth, in effect, nurses Benwick through the worst of his grief. (On the other hand, Mr Elliot, we are told, refused to help the widow of his friend, and by refusing to act as his executor, greatly increased her distress (209).) Harville's tribute has the narrative function of displaying Wentworth as a courageous and enterprising as well as sympathetic man just before the incident which is to present him as very nearly inadequate or impotent, as he faces a crisis of a more complicated sort.

Wentworth's capacity for sympathetic attentiveness (what I have called nursing) is displayed, of course, most fully in his attentions to Anne Elliot herself. If we are to explain 'the deeply *physical* impact' of *Persuasion* we look first, I think, at the intensity of Anne Elliot's responses to her former fiancé's physical presence, and to the indirect, mediated evidence of his awareness of her. Anne and Wentworth are kept apart in the first scenes at Uppercross partly because (as David Monaghan suggests) Anne relegates herself to a peripheral position which the Musgroves do not have the perception or intelligence to see is less than she deserves. Wentworth's lingering resentment and Anne's modesty keep the two former lovers apart, since there is no one with any appreciation of Anne's value to give her the more prominent role that might have brought her to Wentworth's notice. Their intercourse is a minimal one of polite manners and careful avoidance. Wentworth arranges to avoid even the perfunctory physical contact of shaking hands that a formal introduction would require (59). In the subsequent scenes at Uppercross, good manners and politeness, 'the exchange of the common civilities', acts as a barrier to closer intercourse, as the two ex-lovers manoeuvre to keep out of each other's way, even when they are in the same room.

But a child of two has no manners, none of these polite inhibitions, and therefore can be the agency through which the two people whom politeness would have kept 'perpetually estranged' (64) can be brought together. Anne is forced to stay in the room with Wentworth because the sick boy demands her, and imprisoned by the younger child, who 'began to fasten himself upon her, as she knelt, in such a way that, busy as she was about Charles, she could not shake him off', she is rescued by Wentworth's resourceful action: 'In another moment, however, she found herself in the state of being released from him; some one was taking him from her, though he had bent down her head so much, that his little sturdy hands were unfastened from around her neck, and he was resolutely borne away, before she knew that Captain Wentworth had done it' (80). The child is a 'transitional object' to borrow Winnicott's term: Wentworth relieves Anne's body through the agency of his physical contact with the body of the child. The breach of strict decorum is admissible because it appears in the guise of solicitude, and the incident is kept below the level of socially embarrassed consciousness by the silence in which it is transacted. The rescue leaves Anne quite speechless, overwhelmed with confused emotions. They are not due merely to being the recipient of an act of courtesy.

A similar act of solicitude, but this time wholly volunteered by Wentworth and thus showing a fuller attention to Anne, comes in the next chapter where on the return from Winthrop the party meets the Crofts in their gig, who offer a ride to any lady who might be tired. Anne's tiredness has not been dwelt on, though Charles Musgrove's inattention to her has, so that when Wentworth 'cleared the hedge in a moment to say something to his sister' and then, the Crofts having offered a place to Anne, 'without saying a word' turns to her and 'quietly obliged her to be assisted into the carriage' (91) the reader perceives it as a strikingly solicitous action. These deeds may be read as Anne reads them, fully persuaded as she is from the conversation she has just overheard between Wentworth and Louisa, that Wentworth is now indifferent about her: but his detection of Anne's fatigue (the topic has not come up – she has made no complaint) suggests that for a man supposedly courting another woman, his mind is unusually occupied with her. In Highbury misplaced attention to bodily well-being reflects ignorance about or obliviousness to the subject's inner life. In these two instances, in a wonderful twist to the Highbury mode, nursing concern for the body becomes the permissible vehicle in which awakening (or latent) desire can find a plausible and socially sanctioned, because apparently sexually neutral, expression. Anne misreads Wentworth's behaviour in just this way, as chivalry or solicitude without sexual motivation: 'though becoming attached to another, still he could not see her suffer, without the desire of giving her relief'. The irony is far more muted than the irony that attaches to Emma Woodhouse's misconstruings, but Anne's supposition is not unqualified by the narrational circumstances.

In a parallel way, Wentworth's awakened or awakening love for Anne is expressed in his regard for her in that woman's exemplary role as a nurse. It is clear that everyone in the novel values Anne as a nurse, or rather that her value, unrecognised until then, is made visible when she emerges as a nurse, or needs to be used as one, but there is something more to that moment after the accident on the Cobb when Anne, coming downstairs, overhears Wentworth praising her competence:

> ' ... .If Anne will stay, no one so proper, so capable as Anne!'
> She paused a moment to recover from the emotion of hearing herself so spoken of. The other two warmly agreed to what he said, and she then appeared.
> 'You will stay, I am sure; you will stay and nurse her;' cried he, turning to her and speaking with a glow, and yet a gentleness, which seemed almost restoring the past. – She coloured deeply; and he recollected himself, and moved away. (114)

To speak publicly in praise of Anne in the role of nurse is permissible, because of that separation of nursing from sexuality I have described. Whilst the relation is actually one of desire, it is conducted here, once more, according to the canons of solicitude. Wentworth's feeling for Anne can thus be masked by its ideological vehicle. In fact, though, as Anne intuits, he is expressing love for her, and the mutual embarrassment of this passing moment circles round this unspoken, almost unthought, disclosure.

It is through such moments of mutual caring and embarrassment that Anne and Wentworth progress towards their knowledge of each other's heart. Far more to the foreground in the first volume of the novel, though, is Anne's attempt to find solely within herself the resources by which to live through her neglect and isolation, an attempt predicated upon the hopelessness of ever fulfilling her desire. The first volume, after the introduction of the Elliots, comes to focus on the psychology of Anne, as she attempts to school herself into composure and 'reason' when faced with the agitation and distress, as well as awakened desire, brought about by Wentworth's reappearance in her circle. She has 'become hardened' (32) to the affronts of her family, but the wound that opened in her psyche with the rejection of Wentworth, and her recognition that the rejection was a mistake, has not been healed by a second attachment. 'She could not hear that Captain Wentworth's sister was likely to live at Kellynch, without a revival of former pain; and many a stroll and many a sigh were necessary to dispel the agitation of the idea. She often told herself it was folly, before she could harden her nerves sufficiently to feel the continual discussion of the Crofts and their business no evil' (30). To harden her nerves, to inure herself against suffering, is the emotional programme Anne Elliot adopts.

Jane Austen's favourite brother Henry, who published *Persuasion* and *Northanger Abbey* after her death in 1818, delivered during the same year a sermon at 'the chapel of the British Minister at Berlin' in which he spoke of 'the beautiful, the instructive part of Joseph's character' which was, he declared, 'deeply to feel, and strictly to command his feelings'.[25] It is evident from *Persuasion* that Jane Austen shared this ideal of the moral character, for the first volume of the novel consistently depicts Anne Elliot attempting to live the life of the Christian stoic. She feels deeply, but she seeks means, through the exertion of 'reason', to combat her feelings, and to generate, if possible, an independent, autonomous self. 'That man should never suffer his happiness to depend upon external circumstances, is one of the chief precepts of the Stoical philosophy' as Johnson had stated in his sixth *Rambler* essay (1750). He goes on to outline how a Christian can make some use of the stoic ideal, adapting it into a more provisional, more contingent attempt to foster a state of mind which is secure against the destructive invasion of external influences. 'We may very properly enquire', he wrote,

how near to this exalted state it is in our power to approach, how far we can exempt ourselves from outward influences, and secure to our minds a state of tranquillity: for, though the boast of absolute independence is ridiculous and vain, yet a mean flexibility to every impulse, and a patient submission to the tyranny of casual troubles, is below the dignity of that mind, which however depraved or weakened, boasts its derivation from a celestial original.

Like the stoic, Anne Elliot, in Foucault's phrase, 'is called upon to take [her]self as an object of knowledge and a field of action'.[26] The exclusively male ethics and practices developed during the first centuries of Christendom become, in the eighteenth and nineteenth, a means by which the socially disempowered woman converts her powerlessness into self-definition. Though not codified formally, enough features of the stoic regimen are displayed incidentally in the first volume of *Persuasion* to demonstrate that Anne Elliot has absorbed many of the characteristic exercises through which the stoics both guarded and constituted the self. Like them, she 'makes herself familiar with the minimum',[27] thinking, for instance, as Mary and Charles depart, that 'she was left with as many sensations of comfort, as were, perhaps, ever likely to be hers.' 'What was it to her', she asks, 'if Frederick Wentworth were only half a mile distant ... ?' (58) Like them, Anne takes for granted that life will afford her little more comfort than the comfort of a clear conscience. Her attempts to 'harden' herself are a version of the stoic's armour against calamity. Like the stoics, she attempts to argue herself into a state of emotional aloofness from outer hazards, and the most original feature of the novel's prose, as Litz and others have pointed out, is the freedom with which it imitates the nervous swings of Anne's feelings as she struggles to command them, aroused by the sight of Wentworth once again:

'It is over! it is over!' she repeated to herself again, and again, in nervous gratitude. 'The worst is over!'

Mary talked, but she could not attend. She had seen him. They had met. They had been once more in the same room!

Soon, however, she began to reason with herself, and try to be feeling less. Eight years, almost eight years had passed, since all had been given up. How absurd to be resuming the agitation which such an interval had banished into distance and indistinctness! What might not eight years do? Events of every description, changes, alienations, removals, – all, all must be comprised in it; and oblivion of the past – how natural, how certain too! It included nearly a third part of her own life.

Alas! with all her reasonings, she found, that to retentive feelings eight years may be little more than nothing.

Now, how were his sentiments to be read? Was this like wishing to avoid her? And the next moment she was hating herself for the folly which asked the question. (60)

'Reasoning with herself', Anne Elliot takes herself as an object of knowledge, even though, as represented here, her 'reasonings' are a scrambling together of frail defences against the onslaught of unassuaged emotion. But the transparency with which Austen now can present the invasions of feeling – a technical achievement in the development of an open and un-Johnsonian prose – does not, of course, imply revised or fluctuating values: such a telling enactment of the failure of the rational faculty to control or contain the promptings of desire does not impugn 'reason' in itself as an ideal to be striven towards. It is within the ethic of stoicism, too, that Anne's response to hearing that Wentworth has said she is 'so altered that he should not have known her again!' is inscribed. 'These were words which could not but dwell with her. Yet she soon began to rejoice that she had heard them. They were of sobering tendency; they allayed agitation; they composed, and consequently must make her happier' (61). 'Always making sure that one does not become attached to that which does not come under our control'[28] Anne seeks a state of emotional equilibrium or 'composure', not far from the stoic ideal of 'apathia'.

Composure is both an ideal of inner disposition and of social demeanour, and each can foster or augment the other. Sometimes social manners may camouflage an agitated or turbulent mind, as they do most remarkably for Lady Russell who 'had only to listen composedly' on hearing of Wentworth's probable engagement to Louisa Musgrove, 'but internally her heart revelled in angry pleasure, in pleased contempt' at this apparent vindication of her opinion of Anne's former suitor. Usually, for Anne, inner agitation cannot but be expressed physiologically – in tears, in paleness or in blushing – and therefore social devices have to substitute for lack of inner composure. When Wentworth relieves her of the scrambling child, Anne bends over little Charles to hide her face, which otherwise would display her 'confusion of varying, but very painful agitation', before making off to her room to 'arrange' her feelings (80–1). Or a screen for her agitations may conveniently be provided by Mrs Musgrove. When Lady Russell tempts her to accept Elliot by suggesting that Anne would thereby take the place of her mother 'Anne was obliged to turn away, to rise, to walk to a distant table, and, leaning there in pretended employment, try to subdue the feelings this picture excited' (160). In an instance of the symmetry between the lovers that is so consistent in this novel, Anne perceives in, or projects onto, Wentworth, her own typical strategies, as he hides his face after the accident. 'He sat near a table, leaning over it with folded arms, [his] face concealed, as if overpowered by the various feelings of his soul, and trying by prayer and reflection to calm them' (112).

'In *Persuasion* the sense of community has disappeared and the heroine finds herself terribly alone', Litz had written in his earlier book on Austen of 1965.[29] This is another version of the novel as an epochal break with the earlier work, for in it Anne is said to experience the 'despair' of the 'modern "personality"'. The language perhaps belongs rather to the crisis of liberal humanism than to the mood, even the saddest mood, of Anne Elliot, for there is no terror in her comparative emotional isolation, and her self-reflection and self-consciousness are depicted as at least in part a strength, a resource. The attempt to reason herself out of her agitation demonstrates the presence within her of a culture of personal self-determination, but in many ways the most convincing achievement of the novel in this sphere is to show how Anne's 'cultivated mind' is manifested indirectly, not in the self-regulating exercises she performs, but as part of that mind's fabric, in the apparently involuntary and smilingly ironic self-reflection with which she sees the parts she herself plays within her culture.

The novel's dialogue with earlier texts about suffering is carried through two main set-piece scenes, one with Captain Benwick, the bereaved sailor, the other with the crippled and impoverished school-friend, Mrs Smith. Anne and Benwick discuss poetry together, but romantic poetry is presented as dangerously self-absorbing, like the 'sweets of poetical despondence' with which Anne had consoled, and indulged, herself on the walk to Winthrop. Finding that Benwick uses his reading only to amplify his grief, Anne makes 'some suggestions as to the duty and benefit of struggling against affliction':

she was emboldened to go on; and feeling in herself the right of seniority of mind, she ventured to recommend a larger allowance of prose in his daily study; and on being requested to particularise, mentioned such works of our best moralists, such collections of the finest letters, such memoirs of characters of worth and suffering, as occurred to her at the moment as calculated to rouse and fortify the mind by the highest precepts, and the strongest examples of moral and religious endurances. (101)

Some issues of Johnson's periodical, *The Rambler*, especially perhaps number 32, 'on patience, even under extreme misery' would certainly be among those books Anne takes leave to recommend. It was this number of the *Rambler* that was singled out by Boswell in his famous commendation of the work in the *Life of Johnson*, which Austen had, of course, read. 'In no writings whatever can be found *more bark and steel for the mind*, if I may use the expression,' he wrote, 'more that can brace and invigorate every manly and noble sentiment'.[30] This idea of the book as fortifying the male is wonderfully parodied, and perhaps subverted, by the very first sentence of *Persuasion*, conspicuously Johnsonian in its cadence, where Sir Walter Elliot reads the Baronetage to find 'occupation for an idle hour and consolation in a distressed one' and where 'his faculties were roused into admiration and respect ... ' It is subverted once again by the detachment with which, her rather solemn ministrations completed, Anne Elliot views the episode:

> When the evening was over, Anne could not but be amused at the idea of her coming to Lyme, to preach patience and resignation to a young man whom she had never seen before; nor could she help fearing, on more serious reflection, that, like many other great moralists and preachers, she had been eloquent on a point in which her own conduct would ill bear examination. (101)

'That few men, celebrated for theoretic wisdom, live with conformity to their precepts, must be readily confessed', wrote Johnson in *Rambler* 77. 'Do not be too hasty ... to trust, or to admire the teachers of morality: they discourse like angels, but they live like men', Imlac the sage warns Rasselas. Anne's humorous self-inflation is neatly reflected by Wentworth's equally ironic boast later in the novel. 'Like other great men under reverses', he declares, 'I must endeavour to subdue my mind to my fortune. I must learn to brook being happier than I deserve' (247). The novel thus continues a predominantly masculine literary and moral tradition in its presentation of Anne Elliot's care of the self,[31] but it is a tradition which can include too the humorously self-subversive attitudes which frame the heroine's tendency towards earnest idealism. The questioning of stoicism is carried even further in the depiction of Mrs Smith, as well as Anne's propensity to see life – just a little – through the spectacles of books.

Mrs Smith is the first invalid in Jane Austen's novels whose distresses are indubitably real.

> She was a widow, and poor. Her husband had been extravagant; and at his death, about two years before, had left his affairs dreadfully involved. She had had difficulties of every sort to contend with, and in addition to these distresses, had been afflicted with a severe rheumatic fever, which finally settling in her legs, had made her for the present a cripple. She had come to Bath on that account, and was now in lodgings near the hot-baths, living in a very humble way, unable even to afford the comfort of a servant, and of course almost excluded from society. (152–53)

It is Mrs Smith who is to reveal the true nature of the impeccably well-mannered Mr Elliot, an exposure that is, strictly speaking, superfluous since Anne has already made up her own mind not to trust him. She also introduces an element that, given how close the story of Anne comes to romance, is necessary: her story insists on the harsher realities of life. Anne, for example, has elevated notions of the nurse's experience: 'What instances must pass before them', she declares, 'of ardent, disinterested, self-denying attachment, of heroism, fortitude, patience, resignation – of all the conflicts and all the sacrifices that enoble us most. A sick chamber may often furnish the worth of volumes'. The volumes Anne is no doubt thinking of would contain those examples of moral and religious endurances which she had preached about to Benwick not long before, and which in a more self-reflective or tough-minded moment she had seen as contradicted or at least qualified by her own behaviour. Mrs Smith's reply contains a note of astringent realism that serves to dampen the ardour of Anne's romantic and even sentimental claims: '"Yes" said Mrs Smith, more doubtingly, "sometimes it may, though I fear its lessons are not often in the elevated style you describe. Here and there, human nature may be great in times of trial, but generally speaking it is its weakness and not its strength that appears in a sick chamber; it is selfishness and impatience, rather than generosity and fortitude, that one hears of"' (156). One function of Mrs Smith is to anchor the romantic idealism of Anne (to be fully demonstrated in the speeches to Harville which precipitate Wentworth's proposal) to the grim conditions of survival. She restrains the novel's impulse to a day-dream-like wish-fulfilment (the past restored, the rift healed) by setting against it a view of life characterised by day-to-day tenaciousness and an integrity qualified by necessary expediency. The lesson of the sickroom Mrs Smith is to demonstrate is not quite of the elevated kind Anne imagines.

Mrs Smith's liveliness and adroitness are very closely linked to economic advantage and survival. She has had to develop new skills (even literally, like the knitting Nurse Rooke has taught her) in order to survive. She needs tact, address and diplomacy to maximise her possible advantage from Anne's prospective marriage with Mr Elliot. No matter that Elliot has wronged her, no matter that he has betrayed and neglected her, no matter that Anne may be about to marry a cold-hearted villain. To warn Anne is a luxury she cannot afford, to advise caution is the privilege of those whose own economic status is secure. Mrs Smith must adroitly calculate what possible advantages there might be to her in whatever opportunities present themselves. These are the pressing exigencies of the poor. Naturally some readers feel uncomfortable with Mrs Smith's 'cynicism' and with her apparent duplicity towards Anne in concealing what she knows of Mr Elliot, as well as her 'unqualified bitterness' towards him when she is free to speak; they feel that this violates the atmosphere of the novel and that the details of Mr Elliot's perfidy unnecessarily interrupt its progress towards gradual romantic affirmation. But what her presence does is remind us of the social security, as well as the luck, that afford Anne the privilege of her untarnished romantic idealism, and that makes the final fulfilment of her desires such a rare and exceptional apotheosis. 'Prettier musings of high-wrought love and eternal constancy, could never have passed along the streets of Bath, than Anne was sporting with from Camden-place to Westgate-buildings. It was almost enough to spread purification and perfume all the way' (192), is how Austen describes Anne's journey to the interview. In part this is a reflection on the decadence of Bath. 'Oh! who can ever be tired of Bath?' had exclaimed Catherine Morland, the seventeen year old heroine of *Northanger Abbey*. 'Not those who bring such fresh feelings of every sort to it, as you do', replies Henry Tilney. 'But papas and mammas, and brothers and intimate friends are a good deal gone by, to most of the frequenters of Bath – and the honest relish of balls and plays and every-day sights, is past with them' (NA 79). The comment in *Persuasion* is similarly an amused and partly ironic glance at the still-intact and reality-defying ardour of this much older heroine. To spread purification is to imply that the stench of decay might otherwise prevail. In other words, Mrs Smith makes plain that though Anne is a romantic (and it happens miraculously in this instance that her idealism is vindicated and her dreams are fulfilled) Jane Austen is not.

Mrs Smith is surviving, and can be charitable to those poorer even than herself, because she has developed an informal, female network of support, through her landlady and Nurse Rooke, more desperate, more tenuous, but analogous to the mutual support of the sailors. Considering her 'cheerless situation' (worse even than Fanny Price's at Portsmouth) Mrs Smith seems to be astonishingly resilient, and her cheerfulness prompts Anne to an implicit reflection upon her own coping strategies:

Her accommodations were limited to a noisy parlour, and a dark bed-room behind, with no possibility of moving from one to the other without assistance, which there was only one servant in the house to afford, and she never quitted the house but to be conveyed into the warm bath. – Yet, in spite of all this, Anne had reason to believe that she had moments only of languor and depression, to hours of occupation and enjoyment. How could it be? – She watched – observed – reflected – and finally determined that this was not a case of fortitude or of resignation only. – A submissive spirit might be patient, a strong understanding would supply resolution, but here was something more; here was that elasticity of mind, that disposition to be comforted, that power of turning readily from evil to good, and of finding employment which carried her out of herself, which was from Nature alone. It was the choicest gift of Heaven ... (154)

This initial impression is perhaps to be modified, as more is seen of what this adaptability means, and qualified too, by the resentment Mrs Smith is later shown to harbour towards Elliot, but it is clear that Mrs Smith is certainly not 'the Christian Stoic of *Persuasion*'.[32] She is a refutation of the notion that one can retain one's independence within patriarchal society only through the ethic of self-discipline, through patience and resolution and the cultivation of the self. Her 'elasticity', her power of interest in the world about her, and her delight in her imagination, remind us, I think, of another Jane Austen woman who delights to detect the signs of romance in the faces of others. Mrs Smith eagerly constructs from the gossip she has heard and from Anne's bright eyes the hypothesis that she is to marry Elliot:

' ... You need not tell me that you had a pleasant evening. I see it in your eye. I perfectly see how the hours passed – that you had always something agreeable to listen to. In the intervals of the concert, it was conversation.'
    Anne half smiled and said, 'Do you see that in my eye?'
    'Yes, I do. Your countenance perfectly informs me that you were in company last night with the person, whom you think the most agreeable in the world, the person who interests you at this present time, more than all the rest of the world put together.'
    A blush overspread Anne's cheeks. She could say nothing. (194)

The presumption and eagerness of Emma Woodhouse are recaptured briefly in these characteristically emphatic speech rhythms ('perfectly ... perfectly ... all the rest of the world put together'). 'If you prefer Mr Martin to every other person: if you think him the most agreeable man you have ever been in company with, why should you hesitate? You blush, Harriet ... '

(E 53). Mrs Smith's elasticity is related to Emma's spirit – a quality that is a moral anomaly, that offends almost as much as it charms, but that ensures her survival, even in the most defeating conditions of personal deprivation.

Though she tells Anne, in her bitterness at Elliot's betrayal, that her 'peace' has been 'shipwrecked' (196), she has earlier claimed to have 'weathered' the most acute of her distresses (154). It is obvious enough how Austen links, through these metaphors, Mrs Smith's mode of survival in her cramped rooms with Mrs Croft's 'weathered face' and happiness in confined quarters, and links them also with the survival and resiliance of Captain Harville, another crippled victim of hazard and misfortune, and as I have suggested, her informal support system is an underclass reflection of the male bonding of the sailors. What is more, Nurse Rooke's enterprise in wringing from her convalescent patients both useful gossip and charitable donations reflects the commercial imperatives and initiatives that rule the lives of the men the novel asks us to admire. (It is amusing to see critics who unquestionably accept the sailors' right to plunder French frigates getting upset at this 'nurse-accomplice'[33] taking minor advantage of her wealthier clients.)

The accident which forms the climax of the first volume of the novel is its turning point, since Louisa Musgrove's jump and its aftermath supposedly lead Wentworth to rediscover his love for Anne, and at the same time release him from obligations to her. The incident, so he says later to Anne, teaches him a lesson: 'There he had learnt to distinguish between the darings of heedlessness and the resolution of a collected mind': a conduct-book moralism (young ladies should always be prudent) that is best regarded as his attempt to rationalise than as an exhaustive account of the incident's meaning. Certainly it convincingly illustrates Anne Elliot's competence in a medical emergency. Whilst Henrietta faints, Mary has hysterics and Wentworth, overcome with shock, staggers against the wall for support, she thinks quickly, resourcefully, and intelligently, making herself the effective temporary commander of this floundering human ship.

Anne keeps her wits when all about her are losing theirs – and to read some critics, it is this which revives Wentworth's love. The occasion is revelatory, though, not determinant. Wentworth is already, perhaps unknown to himself, in love with Anne Elliot, and the incident is only one of a series of moments which confirm his awakening feelings. Austen pairs this incident on the steps of the Cobb with the equally accidental moment at the same place when the Mysterious Stranger, later revealed as Mr Elliot, looks admiringly at her as she passes by.

> She was looking remarkably well; her very regular, very pretty features, having the bloom and freshness of youth restored by the fine wind which had been blowing on her complexion, and by the animation of eye which it had also produced. It was evident that the gentleman, (completely a gentleman in manner) admired her exceedingly. Captain Wentworth looked round at her instantly … (104)

Wentworth says later that he was 'roused' by the other man's glance (242). Wentworth's preoccupation with Anne – made clear on the Winthrop walk – is here brought a stage closer to consciousness.

A Jane Austen young lady who leaps from a high step and knocks herself out embarrasses everyone, and the critics have accordingly given Louisa Musgrove, 'whose headstrong resolution of course leads to her fall',[34] a good dressing down. Outbidding Austen herself in callousness towards members of the Musgrove family, Mary Lascelles remarked that 'the catastrophe which the spectators think they are witnessing is an illusion. Louisa is not dead – or even injured. True, she has fallen on her head, but it had never been a very good one, and the blow seems to have cleared it …'[35] Tony Tanner also plays with the idea that Louisa is 'improved' by her 'alteration', though he goes on to remark that Louisa's demeanour after the fall 'is not the result of achieved moral poise and indistractability … but the timorous cowering of a nervous wreck'.[36] Even critics who normally read accurately like Stuart Tave and Claudia Johnson attribute a degree of deviousness and guile to Louisa at variance with the suggestions of the text.[37] One can see why they do so; to take the aftermath of the accident seriously, to see that the concussion has totally altered Louisa's personality and future role in life, is to face the problem that the punishment seems monstrously to outweigh any conceivable crime, and it therefore violates the sense, so strong in Jane Austen's novels, that the moral world is coherent and meaningful and ultimately rationally ordered. If sufficient fault can be attributed either to Louisa or to Wentworth, symmetry can be restored, and the vicissitudes of the physical can be seen literally to embody the trials of the spirit.

Of course the accident has been prepared for (one can always see these things with the benefit of hindsight). Louisa is high-spirited, enthusiastic, and has been flattered by the attentions of an unusually attractive and forceful man. Anne Elliot has overheard him, at Winthrop, encouraging her to be resolute. 'Your sister is an aimiable creature; but *yours* is the character of decision and firmness, I see. If you value her conduct or happiness, infuse as much of your own spirit into her, as you can' (88). So she has been 'armed with the idea of merit in maintaining her own way' (94) and encouraged too, to believe herself of special interest to the man who thus flatters her. Reflecting back to Wentworth the qualities he says he values, she avails herself of the physiological latitude and promptitude assigned to him and having been jumped down the steps once, 'instantly' runs up them again.

In all their walks, he had had to jump her from the stiles; the sensation was delightful to her. The hardness of the pavement for her feet, made him less willing on the present occasion; he did it, however; she was safely down, and instantly, to shew her enjoyment, ran up the steps to be jumped down again. He advised her against it, thought the jar too great; but no, he reasoned and talked in vain; she smiled and said, 'I am determined I will:' he put out his hands; she was too precipitate by half a second, she fell on the pavement on the Lower Cobb, and was taken up lifeless! (109)

It is as if Julia or Maria Bertram, in squeezing beside the gate into the Ha-Ha, were to impale herself on a spike. Louisa's moral fault (whether it is recklessness, or, more subtly, to offer herself as an emblem of what another values) immediately precipitates its own physiological punishment.

But it takes two to make the accident, and if the critics have hastened to blame Louisa, Wentworth blames himself. 'It was my fault entirely', he says, 'If I had not been weak, she would not have been headstrong.' 'Oh God!', he cries in the carriage on the way back to Uppercross, 'that I had not given way to her at the fatal moment! Had I done as I ought! But so eager and so resolute! Dear, sweet Louisa!' (116), and he is to reiterate these sentiments later in the novel (183). This is very natural, but the crucial phrase is 'the fatal moment'. To recover meaning out of arbitrary assaults of fortune, fatal or tragic illness and accident, human beings renarrate them so as to locate their origin in some fault of their own, however tenuous the connection of this moral fault may be with the final outcome. By taking to himself the blame for this incident Wentworth is enabled to remaster events, to gain some frail hold over contingency and 'fate', to position himself once more as the dominant and controlling male. Of course, Louisa's spiritedness and Wentworth's hesitation both contribute to the accident: but that does not exhaust its significance in the novel. It is the most crucial of the many fortuitous circumstances[38] which make up the narrative and prepare for the eventual reunion of Anne Elliot and Wentworth, a graphic reminder that human-beings are bodies as well as minds, and that the fortunes of the one are not necessarily congruent with the fortunes of the other.

There is another account of the fall's meaning that ought to be taken notice of. Perhaps it is best considered as an instance of the psychopathology of everyday life:

Falling, stumbling and slipping need not always be interpreted as purely accidental miscarriages of motor actions. The double meanings that language attaches to these expressions are enough to indicate the kind of phantasies involved, which can be represented by such losses of bodily equilibrium. I can recall a number of fairly mild nervous illnesses in women and girls which set in after a fall not accompanied by any injury, and which were taken to be traumatic hysterias resulting from the shock of the fall. Even at that time I had an impression that these events were differently connected and that the fall was already a product of the neurosis and expressed the same unconscious phantasies with a sexual content, which could be assumed to be the forces operating behind the symptoms. Is not the same thing meant by a proverb which runs: 'When a girl falls she falls on her back?'[39]

Louisa's escapade can readily be seen as a partly unconscious aspect of her courtship of Wentworth since it invites him to confirm the self-image he has helped to create, and because she is inspirited by his presence (as by the weather, the occasion, and her own bodily vitality): and his failure to reciprocate can be read erotically too. He is not feeling and responding as she is feeling: their missing each other's hands at 'the fatal moment' is a sign that he cannot 'attach himself' to her which he already unconsciously knows. When Wentworth and Anne are reunited, and he looks back on his 'attempts to attach himself to Louisa', the word itself is used: 'He persisted in having loved none but her ....he had been constant unconsciously, nay unintentionally ... ' As for loving Louisa, 'he protested that he had forever felt it to be impossible' (242). At this moment Wentworth's promptitude in emergencies, that instantaneous movement that is his gift, deserts him. He does not reciprocate, either with firmness or with partnership. Louisa's fall then is not far from a parapraxis, since it does enact each of the participant's unconscious processes.

What seems to be inadmissible is the claim that the event is an adequate representative of deliberate considered behaviour, and therefore that it can function as an adequate sample of Louisa's moral character and offer a tenable parallel to Anne's. If this incident is meant as a contrast to Anne's persuadableness in breaking off the engagement (she interprets the incident, with understandable bias towards herself, this way) then one can only say that it is a bad parallel: delight, even heedlessness, in jumping from a step is hardly analogous to (say) wilfully persisting in carrying through a wrong-headed engagement despite advice. In this instance the meaning that Austen is so skilful in loading into nuances of manners and every-day behaviours has gone awry. The analogy between the mind and the body doesn't work so readily and the moral sense which discovers a narrative rationality in events is now in conflict with the novel's other pervasive reminders of mutability and accident in the course of life. Blame Louisa or blame Wentworth? As well blame the wind that made the high part of the new Cobb unpleasant, so that the party had to go down the steps, the wind that blows through Admiral Croft's cupboard, the wind that blew for four days and four nights and would have done for the poor old *Asp* and for Captain Wentworth, if he had not had the luck to bring her into Plymouth Sound six hours previously, the wind that, only minutes before the accident, miraculously blew new bloom into Anne Elliot's face at the precise moment her cousin was passing by on the Cobb.

It is sometimes remarked how careless Jane Austen has been in providing no motivation for William Walter Elliot to be in Lyme at the same time as the Uppercross party. And indeed a postmodern joke might be Wentworth's remark that 'we must consider it to be the arrangement of Providence, that you should not be introduced to your cousin' when the mourning livery and the hanging of the great-coat over the arms prevents Mary from discovering that William Elliot is staying at the same inn (106). But Heaven and Providence are commonly, and usually seriously, invoked in *Persuasion*, as is often observed, most memorably perhaps in the first full statement of Anne Elliot's feelings and beliefs: 'How eloquent could Anne Elliot have been, – how eloquent, at least, were her wishes on the side of early warm attachment, and a cheerful confidence in futurity, against that over-anxious caution which seems to insult exertion and distrust Providence!' (30).[40] At the same time it is a novel that makes much of this very human capacity for work and for exertion – the capacity that turns Harville's small house into a place of happiness, that helps Anne Elliot live through her deprived life without resorting to Elizabeth's arrogance or Mary's sense of ill-usage. The structure of the second volume of *Persuasion* exactly parallels the first, with Wentworth's re-appearance after six chapters replicating his original introduction after six: and his reappearance elicits a brief re-capitulation of the stoic theme, as Anne says to herself after their first encounter 'She hoped to be wise and reasonable in time; but alas! alas! she must confess to herself that she was not wise yet' (178). They are still much at the mercy of chance, as their meetings and exchanges are criss-crossed, interrupted and thwarted by the intrigues and designs of others. Anne once again tries to believe in her autonomy:

> to dwell much on this argument of rational dependance – 'Surely, if there be constant attachment on each side, our hearts must understand each other ere long. We are not boy and girl, to be captiously irritable, misled by every moment's inadvertence, and wantonly playing with our own happiness.' And yet, a few minutes afterwards, she felt as if their being in company with each other, under their present circumstances, could only be exposing them to inadvertencies and misconstructions of the most mischievous kind. (221–2).

'*Persuasion*', as Judy van Sickle Johnson writes, 'is Jane Austen's most unreservedly physical novel'. Its power, as she describes it, 'resides in Austen's success in sustaining the credibility of a renewed emotional attachment through physical signs. Although they are seemingly distant, Anne and Wentworth become increasingly more intimate through seductive half-glances, conscious gazes and slight bodily contact'.[41] But the problem is, both for the figures and the narration, that these bodily signs are not enough in themselves to achieve the final rapprochement. Wentworth's 'manner and look... sentences begun which he could not finish – his half averted eyes and more than half expressive glance' (185) may give warrant to Anne Elliot's belief in his returned or returning affection, but by themselves they do not inevitably convey the meaning she divines, nor overcome the obstacles that their life in the social world, as well as the inhibitions generated by their past history, present to the articulation or fulfilment of the lovers' desires. In the original climactic chapter, the embarrassment and the self-consciousness that are the recurrent motif of their meetings, he 'looking not exactly forward', her emotion 'reddening [her] cheeks, and fixing her eyes on the ground' (182) become intensified, and the final reconciliation is achieved, in fact, by a scene in which body language is made to seem an effective substitute for the spoken word, and to communicate that full and precise meaning of which the previous manifestations of feeling were scarcely decipherable tokens:

He was a moment silent. She turned her eyes towards him for the first time since his re-entering the room. His colour was varying, and he was looking at her with all the power and keenness which she believed no other eyes than his possessed.

'No truth in any such report?' he repeated. 'No truth in any *part* of it?' 'None.'

He had been standing by a chair, enjoying the relief of leaning on it, or of playing with it. He now sat down, drew it a little nearer to her, and looked with an expression which had something more than penetration in it – something softer. Her countenance did not discourage. It was a silent but a very powerful dialogue; on his side supplication, on hers acceptance. Still a little nearer, and a hand taken and pressed; and 'Anne, my own dear Anne!' bursting forth in the fulness of exquisite feeling, – and all suspense and indecision were over. (258)

The power of the 'dialogue', by its own admission, can only be rendered in language, in words, and therefore this moment, however appropriate a climax to the series of physical signs which have communicated the lovers' feelings to the reader, and however skilfully tumescent emotion is conveyed in the continuous tenses, is bound to seem perfunctory.

Added to this, the machinery creaks by which the two figures are brought together in a room without a third person. The two chapters which replace the original volume II, chapter X are, in their fulness and richness – re-presenting the whole cast of characters in the novel – much superior. By having her speak, and speak eloquently and fully, if indirectly, of her own experience and love, the famous climactic scene at the White Hart Inn grants Anne Eliott a central position for the first time in the novel. At the same moment it keeps to the narrative logic whereby what finally brings the pair together is also an accident, or providential, since Anne speaks from her heart, without being sure whether Wentworth, who is seated in the same room writing a letter, can in fact, with the preternatural alertness of the lover, overhear her.

The length and eloquence of Captain Harville's and Anne Elliot's speeches form a consummate duet, almost operatic in its final affirmative intensity, on the theme of constancy. That their dialogue fulfils the desire, repressed or suppressed throughout the novel, for Anne to speak, to be eloquent, that Anne and Wentworth change their typical narrative positions – she speaking, he hanging on her words, she narrating (if indirectly) her deepest experience of life, actively speaking her passive experience, he the dependent listener, at that moment performing a service for a colleague, whose pen drops whilst she (and Austen through her) affirms the experience of women: these aspects of the scene have been in their turn eloquently commented upon. Anne holds the floor at this point, and finds, in terms of the narrative, her fulfillment. She speaks, he writes. In a reversal of the original intention, the role of bodily communication is minimised; only lips and fingers move, and it is through language, not nervous gesture or looks, that the truth is revealed. Anne's speeches combine the authorising procedures of rational debate with the authenticity of (indirect) confession. The presence of the body is in fact reduced to a metaphor, in this disputatious discourse, but one which brings apparently casually to the surface a theme, or a problematic that can be seen, in retrospect, to be deeply embedded in the novel.

Captain Harville believes in 'a true analogy between our bodily frames and our mental; and that as our bodies are the strongest, so are our feelings; capable of bearing most rough usage, and riding out the heaviest weather'. Anne takes up the analogy, to argue her own position: man is more robust than woman, but he is not longer lived, and if women live longer than men, they also love longer (233). And this relation between bodily frailty and strength of attachment is given a precise enactment in Anne's final contribution to the dialogue:

'All the privilege I claim for my own sex (it is not a very enviable one, you need not covet it) is that of loving longest, when existence or when hope is gone.'

She could not immediately have uttered another sentence; her heart was too full, her breath too much oppressed.

'You are a good soul,' cried Captain Harville, putting his hand on her arm quite affectionately. 'There is no quarrelling with you. – And when I think of Benwick, my tongue is tied.' (235–6)

Is there an analogy, in fact, between the body and the spirit? How is the body to be read, and just how does the body disclose or communicate the secrets of the self? These are questions about which *Persuasion* has circled on a series of occasions. To read from the face and the body to the soul, Lavater claimed, was infallibly possible, but depended upon hermeneutic skills which he did not trouble to impart. How the body feels, still less how the body looks, may be far from a reliable guide to its own condition, and say still less about the inner life. But it is common to assume a parallel or analogy between the two, or to take one for the other, – to read, as Highbury reads, body as access to total self. For Sir Walter and Elizabeth Elliot nothing could be simpler: there is no question of an analogy between the body and the mind or spirit, since questions of spirit or value are resolved merely into questions of the comeliness or otherwise of the body and face. Mrs Smith's name, her address, and her infirmity sit together on a continuum read according to a primitive scale of 'objective' value. Of course, the novel deconstructs this summarily as soon as Sir Walter's disposition to overlook Mrs Clay's freckles and awkward wrist is demonstrated. But the desire to see a correspondence between bodily condition and inner nature, to read one as a sure transcription of the secrets of the other, is strong enough for critics, in their turn, to suggest that Mrs Clay's freckles, for which Sir Walter has recommended Gowland's lotion, are the outward sign of her inner corruption – since Gowland's lotion can be linked to venereal disease.[42]

Enough to say that this novel is sometimes troubled and sometimes amused by the mismatchings that occur between inner being and outer appearance. Simple contrastive irony about body and spirit abounds, for wounded and disabled bodies are pictured as emblems of healthy living and spiritual resource. Wentworth is reported as saying that Anne is 'so altered he should not have known her again', speaking of her appearance after seven years, but she is in fact, unaltered, unchanged in spirit, and this very constancy is not unrelated to her decline in looks. In the first draft of the conclusion, after the *rapprochement*, as the lovers retrace the past, and Wentworth goes over his feelings, Anne is said to have 'the felicity of being assured that in the first place (so far from being altered for the worse), she had gained inexpressibly in personal loveliness'. In the revised version this is amplified to form a little moment of muted comedy: Wentworth tells her that he fled to his brother's after the accident at Lyme:

'He enquired after you very particularly; asked even if you were personally altered, little suspecting that to my eye you could never alter.'

Anne smiled, and let it pass. It was too pleasing a blunder for a reproach. It is something for a woman to be assured in her eight-and-twentieth year, that she has not lost one charm of earlier youth: but the value of such homage was inexpressibly increased to Anne, by comparing it with former words, and feeling it to be the result, not the cause of a revival of his warm attachment. (243)

Anne smiles at the blundering offence against chivalry and it is her feelings rather than Wentworth's that now become 'inexpressible'. In smiling she demonstrates her own maturity and cultivation, her own self-irony, but also acknowledges the erosions of time and the inexact correspondence between human emotions or desire and the physical objects that are their focus and motivation. The first incident was a gratifying narrative of dream fulfilment: in its reworking and rephrasing Austen incorporates within the same moment two themes deeply relevant to her novel – acknowledging both time's depredations and the contingencies of human subjectivity – and thereby authenticates the romance she is simultaneously qualifying.

But the problematic is exposed most thoroughly in Austen's representation of Mrs Musgrove's grief in chapter VIII of the first volume. To quote only part of the notorious passage: 'while the agitations of Anne's slender form, and pensive face, may be considered as very completely screened, Captain Wentworth should be allowed some credit for the self-command with which he attended to her large fat sighings over the destiny of a son, whom alive nobody had cared for' (68). If there were a true harmony between body and spirit, then the dismissal of the body as grotesque could stand for dismissal of the feelings: the problem is that each demands a different, but concurrent, simultaneous, response. Austen cannot resolve the problem of her attitude here. Partly the writing insists there is an analogy, at the very least, between our bodily frames and our emotions, otherwise why describe Mrs Musgrove's sighings as 'fat'? But another part of the intention is to mark the disjunction, the separation between 'deep affliction' and 'a large bulky figure': the fact that appraisal of the body, whether approving or otherwise, can make no claim to knowledge or valuation, none whatsoever, of the inner life. Is Mrs Musgrove's sorrow, then, to be framed comically or tragically? The text is at this point riven between the tone adopted for its introspective, subjective narration of Anne's sufferings, a tone inflected towards the nuanced presentation of internal processes – 'all that was real and unabsurd in the parent's feelings' and which it here extends towards this minor character – and its wish to instantiate, once again, the irony that body and spirit may tell off in different directions. But here the narrative capitulates to that crude reading of the body as a decipherable text which the novel examines and repudiates almost everywhere else. The result is a paragraph of defensive floundering.[43]

The puzzle of relations between body and spirit is brought up once again in the little comic aftermath to the proposal scene. Even after reading Wentworth's passionately penned declaration – which shows him as agitated and nervous as ever Anne has been – her troubles are not finished. Overwhelmed, this time with happiness, her body takes over. What she is feeling is joy, what it displays is illness, and her chance to meet Wentworth on the way home is threatened, momentarily, when the Musgroves notice how she looks:

She began not to understand a word they said, and was obliged to plead indisposition and excuse herself. They could then see that she looked very ill – were shocked and concerned – and would not stir without her for the world. This was dreadful! Would they only have gone away, and left her in the quiet possession of that room, it would have been her cure; but to have them all standing or waiting around her was distracting, and, in desperation, she said she would go home.

'By all means, my dear,' cried Mrs Musgrove, 'go home directly and take care of yourself, that you may be fit for the evening. I wish Sarah was here to doctor you, but I am no doctor myself. Charles, ring and order a chair. She must not walk.' (238)

In this coda to the emotional heights of the declaration scene, the kindly, uncomprehending Musgroves enact a brief farcical replay of Highbury's misplaced solicitude about Jane Fairfax. But for the most part in *Persuasion*, as I have been suggesting, nursing and solicitude, if not 'doctoring', are central and serious matters. Because *Persuasion* is so much more than *Emma* about the miscarriages of life, about suffering and vulnerability, it has also necessarily brought to a finer focus the role, as well as the profession, of the nurse, and advocated more urgently the need, the seriousness of care, coping and support. The novel is shot through with recognitions of the body's fragility and mutability, and of the tenuousness of the emotions and valuations that are forever seeking an anchor in its immanent truths. This is a novel about 'the art of losing', to quote Elizabeth Bishop's very apposite poem, 'One Art': the art of existing without bitterness, despite multiple deprivations, of care of the self, the art of composure that is, for the writer, simultaneously the art of composition. If I have argued, too, that *Persuasion* was no radical revisioning of Jane Austen's social world, and that the historicist dimension of the novel may well be exaggerated, it is impossible to deny that the next work she undertook, to which the thematics of ill health are even more germane, was certainly to focus on contemporary social developments.

CHAPTER 5

Sanditon: *the enjoyments of invalidism*

Anne Elliot's 'whining and spoilt sister Mary', remarks her biographer, Park Honan, is 'one of Jane Austen's funniest people'.[1] Others may differ. 'She is not funny', Tony Tanner declares, 'she is unbearable'.[2] Mary Musgrove's hypochondria is displayed on her sister's arrival at Uppercross. 'It was rather a surprise to her to find Mary alone; but being alone, her being unwell and out of spirits, was almost a matter of course' (P 37). Stretched out on the faded sofa in the drawing room, fancying herself ill and neglected, herself neglecting her children, Mary is scarcely more than a contemptible emblem of the idle gentlewoman's life. Hypochondria has taken many forms in Jane Austen, from Fanny Dashwood's hysterics and Mrs Bennet's nerves, to Mr Woodhouse's biliousness, but it is represented now as no more than one of the banalities of genteel existence. Mary's complaints do not even reach the dignity of a proper name. 'I do not think I ever was so ill in my life as I have been all this morning – very unfit to be left alone I am sure. Suppose I were to be seized all of a sudden in some dreadful way, and not able to ring the bell!' (37), she moans. Her unspecific 'illness' is a psychosomatic substitute for flattery and self-importance, a metaphor for boredom and the sense of ill-usage that corrodes her existence, filling for her those vacuities of the gentlewoman's life which are experienced too, in their different ways, by her sisters Elizabeth and Anne. If Mary's illness is less than amusing it is partly because of the burden she puts on Anne, who, not rich in energy and spirits herself, is called upon to soothe her – Anne, who scarcely loves her sister as Emma loves her father.

Austen demonstrates Mary's hypochondria, and then dismisses it, as Anne's patience and 'forced cheerfulness' work a cure, and Mary leaps up to prettify a nosegay on the other side of the room. Little more is heard of her ill health, though such distresses are alluded to in Mrs Croft's reference to the 'all manner of imaginary complaints' of her winter without the Admiral, with only a brief reminder in Mary's hysterics at the scene of Louisa's accident – enough to denote them as being really not much more than a mode of self-importance, a convention to exact attention from others. Mary is no more successful than was Mrs Bennet at using illness symptoms to compel respect from her husband, but she enlists her body quite successfully as an arm of her claims to the regard of her other relations, to secure the consideration she believes is her due from them. Putting herself forward in place of Anne to nurse Louisa at Lyme, she has of course to be taken in charge: 'she had got books from the library and changed them so often, that the balance had certainly been much in favour of Lyme. She had been taken to Charmouth too, and she had bathed ... all this, joined to the sense of being so very useful, had made really an agreeable fortnight' (130). There is the merest trace of contempt: Mary's self promotion is too commonplace to make much of a fuss over.

In contrast the hypochondriacs who dominate the uncompleted novel *Sanditon* are presented with an amazing inventiveness, brio and zest. There is not just one 'sad invalid' here, but at least three, a trio of health-obsessed people whose activities, whilst absurd and selfish, are regarded with more gaiety and equanimity in this text, through its heroine Charlotte Heywood, because they seem to do harm to no one but themselves. The leading spirit is Miss Diana Parker, the extraordinarily active busybody who at the same time complains of multiple illnesses, extreme lassitude among them. Diana's interfering and misguided activity is regarded with amusement and amazement by Charlotte, a stranger to the family, preserved alike by her robust constitution and her independence of mind from any danger of being influenced. The Parkers do not tax the energies of others, and their illnesses are not a form of social domination, or the covert, indirect, exercise of domestic power. Here, instead, their own bodies have become the grounds for inventiveness and energy, preoccupying their imaginations and becoming the source of sufficient activity to direct the conduct of every hour of the day. Their attention to the body is the perverse expression of energy and initiative, but it is, or so the fragment suggests, merely one extension of a wider cultural beleaguerment by the imagination. Indeed Arthur Parker, the twenty-one year old younger son of the family, able-bodied but idle, whose conversation is about his nerves, his rheumatism and the lining of his stomach, gives an altogether new meaning to the modern term 'illness career'. The Parkers, Diana, Susan and Arthur – as the introduction of the opinion of their brother Sydney before the reading of Diana's letter indicates – are to be laughed at. They do not coerce – indeed, in this fragment no one yet threatens or hurts another: even the would-be seducer Sir Edward Denham is too silly to threaten Clara Brereton, his object, 'who saw through him and had not the least intention of being seduced' and Charlotte herself is amply preserved by her common sense from any danger.

Persuasion's two replacement chapters were finished in early August 1816. In January the next year, Jane Austen began another novel, which the eleven and a half completed chapters seem to indicate was planned as a three-volume project, like *Emma*. This manuscript (called 'Sanditon' by the Austen family, not by the author herself) introduces a far wider cast of characters than any of the previous novels has by this stage (except perhaps *Pride and Prejudice*) and its atmosphere is totally different from *Persuasion*, for it seems particularly untouched by melancholy or concerned with nuances of the inner life.

Given the circumstances of its writing, discussion of *Sanditon* is inevitably imbricated with Austen's biography. This exuberant, outlandish and terrifically animated text was produced by a woman slowly dying of a debilitating disease. The manuscript, 120 tiny pages filled with copperplate handwriting, was given to King's College, Cambridge in 1930–1 and reproduced in a photographic edition by B. C. Southam in 1975.[3] The signs of the writer's fragile condition are inscribed on the manuscript itself, which has the date of its beginning 'Jan. 27 1817' at the head, the date 'March 1st' at the head of the fourth page of the ninth chapter, and finally 'March 18', some way, it seems, into Chapter 12. The handwriting, sometimes bold and confident, is sometimes less so, and some of the text seems to have been written in pencil, 'probably when she was too weak to sit long at her desk, and written over in ink afterwards' as the author of the *Memoir*, in which extracts were first published in 1870, suggests.[4] One can correlate the progress of the manuscript with the record, in the surviving letters of the same period, of the relapses and remissions of her illness, an illness, of course which was not diagnosed, and of which the intermittent and separate symptoms – fatigue, 'rheumatism', fever, 'discharge', biliousness and backache – might be readily ascribed to, and treated as, minor or perhaps even discrete, illnesses. To readers today (who know that Jane Austen was to die in Winchester four months to the day after putting aside the MS) the symptoms suggest progressive and grave disease, but they might well have been compatible with periods of optimism and cheerfulness, and in those intervals, a self-critical watchfulness as regards making too much of them. For there is secondly the paradox that this fragment, which is to us manifestly a work of the ill and dying, is a highly successful and energetic comedy making fun of the so-called sick, in which at one moment the illness symptoms so floridly displayed in the text are attributed roundly to nothing but Vanity.

Critics have articulated the relationship between Austen's own disease and the manuscript in various ways. 'Was *Sanditon* the product of an imagination stimulated in ill-health?' asks Brian Southam, in his monograph on Austen's manuscripts – a curious revival of the romantic myth that associated creativity with disease.[5] For Litz 'the unfinished "Last Work" is essentially a private composition', serving a psychological need for its author as 'a defense against illness and depression'.[6] Others have suggested a direct biographical connection, like Jane Austen's niece Anna Lefroy who was to claim in 1862 that 'members of the Parker family ... were certainly suggested by conversations which passed between Aunt Jane and me during the time that she was writing this story. – Their vagaries do by no means exceed the facts from which they were taken'.[7] More ingeniously, D. A. Miller has ascribed the presence in the text of the 'half-mulatto' Miss Lambe to a displacement of Austen's anxieties about the disfiguring facial symptoms of her own illness, which she describes in a letter as 'black and white and every wrong colour'.[8]

It is indeed difficult to separate this culminating satire of hypochondria from some of the remarks in Jane Austen's surviving letters that bear upon the topic of illness. One thinks particularly of those that refer to her own mother.[9] The letters will have been subject to self-censorship, as well as the later attentions of Cassandra, but there is surely a foretaste of the Parkers in the brief mention of Mrs Austen in a letter to Cassandra of 1798: 'My mother continues hearty, her appetite & nights are very good, but her Bowels are still not entirely settled, & she sometimes complains of an Asthma, a Dropsy, Water in her Chest & a Liver Disorder'.[10] The dead-pan presentation is notable. A year later there is another hint in a letter to her sister:

> It began to occur to me before you mentioned it that I had been somewhat silent as to my mother's health for some time, but I thought you could have no difficulty in divining its exact state – you who have guessed so much stranger things. She is tolerably well – better upon the whole than she was some weeks ago. She would tell you herself that she has a very dreadful cold in her head at present; but I have not much compassion for colds in the head without fever or sore throat.[11]

Hypochondriacs in authority, like parents, have the power to compel others to act as if they took their complaints seriously, so that some dexterity in the exercise of irony may be developed in order to convey just how one actually assesses the situation. But other remarks suggest plainly that Miss Austen was willing enough to attribute her mother's symptoms to psychological causes. 'How can M[rs] J. Austen be so provokingly ill-judging?', she exclaims in 1813, 'Now my Mother will be unwell again. Every fault in Ben's blood does harm to hers, & every dinner-invitation he refuses will give her an indigestion.'[12]

It's perhaps significant that the only glimpses of Mrs Austen in the circumspect *Memoir* of her daughter's life show her on the sofa, where she remained, notoriously, during Jane's illness:

The sitting room contained only one sofa, which was frequently occupied by her mother, who was more than seventy years old. Jane would never use it, *even in her mother's absence*; but she contrived a sort of couch for herself with two or three chairs, and was pleased to say that this arrangement was more comfortable to her than a real sofa. Her reasons for this might have been left to be guessed, but for the importunities of a little niece, which obliged her to explain that if she herself had shewn any inclination to use the sofa, her mother might have scrupled being on it so much as was good for her.[13] (my italics)

My guess is that Jane Austen did not in any way want to identify with her mother. Perhaps the brusqueness and impatience with which mentions of ill health, inevitable in family letters, are often handled, comes from the same source. In such remarks one can usually detect Austen's impulse to assert the supremacy of the will or the moral self over the bodily. Long ago, in his lecture on Jane Austen, A. C. Bradley noted that the novelist 'refuses to express a deeper concern than she feels for misfortune and grief' and that 'there is an occasional touch of brutality in the refusal'.[14] Instances of this habit abound in the letters – as in the notorious comment about the neighbour who has suffered a miscarriage: 'I suppose she happened unawares to look at her husband'.[15] The second Lady Williams, she remarks, 'has taken to her old tricks of ill-health again, & is sent for a couple of months among her friends. Perhaps she may make *them* sick'.[16] In the famous letter in which she describes her own symptoms five days after abandoning the manuscript of *Sanditon*, this linguistic habit is revealed now as a more definitely coping strategy: 'I certainly have not been well for many weeks, and about a week ago I was very poorly, I have had a good deal of fever at times & indifferent nights, but am considerably better now, & recovering my Looks a little, which have been bad enough, black & white and every wrong colour. I must not depend upon being ever very blooming again. Sickness is a dangerous Indulgence at my time of Life'.[17] 'Indulgence', 'tricks': Austen seems to wish in these mentions of ill-health to make it over into a question of will, to bring it by force into the sphere of the moral, just as in *Sanditon* Charlotte Heywood translates or reduces the Parkers' illness symptoms into social devices. But facetiously to assert the sovereignty of the moral life over the bodily is not to disregard or minimise illness and death: it rests rather upon a recognition of the insuperable otherness of the bodily phenomenon.

Death is figured as farce in a text from the other end of Austen's writing life, 'Love and Freindship' (1790). As she dies, Marianne, the heroine of sensibility, issues medical advice. 'My fate will teach you this', she proclaims. 'One fatal swoon has cost me my Life..beware of swoons Dear Laura ... .A frenzy fit is not one quarter so pernicious; it is an exercise to the Body and if not too violent, is I dare say conducive to Health in its consequences – Run mad as often as you chuse;- but do not faint – ' (MW 102). Partly this is a protest against conventional ideas of feminine frailty, but it also burlesques that bodily self-preoccupation, the bizarre logic of amateur medical analysis, which is to be revived in *Sanditon*. The multiple deaths of this early work already question the idea that serious bodily events can easily be ascribed moral significance. In Austen's novels after *Sense and Sensibility*, serious illness or death is rarely treated, and usually banished to the outer limits of the fictional canvas, there to be handled with curt irony, like Mrs Churchill's or Dr Grant's demise, but this is not to demonstrate callousness so much as to acknowledge the inaccessibility of such events to ethical presentation. The only death in Austen's novels which is discussed with full earnestness is paradoxically introduced to emphasise this division of the life of the body from the imagination. Henry Tilney describes the circumstances of his mother's death to counter Catherine Morland's fantasy that she has been murdered:

' ... you infer perhaps the probability of some negligence – some – (involuntarily she shook her head) – or it may be – of something still less pardonable.' She raised her eyes to him more fully than she had ever done before. 'My mother's illness,' he continued, 'the seizure which ended in her death *was* sudden. The malady itself, one from which she had often suffered, a bilious fever – its cause therefore constitutional. On the third day, in short as soon as she could be prevailed on, a physician attended her, a very respectable man, and one in whom she had always placed great confidence. Upon his opinion of her danger, two others were called in the next day, and remained in almost constant attendance for four-and-twenty hours. On the fifth day she died ... ' (NA 196–7)

This account is a sombre reminder of the apparently arbitrary processes of the body and their recalcitrance to the means medicine has developed to cope with them. These are contingencies more chilling, because more everyday, than those of Catherine's Gothic imagination. *Sanditon* deals with all this by leaving it out of account, by presenting no real illnesses, and no genuine doctors, portraying symptoms solely as products of its characters' whims, fantasies or frustrated energies. The irony then is that the text which seeks to contain the body within the powers of will and consciousness is marked by the literal death of the author, the most violent sign of the body as Other.

But *Sanditon* cannot be assimilated to, or discussed in terms of Jane Austen's private life. As Tony Tanner has argued in a brilliant chapter,[18] the fragment is a highly developed, richly inventive, and almost wholly successful presentation, even in its draft form, of an intellectually coherent theme and idea. The novel begins with an accident. Mr Parker, the developer of a new resort on the south coast, has travelled to a remote Sussex village in search of a doctor or surgeon who might be persuaded to settle in practice there and so increase the patronage of the place, which is founded on the supposed therapeutic qualities of its situation, and might well, therefore, attract people in need of other medical attention. Right from the start *Sanditon* establishes that it is concerned with the relations between medicine, capitalism and commerce, and since Mr Parker's carriage overturns in 'the wild goose chace' and he sprains his ankle severely, it seems to be predicted that the relationship will be attended with mishap and mischance. Mr Parker is an irrepressibly optimistic man for whom Sanditon is an obsession. He has more than capital invested in this enterprise, as the liturgical cadences indicate: 'it was his Mine, his Lottery, his Speculation & his Hobby Horse; his Occupation his Hope and his Futurity' (372). At first he makes light of the injury to his ankle, telling his wife that they will set off back home, where he will be quickly cured. 'Two hours take us home, from Hailsham – and when once at home, we have our remedy at hand you know. – A little of our own Bracing Sea air will soon set me on my feet again'. (In the manuscript, 'own' has been inserted above the line – Mr Parker has privatised the sea air.) 'Depend upon it my Dear, it is exactly a case for the Sea. Saline air & immersion will be the very thing. – My sensations tell me so already' (367). 'It is sufficient that I *feel* this power', had exclaimed Samuel Johnson's mad astronomer, who believed that the world's weather had fallen under his control (my italics).[19] Mr Parker is not quite a monomaniac, but his reliance on his 'sensations' as a key to external reality is a sign of the romantic culture that links the various eccentrics in this text, and his subjectivity is matched but also exploded by the remark of his sister Diana who writes, on the other hand, that *her* 'feelings tell me too plainly that in my present state, the Sea air w^d probably be the death of me' (387). But just as, at the other end of Austen's writing career, Marianne Dashwood's conviction that 'the day would be lastingly fair' is abruptly confuted, after the sisters set out to walk, by 'a driving rain set full in their face' (SS 41), the pain of his ankle soon stubbornly begins to assert itself and he is obliged to accept help from the Heywoods, the country family who come to his rescue, and in the end to convalesce two weeks at their house.

Parker's enthusiasm for the curative properties of 'immersion' (a fashionable quasi-medical term) and sea-air on a sprained ankle is extended to every variety of illness or disorder as he attempts to persuade the unreceptive and doubting Heywoods of Sanditon's advantages. His fulsome recommendations pick up what seems to be a frequent contemporary note in praise of the curative properties of the sea. In the *Gentleman's Magazine* for January 1816, for example, there is an engraving of the 'General Sea-Bathing Infirmary at Margate' and an encomium on the advantages of the sea for 'scrofulous infections':

Medicine can effect but little in this distressing complaint. It is now universally advised to have recourse to that Ocean, at once the safeguard and the glory of the Nation, whose healing properties cannot be too much extolled ... The numerous places on the coast that now, at each returning summer, vie with each other in tempting the invalid of the interior to try the efficacy of Sea-Air and Sea-Bathing, are solid and convincing proofs of the importance of the offered remedy.[20]

Mr Parker praises Sanditon, but he also runs down its rivals, especially the neighbouring 'Brinshore'. 'Never was there a place more palpably designed by Nature for the resort of the Invalid – the very Spot which Thousands seemed in need of. – The most desirable distance from London! One complete, measured mile nearer than East Bourne ... ' Brinshore on the other hand: ' ... the attempts of two or three speculating People about Brinshore, this last Year, to raise that paltry Hamlet, lying, as it does between a stagnant marsh, a bleak Moor, & the constant effluvia of a ridge of putrifying sea-weed, can end in nothing but their own Disappointment ... ' (369)

To run down a rival resort had long been a tactic of promoters. Dr Antony Relhan's early *Short History of Bright-helmston* (1761) compares Brighton with Bath and Baiae to its advantage ('exempt from the inconvenient steams of hot sulphurous baths, and the dangerous vicinity of Mount Vesuvius')[21] and praises the excellent 'medicated' air and 'Atmosphere' of his favoured bathing place in just as extraordinary terms as Mr Parker's:

Brighthelmston, thus free from the insalutary vapour of stagnant water, distant from the noxious steams of perspiring trees, and every other cause aiding to produce a damp, putrid atmosphere, seldom sees its inhabitants labouring under those disorders which arise from a relaxed fibre and a languid circulation. Yet, from the vicinity of the sea, and the abundant, but salutary vapour it affords, it is as certain that the complaints that arise from a too rigid and tense fibre are equally unknown. Hence neither dropsical, nor Chlorotic complaints; Pleurises, nor Quincies, nor any other inflammatory ones prevail here.[22]

Mr Parker's rhapsodies catch the same note:

> He held it indeed as certain, that no person c^d be really well, no person, (however upheld for the present by fortuitous aids of exercise & spirits in a semblance of Health) could be really in a state of secure & permanent Health without spending at least 6 weeks by the Sea every year. – The Sea air & Sea Bathing together were nearly infallible, one or the other of them being a match for every Disorder, of the Stomach, the Lungs or the Blood; They were anti-spasmodic, anti-pulmonary, anti-sceptic, anti-bilious, & anti-rheumatic. Nobody could catch cold by the Sea, Nobody wanted Appetite by the sea, Nobody wanted Spirits, Nobody wanted Strength. – They were healing, softing, relaxing – fortifying & bracing – seemingly just as was wanted – sometimes one, sometimes the other. – If the Sea breeze failed, the Sea-Bath was the certain corrective; & where Bathing disagreed, the Sea Breeze alone was evidently designed by Nature for the cure. (373)

Remarkably unmoved by this rhetoric, the Heywoods decide to stay at home, but send their daughter Charlotte (who has nursed the ankle) back with the Parkers, and it is largely through her eyes that the other characters are observed and assessed. Anna Lefroy believed that 'The Heywoods stand in place of the Morelands', the decent, sober country family of Austen's recently abandoned *Northanger Abbey*.[23] Mr Heywood is 'hale', sensible and crisply spoken, and his daughter brings those qualities with her as she enters the newly developing resort of Sanditon, as Catherine brought her family's decency (and much naiveté) into the ancient and fashionable city of Bath. 'New' Sanditon (for there is an old Sanditon a sheltered mile and a half further inland) is a monument to the new affluence, the new leisure and new consumerism. The narrator's account of the Heywoods' reasons for not venturing to Sanditon trenchantly suggests that the illnesses which Sanditon's facilities – among them an Hotel, a Terrace and a circulating Library – were built to cater for might well be fictitious.

> They had very pretty Property – enough, had their family been of reasonable Limits to have allowed them a very gentlemanlike share of Luxuries & Change – enough for them to have indulged in a new Carriage & better Roads, an occasional month at Tunbridge Wells, & symptoms of the Gout and a Winter at Bath; – but the maintenance,

Education & fitting out of 14 Children demanded a very quiet, settled, careful course of Life – & obliged them to be stationary and healthy at Willingden. (373–4)

Sanditon is designed to profit from the leisure activities of an affluent class inspired, as was Mary Musgrove, with enthusiasm for 'immersion', of bathing for health, the culmination of the very widespread promotion of water and sea-bathing as therapeutic measures throughout the eighteenth century. It is devoted to a sophisticated society's preoccupation with its bodily well-being, to the exploitation of the proclivities of the body for profit. Not surprisingly, doctors at sea-side resorts and spas developed an interest in and awareness of 'cures by imaginative conviction'.[24] A book on 'the Imagination, as a cause and as a cure of disorders of the body' gave striking illustrations of rheumatic patients, for instance, finding relief in fake remedies.[25]

Mr Parker's partner in the enterprise of Sanditon, to whom Charlotte is soon introduced, is the friendly local dowager Lady Denham, rich, but penny-pinching, one of Austen's most vivid creations (she is far more memorable than, say, Lady Russell) who hearing, for instance, that a young ladies' seminary is expected to take lodgings, hopes some of them might be consumptive, and want milk from her milch asses – asses' milk being a usual recommendation in cases of TB, though, as physicians noted, it was not always easy to come by, and might therefore be charged for highly.[26] She disapproves of Mr Parker's quest for a surgeon to establish in the town because

'It w^d be only encouraging our Servants & the Poor to fancy themselves ill, if there was a D^r at hand. – Oh! Oh! pray, let us have none of the Tribe at Sanditon. We go on very well as we are. There is the Sea & the Downs & my Milch-asses … and what can People want for more? – Here have I lived 70 good years in the world & never took Physic above twice – and never saw the face of a Doctor in all my Life, on my *own* account. – And I verily beleive if my poor dear Sir Harry had never seen one neither, he w^d have been alive now. Ten fees, one after another, did the man take who sent *him* out of the World. – I beseech you Mr Parker, no Doctors here.' (394).

When the school and its prize pupil the young West Indian heiress turn up, Lady Denham goes to visit their lodgings.

In Miss Lambe, here was the very young Lady, sickly & rich, whom she had been asking for; & she made the acquaintance for Sir Edward's sake, & the sake of her Milch asses. How it might answer with regard to the Baronet, remained to be proved, but as to the Animals, she soon found that all her calculations of Profit w^d be vain. M^{rs} G would not allow Miss L to have the smallest symptom of a Decline, or any complaint which Asses milk could possibly relieve. 'Miss L was under the constant care of an experienced Physician; and his Prescriptions must be their rule'.

But the best joke is in reserve: 'except in favour of some tonic pills, which a Cousin of her own had a Propriety in, M^{rs} G, did never deviate from the strict Medecinal page' (422).

The stridently healthy Lady Denham's low opinion those she calls 'the Tribe' is shared, amusingly enough, by Mr Parker's hypochondriac sister Diana, who is introduced to Charlotte through the reading aloud of her extraordinary letter in chapter V. If readers so often seek to account for this fragment in terms of Austen's biography, this is partly, I think, to deflect the disconcerting quality of its comedy. Dismayed by what they take to be the unsubtlety of the writing, they suggest 'real life' analogues or defend the text as the courageous self-therapy of a dangerously ill writer. But such responses do not really focus the issue, which has to do with the boundaries of what we are pleased to call 'realism'. One way of accounting for the perceived crudity or strangeness of the text is to emphasise that it is, after all, still in manuscript. 'The fragment has a certain roughness and harshness of satire', observed R. W. Chapman, and suggested that this is 'due in part to lack of revision' in which the roughnesses would be 'smoothed'. 'But a degree of savagery would, I think, have persisted', he added.[27] The problem of in what frame – burlesque, caricature, savage or realistic comedy – to put the characters is at its most acute during the reading of Diana's letter.

Brian Southam has argued that, *pace* Chapman, 'the modifications to the characters, especially to the four eccentrics, are not in the direction of toning down, of de-caricaturising, but tend to enforce and heighten their traits and eccentricities' and has convincingly demonstrated this in the case of Mr Parker.[28] It is even clearer if one looks at the amendments – whether made in the course of writing, or at a later time is unclear – to the presentation of his flamboyantly ailing siblings. Diana Parker's dominant idiom is a kind of hypochondriac's hyperbole. 'Had you the most experienced Man in his Line settled at Sanditon, it w^d be no recommendation to us. We have entirely done with the whole Medical Tribe ... '(386). 'Susan never eats, I grant you,' she says of her sister, '& just at present *I* shall want nothing; I never eat for about a week after a Journey' (411). Later, after hurrying about Sanditon, Diana, 'who by her own account, had not once sat down during the space of seven hours, confessed herself a little tired' (414). What makes Diana so risible is the combination of specificity and the wildly improbable, a specificity that suggests both her energy of mind and at the same time the eccentricity of its application.

The revisions to the manuscript show this effect being attained. Mr Parker reads Diana's letter aloud to Charlotte, believing that it shows her 'exactly as she is, the most active, friendly, warm hearted Being in existence, & therefore must give a good impression' (386). Her brother's letter found her, Diana Parker declares, 'suffering under a more severe attack than usual of my old greivance, Spasmodic Bile & hardly able to crawl from my Bed to the Sofa' (386). As to the journey to Sanditon, 'I doubt whether Susan's nerves w^d be equal to the effort', she writes to her brother. 'She has been suffering much from Headache. [and] Six Leaches a day for the last week have relieved her a little'. (Ms 46) The manuscript shows that this is quickly expanded into 'She has been suffering much from the Headache and Six Leaches a day for 10 days together relieved her so little that we thought it right to change our measures'. Susan, after having teeth drawn, 'can only speak in a whisper – and fainted away twice this morning on poor Arthur's sneezing', which is first altered to 'poor Arthur's coughing' and then to 'on poor Arthur's trying to suppress a cough' (Ms 46). This not only suggests Diana's exaggerated solicitousness for the actually robust and selfish Arthur, but the way all three Parkers suffer in concert, reflect and amplify, act and react upon each others' symptoms.

Another example occurs in the same letter. Diana relates how she attended to the sprained ankle of a coachman: 'by the immediate use of Friction alone, well persevered in (& I rubbed his Ancle with my own hand for 4 hours without intermission) – he was well in three days'. In revision, 'well' becomes 'steadily' and 4 hours becomes 'Six' – all too much for the author of the *Memoir*, who restored 'four'.[29] These extraordinary medical achievements and interventions are climaxed in the heroic measures dictated by Diana's own assessment of her sister's constitution:

'Six Leaches a day for 10 days together relieved her so little that we thought it right to change our measures – and being convinced on examination that the Evil lay in her Gum, I persuaded her to attack the disorder there. She has accordingly had 3 teeth drawn, & is decidedly better, but her Nerves are a good deal deranged ....' (387)

One can only (remembering Jane Austen's own description of a visit to an early nineteenth-century dentist[30]) share Charlotte Heywood's amazed response: 'I am astonished at the chearful style of the Letter, considering the state in which both Sisters appear to be. – Three Teeth drawn at once! – frightful! – Your Sister Diana seems almost as ill as possible, but those 3 Teeth of your Sister Susan's, are more distressing than all the rest' (388). Originally this read 'most disturbing to one's imagination' and was altered possibly because of the wish not to associate the term 'imagination' with the very level-headed Charlotte. 'Remembering the three teeth drawn in one day', Charlotte, when eventually introduced to Susan, approaches her 'with a peculiar degree of Respectful Compassion' (413). And indeed the teeth do haunt one's imagination – as if Jane Austen were making a particular point of challenging credulity about what excessive attention to the body can drive someone to. Diana Parker is addicted to extravagant expression, but she is not a liar: by taking her character's behaviour so far to the edge of the grotesque Austen seems to be cultivating a distinct effect, perhaps influenced by Fanny Burney's *Camilla* (1796) to the extraordinary scrapes of whose heroine she pointedly alludes in the text (390). Susan 'talked, however, the whole evening as incessantly as Diana'.

Besides the Parkers, Charlotte is introduced to Lady Denham's relations, among them the Baronet, Sir Edward Denham, forced to stay in one place by his comparative poverty, but in consequence, a great reader of fashionable literature. Sir Edward's literary rhapsodies, the first on romantic poetry, the second on the sentimental novel, are so high-flown and preposterous that they do seem to verge on literary burlesque, a familiar kind of parody in the conservative novel, not so far away, as Marilyn Butler remarks, from the parodies in Eaton Stannard Barrett's *The Heroine*.[31] One is reminded too of the Edward of 'Love and Freindship'. There is, though, a definite thematic link between Sir Edward and the Parkers, between their hypochondria and his own brand of hyperbole. 'Most willingly, Fair Questioner', he replies to Charlotte's request to tell her what novels he likes: 'The Novels which I approve are such as display Human Nature with Grandeur – such as shew her in the Sublimities of intense Feeling – such as exhibit the progress of strong Passion from the first Germ of incipient Susceptibility to the utmost Energies of Reason half-dethroned'. Richardson had Lovelace say dryly 'It is true I have been gay and enterprising. It is in my constitution to be so. I know not how I came by such a constitution; but I was never accustomed to check or control; that you all know',[32] but Sir Edward elaborates a defence of heroes who '(though at the risk of some Aberration from the strict line of Primitive Obligation)' 'hazard all, dare all, atcheive all' in their pursuit of women, in phrases fetched – far fetched – from the poetic criticism of a different age. In Denham's version of Romanticism the body (at least the young and healthy male body) is the sanction of conduct and the source of morality. The heart ('the primitive capabilities of the heart', like Wordsworth's 'essential passions of the heart') is an energising principle that must be obeyed, for the body's promptings give access to a higher morality than that of ordinary mortals. The 'impulses' of 'illimitable ardour' – the phrase occurs in both rhapsodies – are 'sovereign'. The burlesque elements of Denham's speeches are controlled in their first conversation by being set within a precise social moment, by his nervous awareness as he speaks to Charlotte of Clara's proximity, and by Charlotte's prim but eminently sensible responses, but in the second set of speeches, more extreme and preposterous, they are not.

Charlotte's encounter with the youngest of the Parker family, Arthur, in chapter X, though, brings a quite new and successful effect into Jane Austen's writing. Austen creates Arthur, torpid and twenty, as a more physical creature than any other male in her mature work. Though treated by his sisters as a vulnerable weakling, he is in fact 'Broad made & Lusty' (413). 'Heavy in eye as well as in Figure' he is aroused from his sluggish self-absorption, as he sits in front of a blazing fire on a fine summer's day, by Charlotte Heywood's physical proximity: 'he evidently felt it no penance to have a fine young Woman next to him, requiring in common Politeness some attention' and 'fine young woman' – perhaps a clearer measure of Austen's intention – was originally, it seems, 'a good-looking Girl' (Ms 96). (Later he is seen stimulated to some minor physical exercise by the chance of seeing the young Miss Beauforts posing in front of their windows (423).) Arthur is a male of common clay – 'a good deal of Earthy Dross hung about him' – a self-engrossed sensualist with a sodden complexion whose sensuality happens to be turned inward to an anxious attention to his own bodily processes, but who tries awkwardly to court his companion by offering to brew her cocoa and buttering her toast. His small-talk is of his ailments, of being bathed by perspiration after a very short walk in the middle of the day – 'I am very subject to Perspiration, and there cannot be a surer sign of Nervousness', he explains – which makes Charlotte grateful for the interruption brought by the arrival of the tea things, but with a similar obliviousness to the offensive overtones of medical talk he goes on to complain repetitively how unbuttered toast hurts 'the Coats of the Stomach' (417).

Charlotte has no sooner made her assessment of him as a malingerer, one whose 'enjoyments in Invalidism were very different from his sisters – by no means so spiritualized' and the adopter of the sick-role 'principally for the indulgence of an Indolent temper – & to be determined on having no Disorders but such as called for warm rooms & good Nourishment' (418), than she is forced to slightly readjust this opinion. Seeing that she takes another cup of tea, Arthur is amazed:

'What! said he – Do you venture upon two dishes of strong Green Tea in one Even^g? – What Nerves you must have! – How I envy you! – Now, if *I* were to swallow only one such dish – what do you think it's effect would be upon me? – ' 'Keep you awake perhaps all night' – replied Charlotte, meaning to overthrow his attempts at Surprise, by the Grandeur of her own Conceptions. – 'Oh! if that were all! – he exclaimed. – No – it acts on me like Poison and w^d entirely take away the use of my right side, before I had swallowed it 5 minutes. – It sounds almost incredible – but it has happened to me so often that I cannot doubt it. – The use of my right Side is entirely taken away for several hours!' 'It sounds rather odd to be sure – answered Charlotte coolly – but I dare say it would be proved to be the simplest thing in the World, by those who have studied right sides & Green Tea scientifically & thoroughly understand all the possibilities of their action on each other.' (418)

Once again, the MS shows signs of Austen intensifying the idiosyncrasy of the character: 'acts on me like Poison' is added above the line. 'It has happened to me so often that I cannot doubt it' was originally merely 'it has happened to me two times' (Ms 92). It is as if Austen wanted to make a deliberate challenge to one's notions of the possible. Like Charlotte's response to Susan's visit to the dentist, the text seems actively to dwell on, to call attention to, the amazing behaviour of the hypochondriacal body. I do not think the effect of this is accurately defined as burlesque or as a subversion or even questioning, of the realistic parameters that have determined the shape of Austen's mature fiction: what is happening rather is that this writing is bringing out the fact that where relations between the body and the imagination are concerned, ordinary criteria go by the board. Nothing is too amazing to be true about a person's relation to their body: the body is an infinitely labile and plastic medium for the living through and projection of desires and symptoms and ideas, an expandable arena for the imagination and culture to collaborate in the creation of subjective phenomena. In this light Charlotte's own strongly commonsensical response is seen to be a product of her own physical well-being. 'In the boldness of her own good health' she can see nothing in Susan's condition that would not be cured by throwing her drops and smelling salts out of the window (413). But the extraordinary nature of Arthur's claims, like the extraordinary procedures of his sisters, in effect lays siege to, and may even destabilise, Charlotte's stolid and confident moralism.

The alterations in the manuscript heighten the absurdities of the Parkers, but they subdue and restrain the vocabulary of the heroine. When Diana Parker actually arrives at Sanditon, and they meet, Charlotte first described her as 'rather delicate than absolutely sickly' which became 'delicate looking rather than sickly' as if Jane Austen had caught the dramatic highly coloured speech of Diana Parker and had to curtail its momentary overflow into the consciousness of the 'sober-minded' Miss Heywood. Similarly, her originally 'great curiosity to see Mr Arthur Parker' subsides into 'considerable' as the sentence is revised (Ms 93). Charlotte's general reflections on the family open chapter X. 'The Parkers, were no doubt a family of Imagination & quick feelings – and while the eldest Brother found vent for his superfluity of sensation as a Projector, the Sisters were perhaps driven to dissipate theirs in the invention of odd complaints', Charlotte surmises (412). Her thoughts fall naturally into the cadences and vocabulary of the century that has past:

Some natural delicacy of Constitution in fact, with an unfortunate turn for Medecine, especially quack Medecine, had given them an early tendency at various times, to various Disorders; – the rest of their sufferings was from Fancy, the love of Distinction & the love of the Wonderful. – They had Charitable hearts & many amiable feelings – but a spirit of restless activity, & the glory of doing more than any body else, had their share in every exertion of Benevolence – and there was Vanity in all they did, as well as in all they endured. (412–13)

The last sentence of this striking paragraph originally read 'benevolent hearts', and had additional emphasis: 'The disease of activity, & the glory of doing more than any body else, had their share in every exertion of Health, as well as in every inaction of Sickness, and there was Vanity in all they did, as well as in all they endured' (Ms 91). The metaphor has been deleted, because it is precisely *not* as a disease, out of reach of the moral life, that Charlotte is to regard the activities of the Parkers: she wishes to assert the sovereignty of reason, and to read their symptoms and conduct as amenable to moral interpretation. To the same end Austen removes the overemphasis, the hint of Charlotte's own exasperation, in the pompous antitheses.

This is a recovery of the confident rhetoric of a dominant eighteenth-century tradition. '*Nervous* disorders are the diseases of the Wealthy, the Voluptuous and the Lazy', George Cheyne's comment, already quoted, frames them within a discourse of the moral life.[33] 'Illness' from this point of view, is dismissed as a function of increased and deplorable affluence, to be remedied by fresh air, exercise, greater self-control, and above all employment. An anecdote told by Mrs Thrale exemplifies Samuel Johnson's attitude.

We talked of Lady Tavistock, who grieved herself to death for the loss of her husband – 'She was rich and wanted employment (says Johnson), so she cried till she lost all power of restraining her tears: other women are forced to outlive their husbands, who were just as much beloved, depend upon it; but they have no time for grief: and I doubt not, if we had put Lady Tavistock into a small chandler's shop and given her a nurse-child to tend, her life would have been saved. The poor and the busy have no leisure for sentimental sorrow'.[34]

Mary Wollstonecraft extended his observations into the physical sphere. 'What can be a more melancholy sight to a thinking mind', she asked,

than to look into the numerous carriages that drive helter-skelter about this metropolis in a morning full of pale-faced creatures who are flying from themselves! I have often wished, with Dr Johnson, to place some of them in a little shop with half a dozen children looking up to their languid countenances for support. I am much mistaken, if some latent vigour would not soon give health and spirit to their eyes, and some lines drawn by the exercise of reason on the blank cheeks ... might restore lost dignity to the character ... [35]

Under the sign of 'reason' the creative and destructive phenomena of the body are brusquely dismissed as 'indulgence'. Charlotte's position is warranted by her own robustness, but a certain conceptual gulf separates her analysis from the world she is observing.

The body in *Sanditon* thus becomes the site for a particularly sharp confrontation between the ideologies of eighteenth-century rationalism and romanticism. The fragment pits a strong absurdity against a strong common-sense. On the one side this vigorous rationalism, 'excellent health' and realism: on the other romantic ideas, delusions, 'quite fantastic accounts'[36] of illness – and the manuscript breaks off before the tension is resolved. But the last glimpse we are left with of Diana Parker is another manifestation of this dialectic. Mr Parker is concerned for 'the poor Mullins's situation' (though he has left the old estate, he has not abandoned all of the old values) and wants to enlist Lady Denham's help in setting up a subscription for them. He asks his wife to broach the topic when she visits with Charlotte. Diana, who happens to be calling, immediately puts in a claim for 'a poor Woman in Worchestershire', then for 'the establishment of a Charitable Repository at Burton on Trent' and finally remembers 'the family of the poor Man who was hung last assizes at York'. She regrets she is unable to come with Mrs Parker herself:

'but in 5 minutes I must be at Mrs G. – to encourage Miss Lambe in taking her first Dip. She is so frightened, poor Thing, that I promised to come & keep up her Spirits, and go in the Machine with her if she wished it – and as soon as that is over I must hurry home, for Susan is to have Leaches at one oclock – which will be a three hours business, – therefore I really have not a moment to spare – besides that (between ourselves) I ought to be in bed myself at this present time, for I am hardly able to stand … ' (424)

This fantastic proliferation of charitable good works is met by Mr Parker's retraction of his proposal to his wife. '*His* application thus withdrawn, his sister could say no more in support of hers, which was his object, as he felt all their impropriety & all the certainty of their ill effect upon his own better claim' (425). Diana's caricature-like energy is thus contained within the parameters of social realism by being shown to be accessible to considerations of tact and good manners. However extraordinary her activities are, this discourse of extremes is enveloped in and countered by a discourse of propriety.

The fragment *Sanditon* is the logical culmination of Jane Austen's exploration of health and the body through the novels, and especially the three later novels of the Chawton period, since it is concerned with ill-health as a social phenomenon. 'For her the moral human being wages war with the natural human being', writes Marilyn Butler,[37] and it is part of this battle that illness, like death, reminders of the natural and uncontrollable, should not be dwelt on with amplifying sympathy but be treated with the irony, sometimes brusque and flippant, that she had always to hand. Illness was, in the great tradition of comedy, to be made fun of, but was therefore seen, inevitably, in its social relations, as performance. Scepticism about the validity or reality of disease conditions is the only conceivable standpoint for such a comedy, but if illness or (what amounted to the same thing) complaints of illness could be seen as modes of social power, or of domestic coercion, then the treatment of illness, whether professional or amateur, whether doctoring or nursing, could also be seen as part of the politics and economics of the body. In the absence of real power, women find a substitute for it in acts of ostensible medical charity and Diana Parker is a benevolent version of Mrs Norris – the officious, doctoring gentlewoman whose attentions to the servants serve her own psychological purposes. Whilst free of Mrs Norris' odious sanctimony ('Is she not a sister's child? and could I bear to see her want, while I had a bit of bread to give her?' (MP 7)), Diana busies herself in arrangements of enormous ramifications with a similar self-complacency. As she explains the activity on behalf of Mrs Griffith that brings her to Sanditon: 'I hate to employ others, when I am equal to act myself – and my conscience told me that this was an occasion which called for me. Here was a family of helpless Invalides whom I might essentially serve'.

As used here and throughout the fragment the term 'invalid', or rather, 'invalide' seems to have a certain contemporary cachet. 'I know that both you and your Sister are sad sufferers as to health', Charlotte says to Diana Parker, attempting to explain (as it was first put) 'the amazement which she could easily believe to be painted in her face' at Diana's recital of treatments (Ms 86). This is replaced by 'I know what Invalides both you & your sister are', and Diana quickly picks up the implied accolade: 'Invalides indeed! – I trust there are not three People in England who have so sad a right to that appellation' (410). A few pages later, one can just discern from the manuscript that the final 'e' has been added to 'Invalide' in the description of Arthur as 'with no other look of an Invalide than a sodden complexion'. Johnson's *Dictionary* (sixth edition, 1785) gives the word only in this spelling, from the French – it is evidently a fashionable import. The spelling suggests pronunciation with a suitably genteel and mincing air.

Sensibility in the eighteenth-century novel is manifested less in language than in tears and blushes, palpitations and sighs.[38] It has a continuity with illness, for exquisite susceptibility can – as all the sentimental moralists remark – become dangerous, leading to physical decline and collapse. Sensibility is also a sign of withdrawal, the immolation of the sensitive self from the active and political world. In *Sanditon* eighteenth-century reclusive sensibility has become nineteenth-century invalidism: the eighteenth century man or woman of feeling has been transformed into the nineteenth century 'invalide'. Invalidism has now become, as it was to be throughout the century, an advertisement for genteel snobbery and middle-class status. Refinement, exacerbated, is a new mode of defining the self.[39] What is different is that invalidism is no longer merely a private resort (a protest against the world) but the instigator and pivot of economic activity. Around the invalid were to be built the bathing places, the hotels and spas, the sanatoria and hydros of the Victorian age; in her bath-chair the sufferer from delicate health was to reign over a transformation of the coastline and the landscape. Dr Granville's extensive survey of the *Spas of England, and Principal Sea-Bathing Places*, published in the early

1840s, promotes Bournemouth with the same solicitousness for the wealthy and debilitated as Mr Parker promoted Sanditon: 'I hardly need touch upon its superiority as a bathing place to any in the neighbourhood, or along these coasts. It is as an inland sheltered haven for the most tender invalids, however, that I should call your attention to the great capabilities of Bourne... '[40] Mr Parker was right after all: Sanditon was a harbinger of the new age.

But – seeing and representing this new phenomenon – Jane Austen is not more sympathetic to invalidism than she was to sensibility. Both are seen as the result of wealth, compromise formations between the possession of leisure and the need for outlet or activity, the assertion of power. It is thus that *Sanditon* brings to a climax Jane Austen's concern with illness as a cultural phenomenon. The body had always been disposed in Austen's texts as a focus and site of social and economic power relations. Hypochondria is the hostile name given to the manifestations of illness as they present themselves within a leisured, middle-class environment, and manipulation within the limited domestic sphere is perceived to be hypochondria's object. From the beginnings in *Sense and Sensibility* Austen saw illness in the light of its production: the body was not a kind of ultimate, a final cause, self-generating its illness or health, but illness and health were to be read in relation to social circumstances. Jane Austen understood illness then, as I have argued, to be a mode of manners, to be represented in its relation to its context, to economics, ideology and power.

Interwoven with her depiction of the various ways that the body can be a vehicle for ulterior purposes too was a specific concern that linked her with the tradition of 'our best moralists' of which Anne Elliot spoke: of making her texts themselves represent, embody, sanity and healthiness. 'The principle of organisation, and the principle of development, in her work is an intense moral interest of her own in life that is in the first place a preoccupation with certain problems that life compels on her as personal ones. She is intelligent and serious enough to be able to impersonalise her moral tensions as she strives, in her art, to become more fully conscious of them, and to learn what, in the interests of life, she ought to do with them.'[41] This impetus is perhaps most clearly to be discerned, considering the circumstances in which it was written, in Jane Austen's last work. Satire and comedy were, in themselves, inspiriting, salutary, therapeutic. In the letter which she wrote a week after she had put *Sanditon* aside for the last time, describing the symptoms of her illness so clearly that modern doctors feel reasonably confident about making a retrospective diagnosis of Addison's disease, Jane Austen also mentioned a young 'Mr Wildman' whose ideas about novels were as different from hers as those of Charlotte and Sir Edward. 'He & I should not in the least agree of course, in our Ideas of Novels and Heroines', she declared to her niece, and added: 'pictures of perfection as you know make me sick & wicked'.[42] Satiric realism, on the other hand, she implies, could have an energising and bracing effect – of enhancing the life and health of both writer and reader.

Notes

Place of publication is London, unless otherwise noted.

INTRODUCTION

1 *Thraliana*, ed. Katherine C. Balderston, 2 vols., second edn, 1951, I, p. 574, quoted by Mary Poovey, *The Proper Lady and the Woman Writer: Ideology as Style in the Works of Mary Wollstonecraft, Mary Shelley and Jane Austen*, Chicago, 1984, p.14.

2 *The Brontës: Their Friendships, Lives and Correspondence*, edited by T. J. Wise and J. A. Symington, Oxford, 1932, II, p. 18, III, p. 99.

3 D. H. Lawrence, 'A Propos of *Lady Chatterley's Lover*', *Phoenix II*, edited by Warren Roberts and Harry T. Moore, 1968, p. 513.

4 *Jane Austen: The Critical Heritage*, ed. B. C. Southam, [Vol, I], 1968, p. 117.

5 *Jane Austen: The Critical Heritage, Vol. II*: 1870–1940, ed. B. C. Southam, 1987, p. 323.

6 Walter Raleigh, *The English Novel*, 1894, repr. 1919, p. 263.

7 R. W. Chapman, *Jane Austen: Facts and Problems*, Oxford, 1948, p. 202.

8 *Jane Austen: The Critical Heritage*, II, p. 249.

9 Marilyn Butler, *Jane Austen and the War of Ideas*, Oxford, 1975, is of course the most important work. For Locke, see D. D. Devlin, *Jane Austen and Education*, 1975; for Johnson, see C. S. Lewis, 'A Note on Jane Austen', *Essays in Criticism*, 4, 1956, 59–67, Peter L. De Rose, *Jane Austen and Samuel Johnson*, Washington, 1980, and Claudia L. Johnson, 'The "operations of time, and the changes of the human mind": Jane Austen and Dr Johnson again', *Modern Language Quarterly*, 44, 1983, 23–38; for Burke, see Alistair Duckworth, *The Improvement of the Estate* Baltimore, 1971.

10 Claudia L. Johnson, *Jane Austen, Women, Politics and the Novel*, Chicago and London, 1988, pp. xxiv, xxv; Poovey, *Proper Lady*; the precursor of these is Sandra M. Gilbert and Susan Gubar, *The*

Madwoman in the Attic: *the Woman Writer and the Nineteenth-Century Literary Imagination*, New Haven, 1979.

11 *Minor Works*, Volume the Third, p. 209.

12 This is the argument of Drew Leder, *The Absent Body*, Chicago, 1990.

13 See the contributions to Victor Kestenbaum, ed., *The Humanity of the Ill*: *Phenomenological Perspectives*, Knoxville, 1982.

14 Emmanuel Dreuilhe, *Mortal Embrace*: *Living with AIDS*, New York, 1988, p. 8.

15 See *Medical Knowledge*: *Doubt and Certainty*, Open University, 1985, p. 91 for a brief discussion of Marianne under the heading 'Hysteria Furens'.

16 Arthur Kleinman, *Social Origins of Distress and Disease*: *Depression, Neurasthenia, and Pain in Modern China*, New Haven and London, 1986.

17 Arthur Kleinman, *Patients and Healers in the Context of Culture*, New Haven and London, 1980; *The Illness Narratives*, New York, 1988.

18 Susan Sontag, *Illness as Metaphor*, 1978; *AIDS and its Metaphors*, 1989.

19 Mary C. Rawlinson, 'Medicine's discourse and the practice of Medicine', pp. 69–85 in *The Humanity of the Ill*, ed. Kestenbaum.

20 D. J. Enright, ed., *The Faber Book of Fevers and Frets*, 1989, p. 234.

21 *The Kristeva Reader*, ed. Toril Moi, Oxford, 1986, pp. 227–9.

22 Kleinman, *Social Origins*, p. 171.

23 Helena Michie, *The Flesh Made Word*: *Female Figures and Women's Bodies*, New York, 1987.

24 Quoted in H-K. Trask, *Eros and Power*: *The Promise of Feminist Theory*, Philadelphia, 1986, p. 133.

25 *Emile*, chapter 5, quoted in Thomas Laqueur, 'Orgasm, generation and the politics of reproductive biology', in *The Making of the Modern Body*: *Sexuality and Society in the Nineteenth Century*, ed. Catherine Gallagher and Thomas Laqueur, Berkeley, 1987, p. 19.

26 Denise Riley, 'Bodies, identities, feminisms', in *Am I That Name? Feminism and the Category of 'Women' in History*, 1988, p. 103.

27 Jane Gallop, *Thinking Through the Body*, New York, 1988.

28 Elizabeth Grosz, 'Notes towards a corporeal feminism', *Australian Feminist Studies*, 5, Summer 1987, 3–15, p. 7. See also Moira Gatens, 'Towards a feminist philosophy of the body', pp. 59–70, in *Crossing Boundaries*, ed. Caine et al., Sydney, 1988.

29 Grosz, 'Corporeal feminism', p. 9.

30 Kleinman, *Social Origins*, p.146.

31 H. Plessner, *Laughing and Crying*: *A Study of the Limits of Human*

Behaviour, trans. James Spencer Churchill and Marjorie Grene, Evanston, 1970.

32 Oliver W. Sacks, *Migraine: Understanding a Common Disorder*, revised edition, 1985, p. 203.

33 George Eliot to Frederick Harrison, 15 August 1866, *The George Eliot Letters*, ed. Gordon S. Haight, 7 vols., 1954, IV, p. 300. 'I think aesthetic teaching is the highest of all teaching because it deals with life in its highest complexity. But if it ceases to be purely aesthetic – if it lapses anywhere from the picture to the diagram – it becomes the most offensive of all teaching.'

I: SENSE, SENSIBILITY

1 Marilyn Butler offers still the best account of the novel as a thorough and detailed contrast of competing ideologies. 'The entire action is organised to represent Elinor and Marianne in terms of rival value-systems, which are seen directing their behaviour in the most crucial choices of their lives. It is an arrangement which necessarily directs the reader's attention not towards what they experience, but towards how they cope with experience, away from the experiential to the ethical'. *Jane Austen and the War of Ideas*, Oxford, 1975, p. 184.

2 Mrs Dashwood is not discussed for instance in Cathy N. Davidson and E. M. Broner, eds., *The Lost Tradition: Mother and Daughter in Literature*, New York, 1980.

3 Sandra M. Gilbert and Susan Gubar, *The Madwoman in the Attic*, New Haven and London, 1979, p. 157.

4 'Marianne can never keep long from the instrument, you know, ma'am', said Elinor, endeavouring to smooth away the offence, 'and I do not much wonder at it, for it is the very best toned pianoforté I ever heard.' (145)

5 Joyce McDougall, *Theatres of the Body: A Psychoanalytic Approach to Psychosomatic Illness*, 1989, p. 58.

6 Claudia L. Johnson, *Jane Austen, Women, Politics and the Novel*, Chicago and London, 1988, p. 68.

7 Quoted by Everett Zimmermann in 'Admiring Pope no more than is proper: *Sense and Sensibility*', pp. 112–22, in John Halperin, ed., *Jane Austen, Bicentenary Essays*, Cambridge, 1975, p.113.

8 In the novel 'sensibility' of the conventional type is attributed to, of all people, Robert Ferrars. He affects to sympathise with his brother's misfortune, declaring 'I believe he has as good a heart as any in the kingdom; and I declare and protest to you I never was so shocked in my life, as when it all burst forth' (299).

9 J. F. Burrows, *Computation into Criticism: A Study of Jane Austen's Novels and an Experiment in Method*, Oxford, 1987, p. 147.

10 Tony Tanner, *Jane Austen*, 1988, chapter 3, 'Secrecy and Sickness: Sense and Sensibility', p. 85. My discussion is indebted to Tanner's, and overlaps with it here and at other points.

11 Fanny Burney, *Evelina*, ed. Edward A. Bloom, Oxford, 1982, pp. 258, 265, 268.

12 See also pp. 172, 175. Sander L. Gilman, *Disease and Representation, Images of Illness from Madness to AIDS*, Ithaca and London, 1988, chapter 2.

13 'Upon a low matted seat beside the fire sat lady V--; she was in black; her knees were crossed, and her white but emaciated arms flung on one side over her lap; her hands were clasped together, and her eyes fixed upon the fire; she seemed neither to see any thing around her, but totally absorbed in her own reflections, to have sunk into insensibility'. Lady V-- is the erstwhile Julia, passionate advocate of feeling in Maria Edgeworth's *Letters of Julia and Caroline* (1795), *Tales and Novels by Maria Edgeworth*, 1832–3, XIII, p. 348.

14 Wordsworth's 'The Ruined Cottage' was begun in 1797, but not published until a re-written version made part of the first book of *The Prelude* in 1814. Its central figure is like Marianne in her melancholy decline, for Wordsworth presents her gradually increasing misery as due not simply to grief or loss but, like Marianne's, to an intolerable psychological conflict – in her case, the inability to relinquish the hope that her husband will return (*'The Ruined Cottage' and 'The Pedlar'*, ed. James Butler, *The Cornell Wordsworth*, Ithaca, New York, and Hassocks, 1979). Like *Sense and Sensibility*, also begun in 1797 and not published until the second decade of the nineteenth century, it represents a writer, trained in the eighteenth century, remaking a stereotype of sentimentalism into a cogent study of demoralisation.

15 Tanner, *Jane Austen*, p. 81.

16 Arthur Kleinman, *Social Origins of Distress and Disease: Depression, Neurasthenia and Pain in Modern China*, New Haven and London, 1986, p. 178. Tanner makes a similar point, citing Foucault (Tanner, *Jane Austen*, p. 84).

17 Jocelyn Harris, *Jane Austen's Art of Memory*, Cambridge, 1989, p. 59. Claudia Johnson also notes this effect of the allusion (*Jane Austen, Women, Politics and the Novel*, pp. 55–6).

18 Samuel Richardson, *Clarissa, or, the history of a young lady*, ed. John Butt, 4 vols, 1962, IV, Letter LXXXV, pp. 200–1.

19 Margaret Anne Doody, *A Natural Passion: A Study of the Novels of*

Samuel Richardson, Oxford, 1974, p. 171. To underline the point, the death-bed of Mrs Sinclair the bawd is given with ferocious physicality: 'her misfortune has not at all sunk, but rather, as I thought, increased her flesh; rage and violence perhaps swelling her muscular features'. The details of her injuries and mortification are dwelt on with macabre humour (IV, Letter CXXXVIII, pp. 382, 385). Even Lovelace's delirious grief is accompanied by 'starving diet, by profuse phlebotomy, by flaying blisters, eye-let hole cupping ... gallipots, boluses and cephalitic draughts' (IV, Letter CLI, p. 442).

20 Doody, *A Natural Passion*, p. 171.

21 Rudolph M. Bell, *Holy Anorexia*, Chicago and London, 1985, *passim*. This is not in conflict with the view of Austen's contemporaries like Mary Hays and Mary Wollstonecraft, as reported by Claudia Johnson, that 'Clarissa's death is really a twisted testimonial to male power. It reflects the author's conviction that a paragon among women has no reason for being once she becomes damaged property, that only a lesser woman would even want to survive a fate worse than death, which at once deprives her of her virginity, her integrity, and her life force' (Claudia L. Johnson, 'A "sweet face as white as death" : Jane Austen and the politics of female sensibility', *Novel*, 22, 1989, 159–74, p.162).

22 In 'A "sweet face as white as death" ' Claudia L. Johnson gives a list, which includes Inchbald's *A Simple Story*, (1791), Opie's *Adeline Mowbray*, (1805), and Rowson's *Charlotte Temple* (1791).

23 William Buchan, M.D., *Domestic Medicine: or, a Treatise on the Prevention and Cure of Diseases by Regimen and Simple Medicines*, second edition, 1772, reprinted New York and London, 1985, chapter XIII, p.174. In 'Jane Austen: a romantic, systematic, or realistic approach to medicine?', *Studies in Eighteenth Century Culture*, 10, ed. Harry C. Payne, vol X, 1981, pp. 313–26, Toby A. Olshin notes that the nosology of diseases was established by Herman Boerhaave and later elaborated by John Huxham. 'Fever was seen as an illness, not a symptom, and its "putrid" characteristic indicated that it was severe and contagious' (p. 316). Olshin interprets the sequence as an interplay of 'romantic' and 'systematic' attitudes towards Marianne's illness 'in which their interplay serves to diminish the authority of the medical profession'.

24 Buchan, *Domestic Medicine*, p. 265.

25 Buchan, *Domestic Medicine*, p. 175; see also p. 195.

26 Buchan, *Domestic Medicine*, chapter IX, 'Of Infection', pp. 132–38. Buchan describes three types of fever, 'slow or nervous', 'malignant, putrid or spotted' and 'miliary'. He also notes that 'It

sometimes happens, however, that the inflammatory, nervous, and putrid symptoms are so blended together, as to render it very difficult to determine to which class the fever belongs' (p. 248; see also p. 266). See C. J. Lawrence, 'William Buchan: medicine laid open', *Medical History*, 19, 1975, 20–35, especially pp. 25–6.

27 Sir John Pringle, *Observations on the Diseases of the Army* (1752) fifth edition, 1765, p. 82.

28 Buchan, *Domestic Medicine*, p. 132.

29 Johnson, *Jane Austen, Women, Politics and the Novel*, pp. 65–8.

30 A. Walton Litz, *Jane Austen: A Study of Her Artistic Development*, 1965, p. 82.

31 Q. D Leavis notes that in *Sense and Sensibility* 'the masterpiece of meanness is the dialogue between John Dashwood and his wife: this is comedy in the tradition of Ben Jonson', *Collected Essays*, 2 vols., ed. G. Singh, Cambridge, 1983, I, *The Englishness of the English Novel*, p. 156.

32 An exception would be Mrs Gardiner's appraisal of Darcy (PP 258): 'He has not an ill-natured look. On the contrary, there is something pleasing about his mouth when he speaks. And there is something of dignity in his countenance, that would not give one an unfavourable idea of his heart.'

33 I am thus using (and reversing in this instance) the argument of Eve Kosofsky Sedgwick, *Between Men: English Literature and Male Homosocial Desire*, Columbia, New York, 1985. See especially chapter 1, 'Gender asymmetry and erotic triangles', pp. 21–7.

2 'ELOQUENT BLOOD'

1 *Letters*, p. 484 (13 March 1817).

2 'The heart of the condition is apprehension lest attachment figures be inaccessible and/or unresponsive. For these reasons, and especially because it can be expected to enlist sympathy, anxious attachment is the term to be used. It respects the person's natural desire for a close relationship with an attachment figure, and recognises that he is apprehensive lest the relationship be ended' (*Attachment and Loss*, 3 vols., vol. II, *Separation, Anxiety and Anger*, 1973, p. 213). For an alternative reading of Fanny's psychology see Bernard J. Paris, *Character and Conflict in Jane Austen's Novels, a Psychological Approach*, Brighton, 1979, chapter 2, pp. 22–63.

3 *Jane Austen: The Critical Heritage*, ed. B. C. Southam, vol. I, 1968, p. 101.

4 My discussion here is indebted to Laura G. Mooneyham, *Romance, Language and Education in Jane Austen's Novels*, 1988, pp. 78–9.

5 See, for example, 'There was a charm, perhaps, in [Edmund's] sincerity, his steadiness, his integrity which Miss Crawford might be equal to feel, though not equal to discuss with herself' (65), or the remark that Henry's absence at Everingham should 'have convinced the gentleman that he ought to keep longer away, had he been more in the habit of examining his own motives' (114) and Edmund's comment in the chapel at Sotherton on 'the mind which does not struggle against itself'. (88)

6 'Fanny in the first part of the novel is insistently presented as the detached observer', remarks D. D. Devlin, citing this episode. *Jane Austen and Education*, 1975, p. 88. My discussion, and indeed much else in this chapter, is indebted to David Ellis, 'The irony of *Mansfield Park*', *The Critical Review* 12, 1969, 107–19. See also M. W. Fosbery, 'Jane Austen's Fanny Price', *The Cambridge Quarterly*, 8, 2, 1978, 113–28, especially pp. 115–16. I am more generally indebted to Robin Grove, 'Jane Austen's free enquiry: *Mansfield Park*', *The Critical Review*, 25, 1983, 132–150, reprinted in Harold Bloom, ed., *Jane Austen* (Modern Critical Views series), New York, 1986.

7 Vladimir Nabokov, *Lectures on Literature*, ed. Fredson Bowers, 2 vols., New York and London, 1975, I, p. 88.

8 Dr John Gregory, *A Father's Legacy to his Daughters*, 1822, p. 43.

9 Arthur Kleinman, *Social Origins of Distress and Disease: Depression, Neurasthenia and Pain in Modern China*, New Haven and London, 1986, p. 174.

10 Arthur Kleinman, *Rethinking Psychiatry*, 1989, p. 119.

11 Mrs [Elizabeth] Inchbald, 'Preface' to *Lovers Vows*, reprinted in *Mansfield Park*, ed. R. W. Chapman, third edition, Oxford, 1934, p. 478.

12 Claudia Johnson notes this resemblance, *Jane Austen, Women, Politics, and the Novel*, Chicago and London, 1988, p. 110.

13 *Mansfield Park*, ed. Chapman, p. [474].

14 Marilyn Butler, *Jane Austen and the War of Ideas*, Oxford, 1975, p. 248.

15 Moira Gatens, 'A critique of the sex/gender distinction', in J. Allen and P. Patten, eds., *Beyond Marx: Interventions after Marx*, Sydney, 1983.

16 Elizabeth Grosz, 'Inscriptions and body maps: representation and the corporeal', pp. 62–74, in *Feminine/Masculine and Representation*, ed. Terry Threadgold and Anne Cranny-Francis, Sydney, 1990, p. 70.

17 'Her complexion was of the finest texture. It might with truth be said that her eloquent blood spoke through her modest cheek'

('Biographical Notice of the Author' in *Northanger Abbey and Persuasion*, ed. Chapman, p. 5).

18 H. Plessner, *Laughing and Crying: A Study of the Limits of Human Behaviour*, trans. James Spencer Churchill and Marjorie Grene, Evanston, 1970.

19 John Mullan, *Sentiment and Sociability: The Language of Feeling in the Eighteenth Century*, Oxford, 1990, p. 224.

20 Mullan, *Sentiment and Sociability*, p. 88.

21 Terry Castle, *Masquerade and Civilisation: the Carnivalesque in Eighteenth-Century English Culture and Fiction*, 1986, p. 285, citing Patricia Meyer Spacks, *Imagining a Self: Autobiography and Novel in Eighteenth-Century England*, Cambridge, Mass., 1976.

22 Mrs Inchbald, *A Simple Story*, with an introduction by G. L. Strachey, Oxford, 1908, p. 97.

23 Fanny Burney, *Camilla: or, a Picture of Youth*, ed. Edward A. Bloom and Lillian D. Bloom, Oxford, 1972, p. 640.

24 Burney, *Camilla*, pp. 640–1.

25 For instance, Jocelyn Harris, *Jane Austen's Art of Memory*, Cambridge, 1989, p. 145.

26 Ruth Bernard Yeazell, 'The boundaries of Mansfield Park', *Representations*, 7, Summer 1984, 133–52, p. 145.

27 Lionel Trilling, '*Mansfield Park*' reprinted in Ian Watt, ed., *Jane Austen, A Collection of Critical Essays*, Englewood Cliffs, N. J., 1963, pp. 124–40, p. 140.

28 Sandra M. Gilbert and Susan Gubar, *The Madwoman in the Attic*, New Haven and London, 1979, p. 165.

29 J. H. Hubback and Edith C. Hubback, *Jane Austen's Sailor Brothers*, 1906, p. 7.

30 Harold Bloom, 'Introduction' *Jane Austen* (Modern Critical Views series), New York, 1986, p. 7.

31 Tony Tanner, *Jane Austen*, London, 1986, pp.171–2. Alasdair MacIntyre reads Fanny as an instance of Austen's celebration of the virtue of constancy: 'Fanny is charmless; she has only the virtues, the genuine virtues, to protect her, and when she disobeys her guardian, Sir Thomas Bertram, and refuses marriage to Henry Crawford it can only be because of what constancy requires. In so refusing she places the danger of losing her soul before the reward of gaining what for her would be a whole world' (*After Virtue*, Notre Dame, Indiana, 1981, p. 225).

32 Nina Auerbach, 'Jane Austen's dangerous charm, feeling as one ought about Fanny Price', in *Jane Austen: New Perspectives, Women and Literature* (New Series), vol. 3, ed. Janet Todd, New York and London, 1983, pp. 208–21, pp. 210, 212, 218. Julia Prewitt Brown,

Jane Austen's Novels: Social Change and Literary Form, Cambridge Mass., and London, 1979, offers a similar conclusion: 'Fanny and Edmund finally emerge as monsters ... [*Mansfield Park*'s] profundity is malicious ... ' (p. 100).

33 Hélène Cixous and Catherine Clément, *The Newly Born Woman*, translation by Betsy King of *La Jeune Née* (1975), Manchester, 1986, pp. 154, 155. See also *In Dora's Case: Freud – Feminism – Hysteria*, ed. Charles Bernheimer and Claire Kahane, 1985, especially the chapter by Jane Gallop, 'Keys to Dora', pp. 200–20.

34 Carol Pateman, *The Sexual Contract*, Oxford, 1989, p. 206.

35 Samuel Johnson, *The Rambler*, ed. W. J. Bate and Albrecht B. Strauss, *The Yale Edition of the Works of Samuel Johnson*, New Haven and London, 1969, IV. pp. 234–5.

36 George Eliot, *Felix Holt, the Radical* [1866], Edinburgh and London, n.d. p. 21.

37 Mary Poovey, *The Proper Lady and the Woman Writer*, Chicago, 1984, p. 206.

38 William James, *Principles of Psychiatry*, Harvard, 1981, II, p. 1068.

39 *The Standard Edition of the Complete Psychological Works of Sigmund Freud*, trans. J. Strachey and A. Freud, 1963, XVI, pp. 295–6.

40 This is similar to Marilyn Butler's conclusion that 'the exemplary heroine, who speaks to the intellect, and the suffering heroine, who appeals to the emotions, are certainly not easy characters to blend together' (*Jane Austen and the War of Ideas*, pp. 248–9).

41 See Avrom Fleishman, *A Reading of 'Mansfield Park': An Essay in Critical Synthesis*, Minneapolis, 1967, p. 71, and Jane McDonnell, '"A little spirit of independence" : sexual politics and the bildungsroman in *Mansfield Park*', *Novel*, 17, 1984, 197–214.

42 Irwin Ihrenpreis, *Acts of Implication: Suggestion and Covert Meaning in the Works of Dryden, Swift, Pope and Austen*, Berkeley, L. A., and London, 1980, p. 126.

43 Mary Wollstonecraft, *A Vindication of the Rights of Woman* [1792], quoted in Alison G. Sulloway, *Jane Austen and the Province of Womanhood*, Philadelphia, 1989, p. 145.

44 Victor Turner, *The Forest of Symbols: Aspects of Ndembu Ritual*, Ithaca, 1967, chapter IV, 'Betwixt and between: the liminal period in *Rites de Passage*'.

45 Samuel Johnson, 'Pope', in *The Works of Samuel Johnson, LL.D.*, 1820, Vol. XI, *The Lives of the Poets*, p. 156.

46 Alistair M. Duckworth, *The Improvement of the Estate: a Study of Jane Austen's Novels*, Baltimore and London, 1971, p. 78. Fanny, in Duckworth's exclusively ethical reading – he writes of 'the purity of her motivations' – is 'the true trustee of [the house's] traditions'

(p. 72). Avrom Fleishman sees one of the novel's 'central concerns' as 'the selection of Fanny Price as the fit inheritor of a dominant position in the house', *A Reading of 'Mansfield Park'*, p. 59. There are many other examples: Paul Pickrel argues that 'Mansfield makes Fanny worthy of being its spiritual heir at the same time that she makes it worth inheriting ... under her influence the house becomes good as it has always been beautiful', ('Lionel Trilling and *Mansfield Park*', *Studies in English Literature*, 1987, 607- 21, p. 618). Edward W. Said has Fanny as 'the mistress of Mansfield Park' and 'Edmund, the second son, its master', in 'Jane Austen and Empire', *Raymond Williams: Critical Perspectives*, ed. T. Eagleton, Cambridge, 1988, 150–64, pp. 154, 161. F. T. Flahiff, 'Place and replacement in *Mansfield Park*', *University of Toronto Quarterly, A Canadian Journal of the Humanities*, 54, 1985, 221–33, takes issue with such readings (pp. 225–6, 228).

47 Kenneth L. Moler, '"Only connect" : emotional strength and health in *Mansfield Park*', *English Studies*, 64, 1983, 144–52, p. 152.

3 EMMA

1 On education in *Emma*: Mark Schorer, 'The Humiliation of Emma Woodhouse', *The Literary Review*, 2, 4, 1959, 547–563, reprinted in Ian Watt, ed., *Jane Austen: A collection of Critical Essays*, Englewood Cliffs, 1963; R. E. Hughes, 'The education of Emma Woodhouse', *Nineteenth Century Fiction*, 16, 1962; W. J. Harvey, 'The plot of *Emma*', *Essays in Criticism*, 17, 1967, 48–63; Marilyn Butler, '*Emma*', in *Jane Austen and the War of Ideas*, Oxford, 1975, pp. 250–74. On authoring: Claudia L. Johnson, '*Emma*; "Woman, lovely woman, reigns alone" ', in *Jane Austen, Women, Politics and the Novel*', Chicago and London, 1988, pp. 121–43. On reading: Adena Rosmarin, '"Misreading" *Emma*: the powers and perfidies of interpretive history', *English Literary History*, 51, 1984, 315–42; Nancy Armstrong, *Desire and Domestic Fiction: A Political History of the Novel*, New York and Oxford, 1987, pp. 134–60; John A. Düssinger, *In the Pride of the Moment; Encounters in Jane Austen's World*, Columbus, Ohio, 1990, *passim*. On perception: G. Armour Craig, 'Jane Austen's *Emma*: the truths and disguises of human disclosure' in *In Defense of Reading*, ed. R. Brower and R. Poirier, New York, 1962. On epistemology: John P. McGowan, 'Knowledge/power and Jane Austen's radicalism', *Mosaic: a Journal for the Interdisciplinary Study of Literature*, 18, 1985, 1–15. On imagination: Stuart Tave, *Some Words of Jane Austen*, Chicago, 1973, 205–55; Michael Williams, 'Emma, mystery and imagin-

ation' in *Jane Austen: Six Novels and Their Methods*, 1986, pp. 117–53.

2 J. R. Watson, 'Mr Perry's patients: a view of *Emma*', *Essays in Criticism*, 20, 1970, 334–43. See also Albert E. Wilhelm, 'Three word clusters in *Emma*,' *Studies in the Novel*, 7, 1975, 49–60.

3 F. B. Smith, *The People's Health*, 1977, p. 115: 'The pregnant lady's dealings with her doctor began during the fourth or fifth month. In the first half of the century her closest doctor would be the local gentlemanly practitioner calling himself a "pure" surgeon, or a surgeon apothecary like Mr Perry of Highbury in *Emma*'.

4 Mr Weston, who has bided his time before purchasing Randalls, sees the social implications: 'Perry's setting up his carriage! and his wife's persuading him to do it, out of care for his health – just what will happen, I have no doubt, some time or other; only a little premature' (345).

5 Rosmarin, '"Misreading" *Emma*', p. 330.

6 Watson, 'Mr Perry's patients', p. 334.

7 Arthur Kleinman, *Rethinking Psychiatry: From Cultural Category to Personal Experience*, New York and London, 1988, p. 64.

8 *The Diary and Letters of Madame D'Arblay*, edited by her niece, 7 vols., 1854, IV, p. 237 (November 6, 1788).

9 W. F. Bynum, 'The nervous patient in eighteenth- and nine-teenth-century Britain: the psychiatric origins of British neur-ology', in Bynum, Porter and Shepherd, eds., *The Anatomy of Madness: Essays in the History of Psychiatry*, 2 vols., London and New York, 1985, I, *People and Ideas*, pp. 89–102, p. 91.

10 Bynum, 'Nervous Patient', p. 91.

11 George Cheyne, *The English Malady, or a treatise of nervous diseases of all kinds*, (1733), fifth edition, 1735, p. 159.

12 Robert Whytt, *Physiological Essays, II; Observations on the sensibility and irritability of the parts of men and other animals, occasioned by Dr Haller's late treatise on these subjects*, Edinburgh, 1756. See R. K. French, *Robert Whytt: The Soul and Medicine*, 1969, *passim*, and George S. Rousseau, 'Nerves, spirits and fibres: towards defining the origins of sensibility', *The Blue Guitar*, 2, 1976, 125–53.

13 Thomas Trotter, M. D., *A View of the Nervous Temperament*, 1807, p. xvi. The passage is a quotation from Trotter's previous *Medicina Nautica*, vol.III.

14 Trotter, *Nervous Temperament*, pp. 246, 232.

15 Trotter, *Nervous Temperament*, p. 249.

16 Trotter, *Nervous Temperament*, p. 79.

17 I owe this suggestion to an unpublished paper by Professor Gerda Seaman, 'Better sick than sorry: Mrs Mitty meets Lady Lazarus'.

18 Bynum, 'Nervous Patient' p. 90.

19 Alexander Pope, *The Works*, 6 vols, Edinburgh, 1764, II, 'Moral Essay II, Epistle to a Lady', ll. 42–3.

20 Williams, *Six Novels and Their Methods*, pp. 132–3. Williams points out that the 'ogress' might be 'merely the *ad hoc* creation of her nephew's imagination' (p.132).

21 Sandra M. Gilbert and Susan Gubar, *The Madwoman in the Attic*, New Haven and London, 1979, p.173.

22 Watson, 'Mr Perry's patients', p. 339.

23 James Thompson, *Between Self and World: The Novels of Jane Austen*, Pennsylvania State, 1988, p. 168. The term 'idiot' was used by Marvin Mudrick.

24 Avrom Fleishman, 'Two faces of Emma', in *Jane Austen: New Perspectives*, *Women and Literature*, (New Series) vol. 3, edited by Janet Todd, New York and London, 1983, pp. 248–56, p. 248. Fleishman intends this characterisation, of course, to be absurd.

25 I owe this suggestion, as well as much more in this discussion of *Emma*, to my colleague Dr Kay Torney. John A. Düssinger, *In the Pride of the Moment: Encounters in Jane Austen's World*, Columbus, Ohio, 1990, pp. 162–68, notes that Mr Woodhouse fails to decipher the erotic riddle ('Kitty, a fair but frozen maid'), and that this 'appears to conceal a sexual problem of some kind': 'The cost of denying the body is seen not only in his mental block towards anything erotic but more generally in a failure of desire … The Weston's wedding cake was poison to Mr Woodhouse for reasons other than its enzymes' (p. 167).

26 Rudolph E. Siegel, *Galen's System of Physiology and Medicine*, Basel and New York, 1968, p. 184.

27 Maria Edgeworth, *Tales and Novels by Maria Edgeworth*, 1832–33, II, Moral Tales I, 'Forester' p. 35 [1816].

28 Virginia Woolf, 'On being ill' [1930], *The Complete Essays of Virginia Woolf*, 4 Vols., 1969, IV, Hogarth Press, 1967, pp. 193–202.

29 Wayne C. Booth, *The Rhetoric of Fiction*, Chicago and London, 1961, p. 257; Yasmine Gooneratne, *Jane Austen*, Cambridge, 1970, pp. 142–4.

30 Booth, *Rhetoric*, p. 258.

31 *The Philosophical Works of David Hume*, 4 vols., Edinburgh, 1825, IV, p. 345. I take this quotation from S. L. Goldberg's article, 'Agents and lives: making moral sense of people', (*The Critical Review*, 25, 1983, 26–49). My whole discussion of *Emma* (as well as some of my terms), is indebted to the argument of this article, but the claim that 'even subtle moralists like Dr Johnson and Jane

Austen seem ... distant from us in the clear, sharp (and ultimately comfortable) outlines of their moral categories and language' (p. 36) is one I take issue with.

32 Simone de Beauvoir, *The Second Sex* (1949) translated and edited by H. M. Parshley, reprinted Harmondsworth, 1986, pp. 190–92.

33 Susan Sontag, *AIDS and its Metaphors*, 1989, p. 12. See also Sontag's *Illness as Metaphor*, 1979, *passim*.

34 As with Harriet's aborted visit to the Martins: 'Emma could not but picture it all, and feel how justly they might resent, how naturally Harriet must suffer' (p.187). Or her solemn statement '"I shall never marry"': 'Emma then looked up, and immediately saw how it was' (p. 341).

35 L. R. Leavis and J. M. Blom, 'A return to Jane Austen's novels', *English Studies, A Journal of English Language and Literature*, 62, 1981, 313–23, p. 322 note this 'most painful piece of dramatic irony'.

36 Mary Lascelles, *Jane Austen and her Art*, Oxford, 1939, reprinted 1965, p. 176.

37 Arthur Kleinman, *Social Origins of Distress and Disease: Depression, Neurasthenia and Pain in Modern China*, New Haven and London, 1986, *passim*.

38 Kleinman, *Social Origins*, p. 153.

39 Toby A. Olshin in 'Jane Austen: A romantic, systematic or realist approach to medicine?', *Studies in Eighteenth Century Culture*, vol X, ed. Harry C. Payne, 1981, pp. 313- 26, includes Mr Perry in his general condemnation of 'the blind helplessness of the medical profession' in Jane Austen's novels (p. 318). Whilst it is true that Mr Perry is shown to have very few specific remedies (he certainly cannot cure Harriet's putrid sore throat) one may doubt whether, even if persuaded to set up his carriage for his own health, Mr Perry is 'a figure of mockery in *Emma*' (p. 322).

40 See Elaine Showalter, *The Female Malady*, 1989, *passim*.

41 R. W. Chapman, *Jane Austen: Facts and Problems*, Oxford, 1951, p. 203.

42 In 'The feminist depreciation of Austen: a polemical reading', *Novel*, 1990, 303–13, Julia Prewitt Brown, reviewing Claudia L. Johnson's *Jane Austen: Women, Politics, and the Novel*, assembles and takes issue with a number of such formulations (pp. 305–7).

43 Nancy Armstrong, *Desire and Domestic Fiction: A Political History of the Novel*, New York and Oxford, 1987, p. 152.

44 D. A. Miller, 'The late Jane Austen', *Raritan*, 10, 1990, 55–79, p. 59.

45 My 'perhaps' is a recognition of the difficulties surrounding this term in French and English feminist criticism, which are discussed

in Jane Gallop, 'Beyond the *jouissance* principle', pp. 119–24, *Thinking Through the Body*, New York, 1988. The English word 'jouissance' is defined in the OED firstly as 'the possession and use of something affording advantage', and secondly as 'pleasure, delight', etc.

46 Georges Canguilhem, *On the Normal and the Pathological*, trans. Carolyn R. Fawcett, Dortrecht, Boston, London, 1978. This is a translation of the second edition (1972) of *Le normal et le pathologique*, of which the first section is an essay published in 1943, and the second a group of three essays written between 1963 and 1966. The introduction by Michel Foucault, in which he remarks that 'In the extreme, life is what is capable of error ... life result[s] with man, in a living being who is never completely at home, a living being dedicated to "error" and destined, in the end, to "error"', (p.xix) is also relevant. Foucault calls Canguilhem's role in contemporary discussions of science 'rather hidden' (p. xiii).

47 Canguilhem, *On the Normal and the Pathological*, p. 106.

48 Canguilhem, *On the Normal and the Pathological*, p. 108.

49 Canguilhem, *On the Normal and the Pathological*, pp. 115–6.

50 Canguilhem, *On the Normal and the Pathological*, p. 117.

51 Canguilhem, *On the Normal and the Pathological*, p. 143.

52 Canguilhem, *On the Normal and the Pathological*, p. 110.

4 *PERSUASION*

1 See, for example: Laura G. Mooneyham, 'Loss and the Language of Restitution in *Persuasion*' in *Romance, Language and Education in Jane Austen's Novels*, 1988, pp. 146–75; Julia Prewitt Brown, *Jane Austen's Novels: Social Change and Literary Form*, Cambridge, Mass., and London, 1979, p. 148 (Brown notes (pp.179–80) the number of widows and widowers); Alistair M. Duckworth, *The Improvement of the Estate*, Baltimore and London, 1971, p. 180.

2 David Monaghan, *Jane Austen: Structure and Social Vision*, 1980, p. 143.

3 Monaghan, *Austen*, p. 157

4 Mary Poovey, *The Proper Lady and the Woman Writer*, Chicago, 1984, p. 224.

5 Tony Tanner, *Jane Austen*, 1988, p. 211.

6 Tanner, *Jane Austen* p. 225.

7 Penny Gay, 'A changing view: Jane Austen's landscapes', *Sydney Studies in English*, 15, 1989–90, p. 62. See also John Wiltshire, 'A romantic *Persuasion*?', *The Critical Review*, 14, 1971, 3–16.

8 David Spring, 'Interpreters of Jane Austen's social world, literary

critics and historians', in *Jane Austen, New Perspectives, Women and Literature*, (New Series), 3, ed. Janet Todd, New York and London, 1983, pp. 53–69. I have used examples of the same fallacies published later than the examples discussed in Spring's article. See also Daniel P. Gunn, 'In the vicinity of Winthrop: ideological rhetoric in *Persuasion*', *Nineteenth Century Literature*, 41, 1987, 403–18.

9 R. S. Neale, *Bath, 1680–1850, A Social History*, 1981, pp. 193–6.

10 Neale, *Bath*, pp. 207, 205.

11 Neale, *Bath*, p. 246.

12 Patricia Brückman, 'Sir Walter Elliot's Bath address', *Modern Philology*, 80, 1, 1982, 56–60, notes the precision of the novel's assignment of lodgings to its various characters and especially the location of Sir Walter in Camden Place, a never completed, architecturally flawed Crescent. See also Sir Nikolaus Pevsner, 'The architectural setting of Jane Austen's novels', *Journal of the Warburg and Courtauld Institutes* 31, 1968, 404–22.

13 Quoted in Roy Porter, *English Society in the Eighteenth Century*, Harmondsworth, 1982, p. 245.

14 Freud described the primary narcissism parents project upon their infant child: 'Illness, death, renunciation of enjoyment, restrictions on his own will, shall not touch him; the laws of nature and society shall be abrogated in his favour'. Sigmund Freud, 'On Narcissism' (1912) in the *Standard Edition of the Works*, ed. J. Strachey et al, 1957, reprinted 1986, XIV, p. 91.

15 John Caspar Lavater, *Essays on Physiognomy for the promotion of the knowledge and the love of mankind*, trans. Thomas Holcroft, second edition, 4 vols., 1804, I, p. 175. For Lavater's influence see Graeme Tytler, *Physiognomy in the European Novel: Faces and Fortunes*, Princeton, New Jersey, 1982.

16 Barbara M Stafford, John La Puma and David L. Schiedermayer, 'One face of beauty, one picture of health: the hidden aesthetic of medical practice', *Journal of Medicine and Philosophy*, 1989, 213–30. The authors note that Lavater's contemporary, Georg Christoph Lichenberg, opposed his theories, and suggest that 'Lichenberg's most profound insight was that, to be in relationship with anything, be it another person or the world, is by definition to be constantly deformed ... Life erodes geometrical perfection; it distorts edges and roughens contours ... a calibrated central form ... can be maintained only in narcissistic isolation' (p. 224).

17 Lavater, *Essays on Physiognomy*, I, p. 19.

18 A. Walton Litz, '*Persuasion*: forms of estrangement' in J. Halperin, ed., *Jane Austen, Bicentenary Essays*, Cambridge, 1975, p. 225.

19 Litz, 'Forms of estrangement', pp. 223, 228.
20 I am indebted to my colleague Ann Blake for this phrase, as well as much else in this discussion of suffering in *Persuasion*.
21 Claire Fagin and Donna Diers, 'Nursing as metaphor', *American Journal of Nursing*, September 1983, 1362. I am indebted to Meg McGaskill for this reference.
22 Thomas Gisborne, *The Duties of the Female Sex*, second edition, 1797, pp. 11, 12.
23 Duckworth, *Improvement of the Estate*, p. 188.
24 Quoted from his translation of the *Odyssey* by Pope in a letter of 7 Nov. 1725. *The Oxford Book of Friendship*, edited by D. J. Enright and David Rawlinson, Oxford, 1991, p. 192.
25 Rev. Henry Thomas Austen, A. M., *Lectures upon Some Important Passages in the Book of Genesis delivered in the Chapel of the British Minister at Berlin in the year 1818*, 1820, p. 207.
26 Michel Foucault, *The Care of the Self*, (*The History of Sexuality*, Vol. 3), trans. Robert Hurley, Harmondsworth, 1990, p. 42.
27 Foucault, *The Care of the Self*, p. 60.
28 Foucault, *The Care of the Self*, p. 64.
29 A. Walton Litz, *Jane Austen, A Study of her Artistic Development*, 1965, pp. 153, 154.
30 *Boswell's Life of Johnson*, ed. G. B. Hill, revised by L. F. Powell, 6 vols, second edition, 1964, reprinted 1975, I, p. 215.
31 Foucault, *The Care of the Self*, pp. 36–68.
32 Mooneyham, *Romance, Language and Education*. p. 156.
33 Duckworth, *Improvement of the Estate*, p. 192.
34 John Davie, 'Introduction' to World's Classics edition of *Persuasion*, Oxford, 1980, p. x.
35 Mary Lascelles, *Jane Austen and her Art* (1939), Oxford, 1969, p. 78.
36 Tanner, *Jane Austen*, p. 238.
37 'What [Wentworth] does not know is that Louisa's firm powers of mind have been used to eliminate her sister from the competition and leave Captain Wentworth all for herself' (Stuart M. Tave, *Some Words of Jane Austen*, Chicago, 1973, p. 265). Claudia Johnson writes similarly, acknowledging Tave, that 'Louisa, after all, did not disinterestedly supplement her sister's failing powers of mind with the strength of her own. Instead, she took advantage of her sister's persuadability in order to clear the field for Wentworth and herself' (*Jane Austen, Women, Politics and the Novel*, Chicago 1988, p. 156). Austen's stress is repeatedly on 'that seemingly perfect good understanding and agreement together, that good humoured mutual affection' of the sisters (41): Anne Elliot 'did not attribute

guile to any' (82). Anne may of course be mistaken, but the textual basis for assigning guilt, of whatever kind, to Louisa is skimpy.

38 Paul Zeitlow, 'Luck and fortuitous circumstance in *Persuasion*: two interpretations', *English Literary History*, 32, June 1965, 179–95, remains the classic reference for this aspect of the novel.

39 Sigmund Freud, *The Psychopathology of Everyday Life* (1901), in *Standard Edition of the Works*, ed. J. Strachey et al, 1957 reprinted 1986, VI, pp. 174–5.

40 C. S. Lewis remarked on 'the Johnsonian cadence of a sentence which expresses a view that Johnson in one of his countless moods might have supported' ('A note on Jane Austen', *Essays in Criticism*, 4, 1954, 364). Compare, for example, 'that anxious inquietude which is justly chargeable with distrust of heaven' (*Rambler* 2).

41 Judy van Sickle Johnson, 'The bodily frame: learning romance in *Persuasion*', *Nineteenth Century Fiction*, 38, June 1983, 43–61.

42 Tanner, *Jane Austen*, quotes (p. 237) Nora Crook in *The Times Literary Supplement*, 7 Oct. 1983.

43 D. A. Miller, 'The late Jane Austen', *Raritan*, 10, 1990, 55–79, includes a witty analysis of this passage, pp. 60–2.

5 *SANDITON*

1 Park Honan, *Jane Austen: Her Life*, 1987, p. 381.

2 Tony Tanner, *Jane Austen*, 1986, p. 261.

3 *Sanditon, an unfinished novel by Jane Austen, reproduced in facsimile from the manuscript in the possession of King's College, Cambridge*, introduction by B. C. Southam, Oxford and London, 1975. References to this edition will be included in the text.

4 J. E. Austen-Leigh, *Memoir of Jane Austen*, with an introduction by R. W. Chapman, Oxford, 1926, reprinted 1967, p. 192.

5 B. C. Southam, *Jane Austen's Literary Manuscripts: A Study of the Novelist's Development Through the Surviving Papers*, Oxford, 1964.

6 A. Walton Litz, *Jane Austen: A Study of her Artistic Development*, 1965, pp. 164, 165. See also Douglas Bush, *Jane Austen*, 1975, p. 187.

7 Honan, *Jane Austen*, p. 387.

8 D. A. Miller, 'The late Jane Austen', *Raritan*, 10, 1990, 55–79, pp. 55–6.

9 Geoffrey Gorer, 'Poor Honey: some notes on Jane Austen and her mother' (1957) pp. 248–64 in *The Danger of Equality*, 1966. John Halperin notes the connection between the satire on hypochondria in *Sanditon* and Austen's references to her mother in *The Life of Jane Austen*, Baltimore, 1984, p. 328.

10 *Jane Austen's Letters*, collected and edited by R.W. Chapman, Oxford, second edition 1952, reprinted 1969, p. 39.

11 *Letters*, p. 57.

12 *Letters*, p. 329.

13 Austen-Leigh, *Memoir*, pp. 165–6.

14 A. C. Bradley, 'Jane Austen' (1911) in *A Miscellany*, 1929, p. 43.

15 *Letters*, p. 24.

16 *Letters*, p. 304.

17 *Letters*, p. 487.

18 'The disease of activity: *Sanditon*', pp. 250–85 in Tanner's *Jane Austen*.

19 *The History of Rasselas, Prince of Abyssinia* (1759), ed. J. P. Hardy, Oxford, 1968, p. 102.

20 *The Gentleman's Magazine*, 86, Jan. 1816, 17. The Infirmary had recently been extended: the *Gentleman's* had printed an earlier engraving in 1797.

21 Antony Relhan, MD, *A Short History of Brighthelmston, with remarks on its air, and an analysis of its waters, particularly of an uncommon mineral one, long discovered, though but lately used,* 1761, p. 19.

22 Relhan, *A Short History*, pp. 20, 34.

23 Honan, *Jane Austen*, p. 388.

24 William Falconer, MD FRS, *A Dissertation on the Influence of the passions upon disorders of the body*, 1788, p. 23.

25 John Haygarth, MD, *Of the Imagination, as a cause and as a cure of disorders of the body*, 1800.

26 William Buchan, *Domestic Medicine, or a Treatise on the Prevention and Cure of Diseases by Regimen and Simple Medicines*, second edition, 1772, reprinted New York and London, 1985. Buchan recommends that for cases of consumption 'Asses Milk ought to be drunk, if possible, in its natural warmth, and, by a grown person, in the quantity of half an English pint at a time' (p. 225), though he notes 'it cannot always be obtained' (p. 224).

27 R.W. Chapman, *Jane Austen, Facts and Problems*, Oxford, 1948, p. 208.

28 B. C. Southam, *Jane Austen's Literary Manuscripts*, Oxford, 1964, p. 130.

29 *Memoir*, p. 204.

30 *Letters*, pp. 327–8: 'The poor Girls & their Teeth! – I have not mentioned them yet, but we were a whole hour at Spence's, & Lizzy's were filed & lamented over again & poor Marianne had two taken out after all, the two just beyond the Eye teeth, to make room for those in front. – When her doom was fixed, Fanny Lizzie & I walked into the next room, where we heard each of the two

sharp hasty Screams ... It was a disagreable Hour' (16 September 1813).

31 Marilyn Butler, *Jane Austen and the War of Ideas*, Oxford, 1975, p. 288.

32 Samuel Richardson, *Clarissa; or, the History of a Young Lady* (1747–8) 4 vols., ed. John Butt, reprinted 1962, III, p. 399. (Letter XCV).

33 George Cheyne, *The English Malady, or a Treatise of Nervous Diseases of all Kinds*, 1727, p. 158.

34 Hester Lynch Piozzi, *Anecdotes*, in *Shaw and Piozzi, Memoirs of Dr Johnson*, ed. Arthur Sherbo, Oxford, 1974, p. 112.

35 Mary Wollstonecraft, *A Vindication of the Rights of Woman*, (1790), Everyman's Library edition, 1955, p. 160.

36 Tanner, *Jane Austen*, p. 268.

37 Butler, *War of Ideas*, p. 296.

38 John Mullan, *Sentiment and Sociability: the Language of Feeling in the Eighteenth Century*, Oxford, 1988, especially chapter 2, 'Richardson: sentiment and the construction of femininity'.

39 See, among many examples, Ann Douglas Wood,' "The Fashionable Diseases" : women's complaints and their treatment in nineteenth century America', in *Women and Health in America*, ed. J. W. Leavitt, Wisconsin, 1984, pp. 222–38.

40 A. B. Granville, MB, FRS, *Spas of England and Principal Bathing Places*, Vol. 2: *The Midlands and South* (1841), reprinted Bath, 1971, p. 515.

41 F. R. Leavis, *The Great Tradition*, 1948, p. 7.

42 *Letters*, p. 486 (to Fanny Knight, 23 March 1817).

Bibliography

Place of publication is London unless otherwise noted.

Armstrong, Nancy, *Desire and Domestic Fiction: A Political History of the Novel*, New York and Oxford, 1987

Auerbach, Nina, 'Jane Austen's dangerous charm: feeling as one ought about Fanny Price', in *Jane Austen: New Perspectives, Women and Literature*, (New Series), 3, ed. Janet Todd, New York and London, 1983

Austen, Rev. Henry Thomas, A. M., *Lectures upon Some Important Passages in the Book of Genesis delivered in the Chapel of the British Minister at Berlin in the year* 1818, 1820

Austen-Leigh, J. E., *Memoir of Jane Austen*, with an introduction by R. W. Chapman, Oxford, 1926, repr. 1967

Balderston, Katherine C., ed., *Thraliana*, 2 vols., second edn., 1951

Bell, Rudoph M., *Holy Anorexia*, Chicago and London, 1985

Bernheimer, Charles, and Kahane, Claire, eds., *In Dora's Case: Freud – Feminism – Hysteria*, 1985

Bloom, Harold, 'Introduction', *Jane Austen*, (Modern Critical Views series), New York, 1986

Booth, Wayne C., *The Rhetoric of Fiction*, Chicago and London, 1961

Bowlby, John, *Attachment and Loss*, 3 vols., II, *Separation, Anxiety and Anger*, 1973

Bradley, A. C., 'Jane Austen' (1911) in *A Miscellany*, 1929

Brown, Julia Prewitt, 'The feminist depreciation of Austen: a polemical reading', *Novel*, 23, 3, 1990, 303–13

Brown, Julia Prewitt, *Jane Austen's Novels: Social Change and Literary Form*, Cambridge Mass., and London, 1979

Brückman, Patricia, 'Sir Walter Elliot's Bath Address', *Modern Philology*, 80, August 1982, 56–60

Buchan, William, M. D., *Domestic Medicine: or, a Treatise on the Prevention and Cure of Diseases by Regimen and Simple Medicines*, second edn, 1772, reprinted New York and London, 1985

Burney, Fanny, *Camilla: or, a Picture of Youth*, ed. Edward A. Bloom and Lillian D. Bloom, Oxford, 1972

Evelina, ed. Edward A. Bloom, Oxford 1982

[Burney, Fanny], *The Diary and Letters of Madame D'Arblay*, edited by her niece, 7 vols., 1854

Burrows, J. F., *Computation into Criticism: A Study of Jane Austen's Novels and an Experiment in Method*, Oxford, 1987

Bush, Douglas, *Jane Austen*, 1975

Butler, James, ed., '*The Ruined Cottage*' and '*The Pedlar*', *The Cornell Wordsworth*, Ithaca, New York, and Hassocks, 1979

Butler, Marilyn, *Jane Austen and the War of Ideas*, Oxford, 1975

Bynum, W. F., 'The nervous patient in eighteenth- and nineteenth-century Britain: the psychiatric origins of British neurology', in Bynum, Porter and Shepherd, eds., *The Anatomy of Madness*, 2 vols., I, *People and Ideas*, Cambridge, 1975

Canguilhem, Georges, *On the Normal and the Pathological*, trans. by Carolyn R. Fawcett, Dortrecht, Boston, London, 1978

Castle, Terry, *Masquerade and Civilisation: The Carnivalesque in Eighteenth-Century English Culture and Fiction*, 1986

Chapman, R. W., *Jane Austen, Facts and Problems*, Oxford, 1948

Cheyne, George, *The English Malady, or a treatise of nervous diseases of all kinds*, 1727

Cixous, Hélène and Clément, Catherine, *The Newly Born Woman*, trans. Betsy King of *La Jeune Née*, (1975), Manchester, 1986.

Davidson, Cathy N. and Broner, E. M., eds., *The Lost Tradition: Mother and Daughter in Literature*, New York, 1980

Davie, John, 'Introduction' to World's Classics edn of *Persuasion*, Oxford, 1971

De Rose, Peter L., *Jane Austen and Samuel Johnson*, Washington, 1980

de Beauvoir, Simone, *The Second Sex* (1949) translated and edited by H. M. Parshley, reprinted Harmondsworth, 1986

Devlin, D. D., *Jane Austen and Education*, 1975

Doody, Margaret Anne, *A Natural Passion: A Study of the Novels of Samuel Richardson*, Oxford, 1974

Frances Burney, Cambridge, 1988

Dreuilhe, Emmanuel, *Mortal Embrace: Living with AIDS*, New York, 1988

Duckworth, Alistair M., *The Improvement of the Estate*, Baltimore and London, 1971

Düssinger, John A., *In the Pride of the Moment: Encounters in Jane Austen's World*, Columbus, Ohio, 1990

Edgeworth, Maria, *Tales and Novels by Maria Edgeworth*, 18 vols,

1832–3, II, *Moral Tales* I, 'Forester', XIII, *Letters of Julia and Caroline*

Eliot, George [Mary Ann Evans], *Felix Holt, the Radical* (1866) Edinburgh and London, n.d.

The George Eliot Letters, ed. Gordon S. Haight, 7 vols., 1954

Ellis, David, 'The Irony of Mansfield Park', *The Critical Review* 12, 1969, 107–19

Enright D. J., and David Rawlinson, eds., *The Oxford Book of Friendship*, Oxford, 1991

Enright, D. J., ed., *The Faber Book of Fevers and Frets*, 1989

Fagin, Claire and Diers, Donna, 'Nursing as metaphor', *American Journal of Nursing*, September 1983, 1,362

Falconer, William, MD. FRS, *A Dissertation on the Influence of the Passions upon Disorders of the Body*, 1788

Flahiff, F. T., 'Place and replacement in *Mansfield Park*', *University of Toronto Quarterly, A Canadian Journal of the Humanities*, 54, 1985, 221–33

Fleishman, Avrom, 'Two faces of Emma', in *Jane Austen: New Perspectives, Women and Literature*, (New Series), 3, ed. Janet Todd, New York and London, 1983

Fleishman, Avrom, *A Reading of 'Mansfield Park': An Essay in Critical Synthesis*, Minneapolis, 1967

Fosbery, M. W., 'Jane Austen's Fanny Price', *The Cambridge Quarterly*, 8, 2, 1978, 113–28

Foucault, Michel, *The Care of the Self*, (*The History of Sexuality*, vol. 3) trans. Robert Hurley, Harmondsworth, 1990

Freud, Sigmund, *The Standard Edition of the Complete Psychological Works of Sigmund Freud*, trans. J. Strachey, A. Freud et al., 1957 reprinted 1986

Gallop, Jane, *Thinking Through the Body*, New York, 1988

Gatens, Moira, 'A critique of the sex/gender distinction', in J. Allen and P. Patten, eds., *Beyond Marx, Interventions after Marx*, Sydney, 1983, pp.143–160

'Towards a feminist philosophy of the body', pp. 59–70, in *Crossing Boundaries*, ed. Caine et al., Sydney, 1988

Gay, Penny, 'A changing view: Jane Austen's landscapes', *Sydney Studies in English*, 15, 1989–90

The Gentleman's Magazine, 86, Jan. 1816

Gilbert, Sandra M. and Gubar, Susan, *The Madwoman in the Attic: The Woman Writer and the Nineteenth-Century Literary Imagination*, New Haven, 1979

Gilman, Sander L., *Disease and Representation: Images of Illness from Madness to AIDS*, Ithaca and London, 1988

Gisborne, Thomas, *The Duties of the Female Sex*, second edition, 1797

Goldberg, S. L., 'Agents and lives: making moral sense of people', *The Critical Review*, 25, 1983, 26–49

Gooneratne, Yasmine, *Jane Austen*, Cambridge, 1970

Gorer, Geoffrey, 'Poor Honey: some notes on Jane Austen and her mother' (1957) pp. 248–64 in *The Danger of Equality*, 1966

Granville, A. B., MB. FRS, *Spas of England and Principal Bathing Places*, vol 2: *The Midlands and South* [1841], reprinted Bath, 1971

Gregory, Dr John, *A Father's Legacy to his Daughters*, 1822

Grosz, Elizabeth, 'Notes towards a corporeal feminism', *Australian Feminist Studies*, 5, 1987, 3–15

Robin Grove, 'Jane Austen's free enquiry: *Mansfield Park*', *The Critical Review*, 25, 1983, 132–50

Gunn, Daniel P., In the vicinity of Winthrop: ideological rhetoric in *Persuasion*', *Nineteenth Century Literature*, 41, 1987, 403–18

Halperin, John, *The Life of Jane Austen*, Baltimore, 1984

Harris, Jocelyn, *Jane Austen's Art of Memory*, Cambridge, 1989

Harvey, W. J., 'The plot of *Emma*', *Essays in Criticism*, 17, 1967, 48–63

Haygarth, John, MD, *Of the Imagination, as a cause and as a cure of disorders of the body*, 1800

Honan, Park, *Jane Austen: Her Life*, 1987

Hubback, J. H. and Edith C., *Jane Austen's Sailor Brothers*, 1906

Hughes, R. E., 'The education of Emma Woodhouse', *Nineteenth Century Fiction*, 16, 1962

Hume, David, *The Philosophical Works of David Hume*, 4 vols., Edinburgh, 1825

Inchbald, Mrs [Elizabeth], *A Simple Story*, with an introduction by G. L. Strachey, Oxford, 1908

Ihrenpreis, Irwin, *Acts of Implication: Suggestion and Covert Meaning in the Works of Dryden, Swift, Pope and Austen*, Berkeley, L. A., and London, 1980

James, William, *Principles of Psychiatry*, vol. II, Harvard, 1981

Jane Austen's Letters, collected and edited by R. W. Chapman, second edition 1952, reprinted Oxford, 1969

Johnson, Claudia L., 'The "operations of time, and the changes of the human mind" : Jane Austen and Dr Johnson again', *Modern Language Quarterly*, 44, 1983, 23–38

  'The "twilight of probability" ; uncertainty and hope in *Sense and Sensibility*', *Philological Quarterly*, 62, 1983, 171–86.

  Jane Austen: Women, Politics and the Novel, Chicago and London, 1988.

  'A "sweet face as white as death" : Jane Austen and the politics of female sensibility', *Novel*, 1989, 22, 159–74

Johnson, Samuel, *The History of Rasselas, Prince of Abyssinia*, ed. J. P. Hardy, Oxford, 1968

The Rambler, ed. W. J. Bate and Albrecht B. Strauss, *The Yale Edition of the Works of Samuel Johnson*, IV, New Haven and London, 1969

The Lives of the Poets, The Works of Samuel Johnson, LL. D., 12 vols., 1820, vol XI

Johnson, Judy van Sickle, 'The bodily frame: learning romance in *Persuasion*', *Nineteenth Century Fiction*, 38, June 1983, 43–61

Kestenbaum, Victor, ed., *The Humanity of the Ill: Phenomenological Perspectives*, Knoxville, 1982

Kleinman, Arthur, *Social Origins of Distress and Disease: Depression, Neurasthenia, and Pain in Modern China*, New Haven and London, 1986

The Illness Narratives, New York, 1988

Rethinking Psychiatry: From Cultural Category to Personal Experience, New York and London, 1988

Laqueur, Thomas, 'Orgasm, generation and the politics of reproductive biology', in *The Making of the Modern Body: Sexuality and Society in the Nineteenth Century*, ed. Catherine Gallagher and Thomas Laqueur, Berkeley, 1987

Lascelles, Mary, *Jane Austen and her Art* (1939), reprinted Oxford, 1969

Lavater, John Caspar, *Essays on Physiognomy for the promotion of the knowledge and the love of mankind*, trans. Thomas Holcroft, second edition, 4 vols., 1804

Lawrence, D. H., 'A Propos of "Lady Chatterley's Lover"', *Phoenix II*, ed. by Warren Roberts and Harry T. Moore, 1968

Leavis, F. R., *The Great Tradition*, 1948

Leavis, L. R., and Blom, J. M., 'A return to Jane Austen's Novels', *English Studies, A Journal of English Language and Literature*, 62, 1981, 313–23

Leavis, Q. D., *Collected Essays*, 2 vols., ed. G. Singh, Cambridge, 1983

Leder, Drew, *The Absent Body*, Chicago, 1990

Lewis, C. S., 'A note on Jane Austen', *Essays in Criticism*, 4, 1954, 359–71

Litz, A. Walton, *Jane Austen,; A Study of her Artistic Development*, 1965

'*Persuasion*: forms of estrangement', in J. Halperin, ed., *Jane Austen: Bicentenary Essays*, Cambridge, 1975

MacDonagh, Oliver, '*Sanditon*: a regency novel' in *Historical Studies* XVI, *The Writer as Witness*, Cork, 1989, pp. 114–31

MacIntyre, Alasdair, *After Virtue*, Notre Dame, Indiana, 1981

Mary Wollstonecraft, *A Vindication of the Rights of Woman* (1792), edited by Miriam Krannick, Harmondsworth, 1975

McDonnell, Jane, ' " A little spirit of independence" : sexual politics and the bildungsroman in *Mansfield Park*', *Novel*, 17, 1984, 197–214

McDougall, Joyce, *Theatres of the Body*: *A Psychoanalytic Approach to Psychosomatic Illness*, 1989

McGowan, John P., 'Knowledge/power and Jane Austen's radicalism', *Mosaic: A Journal for the Interdisciplinary Study of Literature*, 18, 1985, 1–15

Medical Knowledge: *Doubt and Certainty*, Open University, 1985

Michie, Helena, *The Flesh Made Word*: *Female Figures and Women's Bodies*, New York, 1987

Miller, D. A., *Narrative and its Discontents*: *Problems of Closure in the Traditional Novel*, Princeton, 1981

'The late Jane Austen', *Raritan*, 10, 1990, 55–79

Moi, Toril, ed., *The Kristeva Reader*, Oxford, 1986

Moler, Kenneth L., '"Only connect" : emotional strength and health in *Mansfield Park*', *English Studies*, 64, 1983, 144–52

Monaghan, David, *Jane Austen, Structure and Social Vision*, 1980

Mooneyham, Laura G., *Romance, Language and Education in Jane Austen's Novels*, London, 1988

Mullan, John, *Sentiment and Sociability*: *the Language of Feeling in the Eighteenth Century*, Oxford, 1990

Nabokov, Vladimir, *Lectures on Literature*, ed. Fredson Bowers, 2 Vols., New York and London, 1975

Neale, R. S., *Bath*, 1680–1850, *A Social History*, 1981

Olshin, Toby A., 'Jane Austen: a romantic, systematic, or realistic approach to medicine?', *Studies in Eighteenth Century Culture*, 10, ed. Harry C. Payne, 1981, 313–26

Paris, Bernard J., *Character and Conflict in Jane Austen's Novels*: *A Psychological Approach*, Brighton, 1979

Pateman, Carol, *The Sexual Contract*, Oxford, 1989

Pevsner, Sir Nikolaus, 'The architectural setting of Jane Austen's novels', *Journal of the Warburg and Courtauld Institutes*, 31, 1968, 404–22

Pickrel, Paul, 'Lionel Trilling and *Mansfield Park*', *Studies in English Literature*, 1987, 607–21

Piozzi, Hester Lynch, *Anecdotes*, in *Shaw and Piozzi, Memoirs of Dr Johnson*, ed. Arthur Sherbo, Oxford, 1974

Plessner, H., *Laughing and Crying*: *A Study of the Limits of Human Behaviour*, trans. James Spencer Churchill and Marjorie Grene, Evanston, 1970

Poovey, Mary, *The Proper Lady and the Woman Writer*: *Ideology as Style in the Works of Mary Wollstonecraft, Mary Shelley and Jane Austen*, Chicago, 1984

Pope, Alexander, *The Works*, 6 vols., Edinburgh, 1764

Porter, Roy, *English Society in the Eighteenth Century*, Harmondsworth, 1982

Pringle, Sir John, *Observations on the Diseases of the Army*, (1752) fifth edition, 1765

Raleigh, W., *The English Novel: A Short Sketch from the Earliest Times to the Appearance of Waverley*, (1894), 1919

Rawlinson, Mary C., 'Medicine's discourse and the practice of medicine', pp. 69–85 in *The Humanity of the Ill*, ed. Victor Kestenbaum, Knoxville, 1982

Relhan, Antony MD, *A Short History of Brighthelmston, with remarks on its air, and an analysis of its waters, particularly of an uncommon mineral one, long discovered, though but lately used*, 1761

Richardson, Samuel, *Clarissa, or, the history of a young lady*, in four volumes, ed. John Butt, 1962 [Everyman Library edition]

Riley, Denise, *Am I That Name?, Feminism and the Category of 'Women' in History*, 1988

Rosmarin, Adena, '"Misreading" Emma: the powers and perfidies of interpretive history', *English Literary History*, 51, 1984, 315–42

Rousseau, George S., 'Nerves, spirits and fibres: towards defining the origins of sensibility', *The Blue Guitar*, 2, 1976, 125–53

Sacks, Oliver W., *Migraine, Understanding the Common Disorder*, revised edition, 1985

Said, Edward W., 'Jane Austen and Empire', *Raymond Williams: Critical Perspectives*, ed. T. Eagleton, Cambridge, 1988, pp. 150–64

Sanditon, an unfinished novel by Jane Austen, reproduced in facsimile from the manuscript in the possession of King's College, Cambridge, introduction by B. C. Southam, Oxford and London, 1975

Sedgwick, Eve Kosofsky, *Between Men: English Literature and Male Homosocial Desire*, New York, 1985

Schorer, Mark, 'The humiliation of Emma Woodhouse', *The Literary Review*, 1959, 547–63.

Siegel, Rudolph E., *Galen's System of Physiology and Medicine*, Basel and New York, 1968

Smith, F. B., *The People's Health*, 1977.

Sontag, Susan, *Illness as Metaphor*, 1978
AIDS and its Metaphors, 1989

Southam, B. C. ed., *Jane Austen: The Critical Heritage*, [vol I], 1969
Jane Austen: The Critical Heritage: Vol II, 1870–1940, 1987
Jane Austen's Literary Manuscripts: A Study of the Novelist's Development Through the surviving Papers, Oxford, 1964

Spring, David, 'Interpreters of Jane Austen's social world: literary critics and historians', in *Jane Austen, New Perspectives, Women and Literature* (New Series) 3, ed. Janet Todd, 1983, pp. 53–69

Stafford, Barbara M., La Puma, John, and Schiedermayer, David L., 'One face of beauty, one picture of health: the hidden aesthetic of medical practice', *Journal of Medicine and Philosophy*, 1989, 213–30

Sulloway, Alison G., *Jane Austen and the Province of Womanhood*, Philadelphia, 1989

Tanner, Tony, *Jane Austen*, 1988

Tave, Stuart M., *Some Words of Jane Austen*, Chicago, 1973

Trask, H-K., *Eros and Power: The Promise of Feminist Theory*, Philadelphia, 1986

Trilling, Lionel, 'Mansfield Park', in Ian Watt, ed., *Jane Austen: A Collection of Critical Essays*, Englewood Cliffs, N.J., 1963

Trotter, Thomas, MD., *A View of the Nervous Temperament*, 1807

Turner, Victor, *The Forest of Symbols: Aspects of Ndembu Ritual*, Ithaca, 1967

Tytler, Graeme, *Physiognomy in the European Novel: Faces and Fortunes*, Princeton, New Jersey, 1982.

Watson, J. R., 'Mr Perry's patients: a view of *Emma*', *Essays in Criticism*, 20, 1970, 334–43

Whytt, Robert, *Physiological Essays, II; Observations on the sensibility and irritability of the parts of men and other animals, occasioned by Dr Haller's late treatise on these subjects*, Edinburgh, 1756

Wilhelm, Albert E., 'Three word clusters in *Emma*,' *Studies in the Novel*, 7, 1975, 49–60

Williams, Michael, *Jane Austen: Six Novels and Their Methods*, 1986

Wiltshire, John, 'A romantic *Persuasion*?', *The Critical Review*, 14, 1971, 3–16

Wise, T.J. and Symington, J. A., *The Brontës: Their Friendships, Lives and Correspondence*, 3 vols, Oxford, 1932

Wood, Ann Douglas, "The fashionable diseases" : women's complaints and their treatment in nineteenth century America', in *Women and Health in America*, ed. J. W. Leavitt, Wisconsin, 1984

Woolf, Virginia, 'On being ill' (1930) in *The Complete Essays of Virginia Woolf*, 4 vols., IV, 1967

Zeitlow, Paul, 'Luck and fortuitous circumstance in *Persuasion*: two interpretations', *English Literary History*, 32, 1965, 179–95

Zimmermann, Everett, 'Admiring Pope no more than is proper: *Sense and Sensibility*', in John Halperin, ed., *Jane Austen: Bicentenary Essays*, Cambridge,1975

Index